Pre-publication Review

Mark Krueger, Professor,
Youth Work Learning Center

Like many creative works (oeuvres), *Standing on the Precipice* is a work in progress that captures the development of our field at an important time. As a reader in the field simultaneously looking at and interacting *with* the work, these are my impressions. I am early *in* and already know I like and will be *with* this book for some time as I reread it. With chapters by some of the most creative and experienced writers in the field, it shows (rather than tells) what we have and can become. The insights, ideas, images, and questions the work evokes ring true with child and youth care as I know it to be, and subsequently I am having one epiphany after another.

The book is not just good, creative, mindful thinking and writing, it is good learning of the type many of us search for in our classrooms with students. It is also best practice shown the way best practice can and should be shown—with clarity, creativity, purpose, and ethics, framed with questions and curiosity about where to go next. No foolish certainties to be found here, as novelist Milan Kundera said about the good novel. The authors—as one of the field's leading thinkers, Jerome Beker, urged us to do a few years ago—are trying to hear it deep and look for the questions that do so much to determine the soul of the work. They are also, as another leader, Henry Maier, once said about good developmental care, "in the thick of it."

Shining through for me amidst the multiple contexts and complexities, and the constructing, modelling, and deconstructing that attempts to find and show "simplicity on the other side of complexity," is what I like to think of as the dance, or "lunch." I can see relational work in the verbs, prepositions, actions, interactions, and doing from my precipice as I reflect on child and youth care unfolding in the lived experience. I can also see the messy, nitty-gritty, everyday nature of the work that makes it real, at least for me. I can't wait to get it in the hands of students so I can hear how they see it from where they stand.

There is so much here to see and think about. The view is mostly postmodern, but it is also very practical. The takes, models, and dialogues show us meaning making, relating, and development in everyday contexts. If, like the authors, readers are nimble and creative, I am sure they will see and feel the child and youth care they know in a new light that they can then shine on their practice.

Perhaps what I like best about the book is that it locates child and youth care in the writers' presence. They show up and have become what they write about, and write about what they have become as Karen VanderVen, another leading thinker, encouraged us to do a few years ago in her writing about activity. Each author has his or her own voice and slant, but all are in search of the core of care in relational, contextual, inter-subjective, developmental, gut-wrenching, heartbreaking, heartening, sad, joyful, co-created child and youth care.

At times while reading it I get so excited that I work among these caring thinkers; I lose my place and must read again to see where I am, and what I will find next. If you read this book with a similar mindset, I am sure you will have your own experience of discovery, and be better at what you do because of it. You will also have a better grasp of where the field has been, where it is, and what it can be in the eyes of those who see it with hope for the future. This is a brave book written in the spirit of a child and youth care that always wants to be more for children, youth, and adults. Thus it *is* child and youth care, and one of the most significant contributions to the development of our field in recent years.

standing on the precipice

inquiry into the creative potential of
child and youth care practice

Relational inquiry is something that arises
in the midst of your experience—
as part of your experience, not separate from it.
It is a dynamic process of always
opening and opening and opening
your consciousness, your soul,
endlessly and freely.

standing on the precipice

inquiry into the creative potential of
child and youth care practice

edited by
Gerard Bellefeuille
Frances Ricks

MacEwan
Press

MacEwan
Press

Standing on the Precipice: Inquiry into the Creative Potential of Child and Youth Care Practice
Copyright © 2008, MacEwan Press, Grant MacEwan College

Published in 2008 by MacEwan Press
                      Grant MacEwan College
                      10700 – 104 Avenue
                      Edmonton, Alberta T5J 4S2

ISBN: 978-0-9780453-2-6

1 2 3 4 5 6 7 8 9 10

"The Knowing, Doing and Being in Context: A Praxis-Oriented Approach to Child and Youth Care," by Jennifer White, is reprinted here by the kind permission of Springer Science and Business Media and the original publisher, *Child and Youth Care Forum*, 36(5/6), 2007, 225–244.

Interior design and layout: Carol Dragich, Dragich Design
Cover design and illustration: Lindsay Kirstiuk
Copy editor and proofreader: Brendan Wild
MacEwan Press coordination: Scott Day

Library and Archives of Canada Cataloguing in Publication
Standing on the precipice : inquiry into the creative potential of child and youth care practice / [edited by] Gerard Bellefeuille, Frances Ricks.

Includes bibliographical references.
ISBN 978-0-9780453-2-6

     1. Children—Institutional care. 2. Youth—Institutional care. 3. Social service—Practice. 4. Social work with children. 5. Social work with youth. I. Bellefeuille, Gerard II. Ricks, Frances

HV713.S78 2008   362.73   C2008-905946-8

Printed and bound in Canada by Marquis

This book is printed on acid-free paper that is 100% ancient forest friendly (100% post-consumer recycled)

Contents

Acknowledgements

This book was made possible through the generous support and resources of Grant MacEwan College. We extend our sincere thanks and appreciation to Elaine Kirschner and Sharon Hobden for their vision, leadership, and can-do attitude. We acknowledge Scott Day and Lynn McKinnon for their assistance and advice on publishing and copyright matters, Lindsay Kirstiuk for designing the cover, and Brendan Wild for his diligence in editing. We are also grateful to marketing consultant Charlene Barrett and instructional designer Lynn Feist for their support and guidance. Finally, we thank the authors for their commitment and contributions. In their respective chapters, each has demonstrated reflection and inquiry into a crucial aspect of Child and Youth Care practice, and all are thus *standing on the precipice*. We are most grateful for their participation in the co-creation and evolution of conversations that will emerge from the reading of this book.

Contributors

Gerard Bellefeuille, PhD held the position of Associate Professor at the University of Northern British Columbia before joining the Bachelor of Child and Youth Care program at MacEwan in 2006. Gerard has spent over 25 years working in the human services field as a front-line practitioner, the executive director of non-profit agencies, Provincial Director of Community Development, and organizational consultant. Gerard has co-authored two books, entitled *Breaking the Rules: Transforming Governance in Social Services* and *All Together Now: Creating a Social Capital Mosaic*, and has delivered keynote addresses and academic papers in India, Brazil, New Zealand, Sweden, Italy, the United Kingdom, the United States, and across Canada on a variety of human service issues.

Jennifer Charlesworth, PhD is a Child and Youth Care (CYC) practitioner, facilitator, consultant, trainer, and researcher with 31 years' experience. Her practice has been focused on the interests of children and youth within the context of their families and communities. She has worked as a front-line CYC practitioner in both residential and community settings, child protection worker, supervisor and senior manager within government ministries, and as a lecturer at the University of Victoria's School of Child and Youth Care. For 14 years she has been a consultant and facilitator in private practice working with a wide range of communities. Soon after completing her PhD by special arrangement in Child and Youth Care at the University of Victoria, Jennifer became the Executive Director of the Federation of Child and Family Services of B.C., where she continues to advocate for and serve children, their families, and communities.

Thom Garfat, PhD received his PhD in the School of Child and Youth Care at the University of Victoria in Canada. Since beginning as a front-line worker, Thom has had the opportunity to be involved in almost every aspect of CYC practice. Thom notes, "In the end, no matter the location, the context has always been similar: self and other finding a satisfying way to be together." The details of Thom's working life can be found at: www.cyc-net.org/transformaction.

Mark Greenwald, BA recently retired from 32 years of teaching and supervising in The Special Care Counseling Department at Vanier College in Montreal, Canada. Throughout his career he has published and presented papers, participated on panels, and conducted workshops at many local, national, and international CYC conferences. His professional interests include activity programming, expressive activities, creativity, CYC curriculum development, counselling, identity, and ethics. He and his wife, Heather, live in eastern Ontario, in a 150-year-old log farmhouse where they raised their two children. In addition to contributing to the CYC field, Mark plans to return to earlier interests in photography and mask making.

Marie L. Hoskins, PhD is a professor in the School of Child and Youth Care at the University of Victoria in Canada. Her teaching and research is informed by social constructionist and constructivist ideas. She has applied these theories in her research on adolescents and disordered eating, an inquiry into the shifts in constituting identities while engaged in workplace conflicts, and an exploration of the co-construction of identities surrounding the use of crystal metaamphetamines among adolescent girls. Marie has authored and co-authored numerous articles, published in *Constructivist Psychology, International Women's Quarterly, Child and Youth Care Forum, Mediation Quarterly*, and *Qualitative Inquiry*, and has co-edited a book entitled *Working Relationally with Girls: Complex Lives/Complex Identities*. She is currently a Senior Advisor to the U.N. Child Soldier Initiative, led by Senator Romeo Dallaire.

Donna Jamieson, MEd has been working in the field of Child and Youth Care since 1981. She became a certified Child and Youth Care Counselor in 1984, and was a Registered Psychologist from 1981 to 2007. Donna is currently the chair of the Grant MacEwan College Child and Youth Care Program in Edmonton, Alberta. Donna began teaching part time at Grant

MacEwan College in 1996, and in 2003 she became a full-time instructor at the college. Prior to coming to MacEwan, she headed the Yellowhead Family Support Program, an in-home community-based program that employed Child and Youth Care Counselors to provide support, education, and counselling to families referred by Alberta Children's Services. She was part of this program, which developed and provided services for children, youth, and families, for over 20 years. Before this, she worked at Yellowhead Youth Centre, in various school systems, and at Alberta Hospital. Donna continues to provide workshops and training for community agencies.

Tam Lundy, PhD is a consultant, educator, and mentor in the field of human and social development, with extensive professional experience in government, community, and educational settings. She introduces integral thinking and practice approaches to policy makers and practitioners in diverse disciplines and sectors, such as health promotion, planning, governance, organizational development, community development, engagement, and capacity building. Tam also develops innovative practice tools such as the Integral Map of Community and the Integral Capacity Building Framework, adopted by B.C. Healthy Communities as a foundation of the healthy communities approach. Tam's academic affiliations include a position as Lecturer in the School of Holistic Studies at John F. Kennedy University.

Jack Phelan, MS has been teaching CYC work for many years and has been involved as a CYC practitioner and supervisor in a variety of agency settings. He has travelled internationally to study CYC practice in North America, Europe, and Africa for the past 15 years and has shared the Canadian CYC experience with others. The focus of his writing is on applying theory in practical CYC life space situations and on developing CYC program ideas that meet the complex needs of the youth and families we serve.

Frances Ricks, PhD is an Emeritus Professor in the School of Child and Youth Care at the University of Victoria. Her topics of research and education/training include case management, working with families, ethics in social services, mentoring, building capacity in aboriginal communities, sexual abuse, self awareness in practice planning, and post secondary pedagogy and curriculum. In addition to numerous published articles and research awards, she and co-authors have published the following books: *Accountability Case Management, Breaking the Rules, All Together Now: Creating a Social Capital Mosaic*, and *Emergent Practice Planning*. Frances has received the Women of Distinction award in Education, Training, and Community, and has recently designed training materials with Community Living B.C. (CLBC) on Discovery Goal-Based Planning for persons with disabilities and their families.

Carol Stuart, PhD is an Associate Professor in the School of Child and Youth Care at Ryerson University in Toronto. Carol began her career in Child and Youth Care in Ontario, Canada, and has 30 years of experience across three provinces. She has worked in community and residential-based Child and Youth Care organizations providing services to children and youth at risk and is certified in CYC in Alberta and Ontario. She is a faculty member in the undergraduate program at Ryerson University and is an adjunct member of the School of Child and Youth Care at University of Victoria. She works with graduate students in both universities. Carol's current research interests include professional practice standards, integrated service delivery, residential and group care, youth resilience, and youth at risk. Carol has played a significant role in developing competencies and certification exams for professional CYC workers and is involved in developing accreditation for educational programs.

Jennifer White, PhD is an Assistant Professor in the School of Child and Youth Care at the University of Victoria. She has an MA in Counselling Psychology and an EdD in Educational Leadership from the University of British Columbia (UBC). Jennifer has worked in the human services sector for 20 years. She began her professional career as a CYC practitioner in a large residential treatment facility in Calgary. She has also practiced as a clinical counsellor, educator, policy consultant, researcher, and community developer. Jennifer has a specific interest in the issue of youth suicide prevention, and she has written a number of professional articles and practical documents to support communities' development of comprehensive prevention strategies that capitalize on their own local strengths and resources. Her current research interests are in the area of practitioner knowledge, ethical reflection, practical judgment, and praxis.

Expanding our Creative Potential

Gerard Bellefeuille, PhD, and Frances Ricks, PhD

The first of its kind, this collection of articles challenges students, practitioners, and educators to look beyond the traditional boundaries of Child and Youth Care practice. Taken together, the chapters in this book represent a compendium of innovative and creative thinking on doing the relational work of Child and Youth Care in our rapidly changing world, which is ever-more technologically and socially complex. In such a world, where we have little idea what the needs of children, youth, and families will look like even five years down the road, creativity supported with ongoing inquiry is of paramount importance in promoting and maintaining effective Child and Youth Care practice.

Child and Youth Care is not a static profession located in a specific moment of time; rather, it is a highly creative discipline rooted in a continuous process of being and becoming, the horizons of which are ongoing. Viewing Child and Youth Care as an endless process of becoming implies, rather obviously, an openness to inquiry and other modes of thought. The persistent evolution of Child and Youth Care as a profession is dependent upon unleashing the creative potential of practitioners in the field to engage in bold and imaginative thought.

The experienced and mindful writers featured in this collection have a long history of being engaged in creative practice and education in the field of Child and Youth Care. Each of the nine chapters prompts Child and Youth Care professionals to rethink their understanding of practice challenges and opportunities. As a whole, the book offers a valuable resource for our lifelong journeys as Child and Youth Care practitioners.

The book is divided into three parts: relational practice, critical aspects of relational practice, and complexities of relational practice. Part One, Crafting a Mindful Approach to Relational Practice, opens with Thom Garfat's chapter, "The Inter-Personal In-Between: An Exploration of Relational Child and Youth Care Practice." In this chapter Garfat provides an overview of the evolution of Child and Youth Care practice from its initial focus on *having* a relationship to *being in* relationship. Garfat's chapter sets the stage for Bellefeuille and Jamieson's inquiry into "Relational-Centred Planning: A Turn to Creative Potential and Possibilities." Bellefeuille and Jamieson explore relational practice as a means of unblocking creative potential and finding possibilities in the process of doing assessment and planning. In Part One's final chapter, "Building Developmental Capacities: A Developmentally Responsive Approach to Child and Youth Care Intervention," Jack Phelan outlines the parameters of a developmentally responsive approach to Child and Youth Care intervention. Phelan explains the *developmental stuckness* that underpins the lives of vulnerable youth and families and discusses the developmental process that Child and Youth Care practitioners must progress through to build their capacity to work developmentally. Phelan proposes a developmentally responsive framework that illustrates the core components of good developmental practice.

Part Two, Understanding Critical Aspects of Relational Practice, contains three chapters, each of which addresses a critical aspect of relational Child and Youth Care practice. In chapter 4, "The Knowing, Doing and Being in Context: A Praxis-Oriented Approach to Child and Youth Care," Jennifer White challenges us to think of *praxis* as a mediation between action and consciousness. White defines *praxis* as ethical, self-aware, responsive, and accountable action. She invites the reader to consider praxis as a central tenet of his or her practice and offers a series of questions to provoke critical self-reflection of the practitioner's experience of working with children, youth, and families. In chapter 5, "Shaping the Rules: Child and Youth Care Boundaries in the Context of Relationship. *Bonsai!*" Carol Stuart uses the metaphor of a fence to guide a personal inquiry into the meaning of boundaries and explore how boundaries are expressed in professional practice. The chapter models the author's own process of inquiry into the space between self and other, which is the ultimate focus of boundary setting. Part Two concludes with "The Virtuous Child and Youth Care Practitioner: Exploring Identity and Ethical Practice" written by Mark Greenwald, which investigates the ethics of relational Child and Youth Care practice. He examines the relationship between identity and ethical Child and Youth Care practice by presenting a conversation between a supervisor and a front-line Child and Youth Care practitioner.

In Part Three, Becoming Aware and Challenged by the Complexities of Relational Child and Youth Care Practice, Tam Lundy explores ground-breaking thinking and practice approaches for catalyzing effective and sustainable change—in people, in organizations, and in communities. She investigates the following lines of inquiry: What does it mean to *be the change*? What do we see in the world? How do our inner experiences come to life in our actions and behaviours? In other words, how does our *being* shape our *doing*? How does paying attention to our inner development make our actions more effective? And how does this enhance our professional capacity as Child and Youth Care practitioners? In chapter 8, Jennifer Charlesworth discusses issues of using voice in Child and Youth Care practice. She identifies what is meant by voice, specifies how the absence of voice shows up in practice, and offers the opportunity to examine one's presence/absence of voice. Jennifer explores strategies that can be used by practitioners to overcome barriers to voicing. The collection's final chapter, "Experiencing Differences: The Challenges, Opportunities, and Cautions" by Marie Hoskins and Frances Ricks, proposes an approach for understanding and managing the occurrence of menacing differences in the context of Child and Youth Care practice. The authors suggest ways to think about experiencing differences and how differences are perceived and created by us; they present a reflective strategy to guide Child and Youth Care practitioners to function at a higher level of consciousness when differences surface within their personal and professional relationships.

Crafting a Mindful Approach to Relational Practice

Part One introduces the basic assumptions, values, guiding principles, and lexicon of relational Child and Youth Care practice. The three chapters that comprise Part One are intended to expand readers' explorations of the relational core of Child and Youth Care practice as expressed in terms of being-in-relationship—a relational process in which understanding and multiple perspectives are shared and co-created. Relational practice is complex and demands a high degree of ingenuity, creativity, and openness on the part of the Child and Youth Care practitioner. It requires "being with" and "being in the moment" with others, and it provides a way of understanding and listening to others, and it reassures them of their special place in the world.

CHAPTER 1

The Inter-Personal In-Between

An Exploration of Relational Child and Youth Care Practice

Thom Garfat, PhD

ABSTRACT

Child and Youth Care practice has always focused on relationships.
As the field evolved, this focus shifted from simply having a relationship
to being in relationship with other. This chapter briefly describes
this evolution and then turns to the current focus on contemporary
Relational Child and Youth Care practice, which emphasizes the
in-between between self and other. A description of some of the
characteristics and process of Relational Child and Youth Care practice
is then offered in a beginning exploration of this new development
within the field.

INTRODUCTION

Relational Child and Youth Care (CYC) practice exists in the in-between (Garfat, 2007a); the in-between between self and other. There is no place else it can be. For without our presence in the in-between, there is no opportunity for a co-created, connected experiencing to occur. The co-creation of the in-between between us is central to Relational CYC practice.

While it may seem early in this chapter to pause and reflect, it is essential to do so, for the comments in the opening paragraph set the foundation for all that is to follow. Let us linger for a moment over these reflections.

Where is the In-between?

It may seem strange to wonder about "where" it is, before discussing "what" it is, but it is appropriate because in many ways the rest makes more sense once we discover the "where."

In contemporary Child and Youth Care practice we find constant reference to such concepts as engagement (Gannon, 2001), connection (Krueger, 1994), and being together (Fewster, 1990; Krueger, 2004) in moments of rhythmic harmony (Fulcher, 2004; Maier, 1992). Inherent in these concepts is the idea that there is a joining together of self and other (Charles & Garfat, in press; Fewster, 2004; Krueger, 1998; Ricks, 2001). It is this joining together that creates the in-between between us. It is in this area of joint connectedness where Relational CYC practice occurs.

Imagine for a moment standing inside a small circle and facing another person who is also standing inside his or her own small circle. Now imagine another circle between the two of you that touches each of your independent circles. That central circle represents the in-between between self and other.

Figure 1.

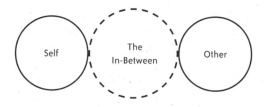

As our relationship with the other develops and we become more familiar, more secure, more intimate, and more vulnerable, the space between us changes. The in-between changes as we "step into the in-between," as we see in the diagram below. Gradually, the in-between becomes composed of us. We become a part of the interpersonal in-between while still maintaining our selves.

Figure 2.

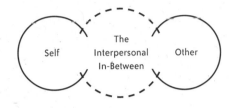

Instead of just imagining this in the abstract, stand in front of another person—preferably one with whom you are not intimate. Move back and forth until you find a distance from one another that is comfortable for both of you. Look at the space between you. This, the space between you that allows you both to be comfortable, is also the in-between. While it is not, really, a physical space, it is a space defined by the momentary boundaries of comfort for each of you. As your relationship changes, so might this space. Notice in your life, for example, how with some people you feel safe when close, and with others you only feel safe with distance. This physical representation mimics the experiential boundaries of self in relation with other. It is only a metaphor; treat it as such: interpret it for what it means in terms of non-physical interpersonal relations.

What is the In-between?

Eventually, the interpersonal in-between, under the conditions of security, vulnerability, caring, and engagement, becomes what some have called the place of "us" (Mann-Feder, 1999), where "connected experiencing" (Garfat, 1998) occurs, the opportunity for the co-creation of reality (Peterson, 1998) is available, and relational practice (Garfat, 2003a, 2003b) takes on full meaning. In this state we (self and other) are the interpersonal in-between. It is here, in this interpersonally co-created place, that Relational CYC practice occurs; and so, it is this that we work towards in our interactions with others.

Figure 3.

You and Other
Are the
Interpersonal
In-Between

In Relational CYC practice, the interpersonal in-between is the place of connected engagement (Garfat, 1998) in which we are in-relation with other. It is the space and place created by our interconnectedness where we are in the flow of the stream of immediacies (Guttman, 1991). Imagine dancing in full synchronization with another person to the extent that you have the experience that *we* are dancing. That is connected experiencing: when self and other are *in* the experience together.

The space between us changes as we develop greater intimacy. Intimacy involves more than simply what we talk about. It defines how we are together. The in-between is the place of relationship; in essence, it is the context of the relationship. Thus, when we talk about "being in relationship," we are talking about being in the in-between. The in-between, then, is the container for the relationship between self and other as well as the space created by the relationship.

Checking-in

Can you accept what has been said so far? Can you make sense of it in a manner that will allow you to continue with an open mind? This is where you, the reader, need to reflect on your self: who you are, how you know yourself, and what limits you bring to your own experiencing of things. When you turn your reflections on your self, what do you experience?

Ultimately, Relational CYC practice begins with knowing and reflecting on self in all its glory and all its ugliness: being unafraid to experience the fear of looking in on your self in the moment. As Fewster (1999) noted, "our own sense of Self is our primary professional resource" (p. vi).

Relational CYC practice is, by definition, reflective practice, and while we reflect on knowledge and experience and how they impact what goes on in the in-between, we also reflect on self. For as Ricks (1993) has said, self is the lens through which we view the world and our experiences in, and of, it. It is through this "perceiving self" that we structure and give meaning to our experiencing in the world. As I have said elsewhere (Garfat, 2002), one makes a decision about what one believes about reality, and in applying this lens-of-belief, one acts in a particular fashion, all too frequently closing one's mind to alterative ways of seeing things (Watzlawick, 1990). Self, then, creates experience, including the experience of self, other, and the in-between. So here are two questions for reflection:

- How do you limit your own openness to others, to connecting, to being with other?
- How do you explain these self-imposed limits?

These are not simplistic questions to be passed over lightly in your rush to move on. These questions are worthy of your time, for they are questions that invite you into your self, a place with which you need to be, or become, both familiar and comfortable if you wish to practice Relational Child and Youth Care.

Relational CYC practice attends to the in-between, for it is only in the in-between that we find the context for healing (Fewster, 2005). The purity of self that is present in the in-between is not devoid of all the characteristics of our "shelled self" (Garfat, 2007a); that purity lies in recognizing, accepting, and embracing them. In the interpersonal in-between there exists only what Fewster (2005) has called the unadorned self of me and you, comprising all that we are, connected. In the interpersonal in-between, you are only who you are. Nothing more and certainly nothing less—for if you are either, you are not in the in-between. What we seek here, in this interpersonal in-between, is what Fewster (2005) has called "self to self contact."

With that somewhat esoteric introduction, we turn to the history that brought us to this place, for Relational Child and Youth practice did not simply emerge full blown as a new idea. It grows out of the history of our field.

THE EVOLUTION OF RELATIONAL CHILD AND YOUTH CARE PRACTICE

"...children and staff have to achieve some sort of relationship."

– Beedell, 1970, p. 84

Relational Child and Youth Care practice evolved, as the name suggests, from the field's historic focus on relationship. In one form or another, relationship has always been essential to any interpersonal healing, even in the olden days of orphanages and, too, long before that (Charles & Garfat, in press). But that history is in many ways not relevant here because it is so long in the past. Rather than go that far back, we shall contain ourselves to the past 50 years or so, because it is during this time that the meaning and importance of the role of relationship developed as a central focus in CYC practice (Beedell, 1970; Brendtro, 1969; Burmeister, 1960; Redl, 1959).

This focus on relationship was not, of course, specific to the field of Child and Youth Care. Rather, it was a reflection of the conceptualization of healing encounters in other forms of helping. Carl Rogers expressed, for example, in 1961, his belief that if the helper was able to "provide" a certain type of relationship, the other person would be able to use that relationship for personal growth and development. The astute reader will notice in this reference from Rogers a focus on *providing* a certain type of relationship, as though the development of a relationship were somehow a one-way process; this implies the helper can, in fact, create the relationship as he or she would have it be. While contemporary CYC practice holds a focus on being in relationship (Fewster, 1990), earlier writings reflected the same orientation espoused by Rogers, depicting the creation of the relationship by the helper. It is as if somehow, standing "out there," the worker, from the outside, creates the relationship between self and other. As Maier (1987, p. vi) noted, "The act of making connections and forming a bond was seen in the hands of the worker with regard to the residents."

Larry Brendtro, who is frequently identified as encouraging our field to focus specifically on the relationship between worker and young person, said the following in his landmark article "Establishing Relationship Beachheads": "it is not enough for the worker to establish a 'relationship' with a child, but he must also see to it that he uses the 'relationship' in a therapeutic manner" (p. 56). While Brendtro's focus has moved from this position to one of mutuality in the interpersonal interaction (Brendtro, Brokenleg, & Van Bockern, 2002; Brendtro, 2004), this early articulation reflects the position of the field at the time.

Thus we see how Child and Youth Care practice followed closely in the wake of developing knowledge in other helping fields. This is not to suggest a criticism of the field; rather, it is to note how the field, in spite of its fledgling development, evolved along with other fields. In this regard it paralleled the thinking of the times. As we shall see later, the field has moved from a position of following other fields to being on the leading edge of such developments.

From this initial position of "having and using a relationship," as if it were some simple tool in the bag of magical tricks the worker carried to the floor, the field moved on. The introduction of an intense focus on self, coupled with a phenomenological influence on how one experiences and how one creates that experiencing (Garfat, 2002), eventually led the field to consider that "being in relationship" is different than, and preferable to, "having a relationship." As Fewster (2004, p. 3) notes, "Being in relationship means that we have what it takes to remain open and responsive in conditions where most mortals—and professionals—quickly distance themselves, become 'objective' and look for the external 'fix.'"

What Does Relationship Mean?

Before we go any further with this discussion, take a few minutes to reflect on the following questions:

- What does the word *relationship* mean to you—not a *good relationship*, nor a *therapeutic relationship*, but just *relationship*?
- Now, find someone else and ask them the same question. Compare your two responses. How are they the same? How are they different?

Chances are, if you were to ask a dozen different people to answer the questions, all twelve would vary in some important manner. As Brendtro (1969) said, almost everybody agrees that "relationship" is important, yet there is little agreement on what this term means. This statement seems to be as true today as it was fifty years ago. As Beedell (1970) remarked, "relationship is a dangerous and curious word. It can be used to cover a multitude of interactions, shallow or deep, profitable to the individuals concerned or perhaps even damaging" (p. 85).

Moving forward in time (and staying within our field), we find that Maier, in 1987, had this to say: "There is neither 'a relationship' nor a state of a relationship. Relationship is actually a popular term for innumerable forms and degrees of mutually achieved processes of interactions, and these might utilize, simultaneously, affective, behavioral, and cognitive components" (p. v). And perhaps, in some ways, that is as good a definition as any, although there are certainly others. What we might notice in Maier's definition, however, is the use of the phrase "mutually achieved processes of interaction," because earlier definitions did not indulge the concept of mutuality. Relationship was seen as an end, not a process. In the writings of this time about what is meant by *relationship*, we see, then, a movement towards some kind of co-created experience or entity: relationship as mutually formed. Maier (1987) had this to say:

> The once held notion of forming a relationship as a prelude to work is being replaced by an awareness that relationships are formed by the interactive process of investing energy and struggling together from the onset of the encounter. Most important is the fact that relationships change with the process of interactions rather than interactions changing with the progress in relationships. (pp. v–vi)

And still the field continued to advance. In the mid 1990s, strongly influenced by systems thinking, the field emphasized a focus on "connectedness in relationship" and of further deepening the idea of mutuality, to the extent that people spoke of the co-creation of experience (Peterson, 1993) and connected experiencing (Garfat, 1998).

Today, perhaps one of the most common understandings of the meaning of relationship is "to be in a state of connectedness with other," for as Susan Leaf (1995) observed, "a 'relationship' means connection, on some level" (p. 16), and this common, everyday definition offers much food for thought—what does it mean, for example, to be "in a state of connectedness"?

- This is not a rhetorical question. Stop for a moment and ask yourself, "What does it mean to be in a state of connectedness?"

Without establishing a firm definition, which we will attempt later, I suspect that all readers have an almost instinctive way of understanding the idea of "being in a state of connectedness," for surely we all feel this sense of connection with those we love, the children and families we work with, and, yes, even the plumber, the bank clerk, or the landlord. Contemporary CYC practice, as indicated above, however, suggests that this state of connectedness can only arise when both parties are engaged in the relationship development process.

In the broad sense, to be in relationship is to be in a state of co-created connected experiencing with other. It is this being in a "state of co-created connected experiencing with other" that we must explore if we are to understand the meaning and actualization of relational practice. However, before we go there, it is perhaps important to explore a few other concepts that have been associated with relationship within our field—specifically, the notion of the "good" relationship and the "therapeutic" relationship, both of which are common, if misleading, expressions within our field, and both of which have had tremendous influence on practice.

What is a "Good Relationship"?

> *"It is easy for the uninitiated adult to misconstrue an initially cooperative attitude as the beginning of a good relationship."*
>
> – Brendtro, 1969, p. 62

Many, many times in my work with teams, I have heard people say that they have a "good relationship" with the young people with whom they work. Usually what is meant by this is either (a) the young person seems to like the staff, or (b) the young person does as the staff asks, or (c) there is a lack of tension in the relationship—it is easy and even relaxing. However, in our field a good relationship must have a different meaning, for surely the relationship we have (or should have) with young people and/or families is more complex than this simple "works for me, feels good" assessment. If we reach back, once again, to Beedell (1970), we find the following:

> We can recognize a good relationship between two people
> when they can be, to some extent, less defended with one
> another than is generally the case in their social interactions
> and when this leads to a situation in which there is some
> mutual recognition, implicit or explicit, of their actual or
> potential value and threat to one another. (p. 85)

Again, we see the early indicators of the possible evolution of the idea of mutuality, even, in this case, before Maier mentioned it. Although it was to be years before this notion of mutuality, as we have seen, became common in the field, we do notice this early indicator that a good relationship involved some kind of mutual value, even if only the potential of that value.

So, as we see, the field over 30 years ago was moving forward from the idea of simply having a relationship to that of having a good relationship with the young person—a good relationship was a radical departure from previous thinking that one simply needed, developed from the outside in, a "relationship," albeit a "relationship of influence" (Redl, 1959) with the young person.

While it seems commonplace today to think of the qualities of a relationship (e.g., those characteristics that would define it as good), at the time the field was discussing the idea that there are influencing characteristics to a relationship. This idea was, in and of itself, new and challenging, for it caused people to think about what was meant by the terms *good* or *effective*, or even *helpful*. And what were some of these characteristics of a good relationship?

- privacy that allows for undefendedness and a perception of self and other as separate but related (Beedell, 1970)
- approval and acceptance by other (Pringle, 1975)
- appreciation of and respect for the way in which the other person perceives self and the world in general (Burns, 1983)
- genuineness (Heslop, 1992)
- respect, honesty, availability/presence (Leaf, 1995)

Well, the list could go on, but the point is this: as even this limited list shows, our focus on the relationship was changing as the field developed. Child and Youth Care began to focus on the relationship between worker and child. Why? Because families were not much considered back then (Garfat, 2007b). The characteristics of the relationship began to develop greater significance as we began to recognize that the qualities of the relationship were central to the effectiveness of the helping process. Thus, our definition of a good relationship was constantly changing: it moved from one in which the young person did as asked, towards one that involved the young person liking the staff, and then further towards one that involved acceptance, genuineness, respect, honesty, and presence. In this list of characteristics we see the beginnings of what was to be called the "therapeutic relationship," a relationship in which the characteristics of both self and other were important. This evolution was sparked by the recognition, however slow it was to evolve, that a helping relationship is, in essence, a two-way process of relationship development.

The Therapeutic Relationship

After acknowledging that relationship was important, the field turned to concerns about the qualities of a good relationship. Following this stage, we began to focus on the elements of not just a good relationship but a therapeutic relationship, and then, only later, did we become concerned with "being in relationship" after moving from "having a relationship"—regardless of the characteristics.

As the field evolved, CYC practitioners, educators, and scholars attempted to define the importance and characteristics of a therapeutic relationship, one that was formed for the benefit of the young person in an attempt to facilitate the meeting of that young person's needs. As Masud Hoghughi (1988) observed, "'Therapeutic relationships' have been generally regarded by everyone as being crucial prerequisites of all treatment" (p. 37). Going further, Lahn Jones (2007) recently asserted that the theoretical basis for CYC is the creation and maintenance of the therapeutic relationship from within the life space of the client. In this statement we find a clear linkage between a therapeutic relationship and a "theoretical basis," which indicates how this idea has become a part of the foundational philosophy of our work.

Before going further, let us reflect for a moment on the comments and quotations that have led us to this point. While the foregoing has been divided into discrete sections, it is obvious that throughout the evolution of relationship work in our field, elements, or characteristics, of the relationship have been mentioned but have not been taken up immediately as the objects of ongoing writing and investigation. We see, for example, that mention has been made of mutuality, co-creation, the awareness of what the other brings to the relationship, and an awareness of how the other perceives the world. But upon introduction, these ideas were not pursued further by the field. Yet at some point, these emergent characteristics became more important, more the focus of our relationship work. In fact, as Maier said in 1987, "...the once held notion of forming a relationship as a prelude to work is being replaced by an awareness that relationships are formed by the interactive process of investing energy and struggling together from the onset of the encounter" (p. v).

From this evolving history, then, we have moved to a place where the field easily states "your job is to establish a therapeutic relationship with each child" (Cavalier, 2006, n.p.). The question of how one does so, however, still lingers.

However, like the good relationship, and the simple relationship before it, the therapeutic relationship remained undefined in the field, although one does find frequent reference to the term in the literature, written, it seems, as though everyone had a full understanding of the meaning. In reality, there was, and is, no common definition available.

Yet, throughout the years, something was evolving within the field; something that was, I suspect, hinted at by these attempts to define the relationship, relationship-based work, and the like. For parallel to these indications in the literature, a deepening awareness was also evolving of these elements:

- the presence and role of self (Kostouros & McLean, 2006; Ricks, 1989, 1993)
- an awareness of the experience of other (Fewster, 1990)
- an acknowledgement of the importance of context (Krueger & Stuart, 1999; VanderVen, 1991)
- the relevance of connection and engagement (Leaf, 1995; Maier, 1992)
- an evolution of the importance of boundaries in practice (Mann-Feder, 1999)
- an acceptance that reality is constructed by the individual (Garfat, 1998)
- an emphasis on being in relationship (Fewster, 1990)

So, what was that "something" that appears to have been evolving? And how is it the same or different from that which came before?

From recent writings (Fewster, 2001, 2004; Garfat, 2003a, 2003b; Krueger, 1998, 2004; Molepo, 2004; Smart, 2006; Smith, 2007), it would appear that the thing that was evolving, unbeknownst to all of us, was Relational Child and Youth Care practice. And it is to this we now turn in our attempt to understand what is meant by Relational Child and Youth Care.

CHARACTERISTICS OF RELATIONAL CHILD AND YOUTH CARE PRACTICE

"An effective relationship depends upon many things."

– Ernie Hilton, 2005

How or why Relational Child and Youth Care practice came to be is, essentially, irrelevant. At some point, someone, inspired by whatever muse, decided to coin the phrase to reflect the changing focus of the field, and thus we have, today, Relational Child and Youth Care practice—as witnessed, for example, in the journal of the same name. At this point, however, it is important to note how the word *relational* is frequently used.

It is not uncommon these days, when reading the literature of our field, to encounter the word *relational* in phrases such as "the relational dynamics," "relational values," "relational research," "attending to the relational," and even "a relational perspective." When we look closely at the writings, we discover that what is being referred to, in general, is a focus on aspects of the relationships one has with others. Probably the most common phrase we encounter is "a relational approach," which people use to refer to how they work with young people and/or families. While focusing on the "aspects of relationship" substantiates the claim that one is using a relationship-based approach, it is my contention that the terms *relational approach* or *relational practice* refer to something different, deeper, and more complex. While I accept that everything that occurs does so in the context of relationships—after all, we have long accepted that everything, and everyone, is connected in relationship to other people and things—just because one acknowledges involvement in relationships, however, does not make one's approach relational.

It is the goal of this section of this paper to try to explain just what a relational approach and Relational CYC practice might entail.

- To begin, think of a relationship you have with someone else.
- Now describe that relationship.

Relational Practice Focuses on the Relationship

Now, I would like you to consider two types of responses to this reflection. You might, for example, have answered in a manner similar to the following:

- She is the teacher and I am the student.
- She likes me.
- He is the one who has the power, and I have none.
- We are friends.
- She is my aunt.

Alternatively, you may have answered in a manner similar to the following:

- It is safe.

- It is a place where we can explore alternatives.
- It is intimate.
- It is scary.
- It is full, warm, accepting, loving, and so forth.

In the first case, you might notice that we are referring to the people or roles in the relationship, and in the second case we are referring to characteristics of the relationship.

Relational practice involves a focus on the relationship, while recognizing and respecting the characteristics of the individuals involved in that relationship. Relational work, in contrast, attends to the relationship itself.

At first glance this may seem like a simple difference, but the implications are profound. When I say, for example, that a relationship is safe, I am referring to how we each, self and other, experience ourselves in the context of this relationship: we both "feel safe," psychologically, emotionally, physically, and spiritually. I am referring, though, to the fact that this relationship is a place where I feel secure and able to risk without fear.

In this example (for safety is only an example), my work—my job, if you like—is to be in this relationship in a manner that contributes to the experience of safety for both of us.

There is a question of balance here: a balance between my own experiencing and that of the other; a balance between my actions and those of the other.

Relational Practice Focuses on Balance

I want to offer up a metaphor for consideration that may seem somewhat unusual, and in doing so I would ask the reader to remember that a metaphor is simply a vehicle to convey meaning and understanding.

> A seesaw (teeter-totter) is a long board balanced over a raised bar in the middle. One person sits on each end, and typically they pump their feet up and down at ground level so that as one end goes up the other goes down.
>
> Remember how, as a child, you sometimes played on what we call a seesaw. Sometimes, as you played, one of you would move closer to or away from the centre. As you did so, the other person continued to move up and down. If you

moved in too quickly, however, the person on the other end might crash suddenly to the ground. If you moved away from the centre, the other person would rise more quickly into the air.

Probably, sometimes, you played with balance. You might have tried to get the seesaw to balance equally in the middle, with both you and the other suspended in the air, with neither of you having your feet on the ground. Or you might have balanced the board so that one of you was higher in the air than the other. To obtain this balance you were required to pay attention to one another, moving in and out, closer together or farther apart as, together, you worked towards achieving balance; at the same time you were attentive to your safety—not moving too quickly lest the other be surprised and fall off, possibly injuring herself (or you).

And perhaps you remember how, as a child playing on the seesaw, you would move slowly closer to the other and she, wanting to maintain the balance, would move a little closer towards the centre as well. But sometimes, if one of you moved closer too quickly, the other would become anxious or frightened and move suddenly forward or back, causing you to have to quickly adjust yourself to avoid falling to the ground.

And sometimes, while playing on the seesaw, the two of you would agree to change the characteristics of the balance between you, and one might move a little forward, upsetting the balance by agreement, and, once that person was settled in the new position, the other would slowly adjust herself to find that place of agreed-upon balance between you, arriving by mutual agreement at a new, closer point of balance in your relationship.

In some respects, relational practice is like a seesaw. Sometimes as a relationship develops, for example, one or the other moves too quickly towards the other (for example, seeking greater intimacy) before the other is ready, and the other, startled, moves back in reaction, creating greater distance in the relationship.

We attend to the balance in the relationship between self and other; we move in and out, adjusting as necessary to maintain this balance. We are careful not to surprise or upset the other, except as we might do intentionally. When we look at the possible characteristics of the relationship, we realize there are many areas in which we may wish to work towards balance: safety, intimacy, caring, connectedness, and so on. It is almost as if relational practice is a carefully orchestrated chorus of seesaws, connected by the balancing of "selves in relationship."

- But like I said, this is just a metaphor. Your job is to translate it. Do that now.

Relational Practice Recognizes that the Relationship is Co-created

As early as 1988, Raymond Peterson introduced the idea of co-created experiencing, referring to the idea that all of our experiences with young people are the result of a process of mutual construction. If something is co-created, then it exists between us, and it exists only because of the contributions of both of us. It is "ours": not your relationship with me, or mine with you, but "our" relationship—created by and belonging to the two of us. This relationship is not a one way street, a connectedness that is created by only one of the parties to the relationship. Just as it takes two to tango, it also takes two (or more) to form a relationship—for while a relationship may always exist, even if it is a relationship of distance and fear, both parties participate in creating it.

This notion of the co-created or co-constructed relationship between self and other is a radical departure from earlier notions expressed in the literature that it was the worker who created a relationship with the young person and then used that relationship to manipulate the young person towards pre-determined appropriate actions. Indeed, as Fletcher (1998) has said, relational practice differs from the dominant discourse in which emphasizing connection has been characterized as a weakness, probably due to the absence of the exercise of "power over" the other. For if a relationship is co-created, then one cannot hope to manipulate the other; one can only influence the other through how one is, oneself, in the relationship. As Glasser (1984) has said, we cannot change anyone; we can only change how we are with a person, grounded in the belief that if we are different in relationship with the other, that person, in turn, will be different with us. This emphasizes the mutuality of process. The only person over whom I have control in a relationship is me.

However, we come back to the issue of balance, and the type of balance we wish to encourage in the in-between. In some cases we may participate in a relationship that is out of balance, one in which, for example, one person holds all the power and the other feels insignificant. Imagine, again, the seesaw, with one person solidly grounded, and the other held precariously high in the air. This is not the kind of co-created relationship we desire if we seek to be truly therapeutic. We desire a relationship in which both parties can achieve an agreed balance on many important characteristics and within which both persons recognize their equality of influence.

Relational Practice Focuses on "Us"

> "How are we doing?" I ask after a particularly stressful discussion with a woman with whom I have been working for a few days now.
>
> "We're fine," she responds with curiosity in her voice.
>
> "And how is our relationship doing?" I ask.
>
> "Fine," she laughs. "How do you think it is doing?"
>
> I laugh with her for a moment, reflecting. "It feels more open than before. I know I feel more relaxed in it. It feels a little like a safe place; a bit more like us, rather than just you and me."
>
> "Me too," she responds. "I can feel it changing. I didn't think of this before."
>
> We have had this conversation many times before, even in our short two days.

Fletcher (1998) said that it is the emphasis on connectedness, rather than individuation, that distinguishes relational theory—the foundation of relational practice. There is, therefore, an important focus on the manner in which individuals are connected, and their experience of connectedness, in relationship.

In relational practice we are constantly monitoring the in-between of our connectedness. As a part of monitoring the co-created relationship, we check-in with self and we check-in with the other, discuss our relationship and keep it present in our focus, monitoring the shifts and changes that occur as we move through our experiences together. The question "how are we doing?" invites us both to attend to what Varda Mann-Feder (1999) identifies as the "us," the jointly created experience of self and other in connection, which is an important element in development. In doing so, we are attending to the relational, noticing not just that we are connected, but how we are connected.

By constantly monitoring the connection with the other, we are paying attention to how each of us is making sense of this relational experience. If, after such an exchange, we find the relationship between us to be less than before, or if we find we are having different experiences of it, we focus on what it is we need to do to restore or enhance the experience of relationship each of us is having and to achieve balance.

Relational Practice Focuses on Meaning-Making by Self and Other

> "When you yelled at me, I thought it meant you did not like me any more," he said, asking, I knew, if I still liked him after our argument.
>
> "So," I wondered out loud, "is our relationship feeling unsafe for you? Do you feel threatened in it?"
>
> "No. But I feel worried."
>
> "Do you want to know what I was thinking when I yelled at you? Or would you like to know how I feel in our relationship?"
>
> Notice that the question is about how I feel *in* our relationship, not how I feel *about* it.

Each of us has to make sense of that which we experience, and the meaning that we make of an experience may be different than the meaning made by the other. The meaning that we make structures our experience of self and other (Garfat, 2001) and, ultimately, the relationship between us.

When a young person and a CYC worker encounter one another, both go through a process of making meaning of that encounter. When we are engaging with the other, we wonder about what sense that other is making of what we say and do, just as we wonder about the meaning we, ourselves, are making. It is too easy to assume that we know what something means to the other, and to make such an assumption creates the pathway to misunderstanding. We always, therefore, check-in with the other to help us understand their experience, and in doing so we open the pathway for wondering what impact this is having on "our" relationship.

Here is a simple exercise for you.

Walk up to someone and do something. It does not have to be a complicated something—say hello, reach out and touch them, bump into them, walk around them, don't look at them. Once you have done this, sit down together and discuss what your action meant to each of you.

Notice the similarities and differences in how you made sense of what you did.

In this simple exercise, we find that the essence of meaning-making in relational work—and its importance for every experience of the other, no matter how small—holds meaning. Relational practice involves focussing on how the participants are making meaning of their experiences together and how that meaning-making influences the relationship.

Relational Practice Focuses on Self in Relationship

How I am who I am, and how you are who you are—as these influence the creation of the in-between between us—is a focus of relational practice. This is true for two reasons: who we are impacts how we are together, and how we are together affects how we are who we are.

The in-between between us is the place where we develop, and discover, who we are. Without relationships we have no way to know who we are. As Frances Ricks (2001) said, "without self, there is no other" (n.p.). We evolve and grow in the context of these relationships: the in-between is the place of our becoming. Self evolves in the context of the relationship (Fewster, 2001), and thus relational practice attends to the self—of self and other.

When I ask the question "how are you?" with an emphasis on the verb *are*, I am asking about your self; I am asking about your being. And that can only be contextualized by your experiencing of yourself in this moment of being with me, in our relational place. For when you are with me, that is the only experience of self that is available to you at that moment, regardless of what else, or other, or experience might be influencing your experience of self beyond this moment of being in the in-between. This is why we can feel safe when we are with one person, even though all the other events in our lives may be contributing to our feeling otherwise.

> "How are you doing?" I asked Caroline, who was, I knew, going through a grieving process.
>
> "I'm okay," she replies.

> "I thought you might be sad or angry," I probe.
>
> "Well, I am. I miss my mother."
>
> "So, if you are missing your mother, how can you say you are 'okay'?"
>
> "I mean, right now, I feel okay."
>
> "So, I am wondering, can you let the sadness come in here for the moment?"

By inviting the other to bring other experiences of self into our relational moments, we create, all things being well, a place of safety and security for experiencing things that might otherwise be overwhelming. In this context we find ways in which to deal with some of these other experiences. In a safe place, all experiences are possible.

In this context of the in-between, we also have the opportunity to notice the evolution of our own self. As the other, for example, takes risks with us, we learn about how we deal with risk-taking by the other. And as we, in our quest to be helpful, take risks with the other, our own self evolves; both of us growing safely in the context of the in-between. And as we co-create this experience between us, we come to know who we are. For, as Fewster (2001) noted, "only through the process of co-creating relationships can we come to know our Selves" (n.p.).

RELATIONAL CHILD AND YOUTH CARE PRACTICE

So far we have discussed some of the characteristics of relational practice. But what does it mean to talk about the specific approach that is of interest to us: Relational Child and Youth Care practice. It means, in essence, to focus on the relational while paying attention to the characteristics of effective CYC practice. While there is no absolute agreement about the characteristics of a Child and Youth Care approach, there seem to be some common themes in the literature that we can assume represent contemporary practice. Krueger (1991), in writing about central themes in practice, has identified some of these characteristics, and elsewhere I (Garfat, 2004) have identified others. While these two lists do not, of course, fully define a CYC approach, together they do represent a majority of the themes of practice identified in both the literature and practice. The following list, which combines these two sources, yet abbreviates them for the purpose of this discussion, identifies some of these characteristics:

- doing with
- engagement and connection
- flexibility/individuality of approach
- interventions focused on the present
- attention to meaning-making
- being there/in relationship
- coming from your centre
- meeting them where they are at
- interacting together
- discovering and using self

It is not my intention to discuss all the characteristics of a Child and Youth Care approach as they relate to relational practice (that has been done elsewhere; see, for example, Garfat & McElwee, 2006); rather, I wish to indicate, using some of these characteristics, how Relational Child and Youth Care practice might look.

First, however, the reader might have noticed the compatibility between many of the characteristics listed above (and others that one might find in the field) and relational practice as it has been discussed so far in this chapter. We see, for example, an emphasis on connection, engagement, being with the other in interaction, a focus on the immediate, on what is occurring for the other in the context of the moment, and the importance of interaction with an emphasis on the self of the individual. So, at first glance it appears obvious that relational practice is a fit with a CYC approach.

Imagine, if you will, the following scenario:

> I step into the room where I know Sharon is hiding herself
> away from a situation that has just occurred. She has been
> with us in this program for a while, now, and we have spent
> many moments together as a part of her experience here. It
> would be inaccurate, however, to say that we have a good
> relationship (remember the previous discussion) because
> so far our relationship, in my experience, has been one of
> distance, uncertainty, and insecurity. She lives in the world
> as an angry 15 year old, abused by men in her family, and
> leery, therefore, of contact with other men. Our relationship

is hesitant, uncertain, and tentative in spite of the time we have spent together.

"Sharon?" I inquire as I step into the room. The inquiry is a question that asks, essentially, if she is willing (able) to engage. It is not the demand for engagement that a phrase such as "we need to talk" might convey. It offers her, I hope, some little feeling of power in the moment. I know that if we are to truly engage she must also make that commitment.

"What do you want?" she demands, throwing up, for me, a wall of defensiveness.

"I am wondering, how you're doing? I know you just had an argument with the other staff." The emphasis is on her, on how she is doing in the moment, not on what she might have done. I want to connect with who, and how, she is. The question addresses self, not behaviour. Because the truth is I do not, at this moment, care about her behaviour. And at the same time, I am wondering "how am I?" and "what am I doing to create this experience of her, of us. How am I contributing to the in-between?" Because from the moment of first contact, at the beginning and each and every time after that, everything we do contributes to the joint construction of our experiencing.

"Ya. So what!" It is a statement more than a question, but I choose to think otherwise. I see the mistake in my approach. By going beyond the "wondering how you are doing," I shifted the focus to what she did rather than how she is doing. This is, I think, probably an approach with which she thinks she is familiar: blaming, demanding, accusatory. I wonder why I went there and how it is affecting the in-between beyond my immediate noticing that it has contributed to distance in our relationship.
"So, I wanted to know, how *are* you?" I know I have to connect with her for anything meaningful to happen here. We have to move away from the behaviour and into her experiencing of self in this moment. If we do not engage, nothing meaningful will happen.

Sharon looks at me like I was a plate of the wrong food served at the wrong time. "Why are you always asking me that?" There is an opening here, I think, a possibility to move closer in connection, to develop the in-between between us. I notice how I am interpreting her statement and non-verbal actions and mark it for my own reference.

"Because I am always wondering how you are doing whenever we meet," I respond, as clearly as I can. "And I think that if I am going to be helpful at all, we need to be connected while we talk. So I think that by asking how you are, we might connect a little closer than if I start right away to ask about your behaviour, which is really of less concern to me right now than how you are doing."

I want Sharon to know that caring and connection are the foundation of our relationship, and that I am interested in beginning with a focus on the present, the immediate, the *now* of our interaction. I also want to let her know how I interpret my behaviour, what it means to me in this moment of encounter so as to challenge any other meaning she might be attributing to it. But I feel her pull back a little, the distance in our relatedness expanding rather than shrinking. I feel less connected than I did just a second ago, and I remember her experiences with the men in her family. I am thinking that perhaps it is because of the meaning she makes of the word *closer*, which may imply something different than what I intended. In response, I move myself a little further away from her physically, striving for balance, and I make sure I am not blocking her exit should she decide she needs to leave this encounter. I sense her relax; there is a little less tension in the in-between. I feel the tension leave me, without having realized it was present. But I want us to move closer. What's that about, I wonder?

"When I was your age, I used to get into trouble a lot," I say, hoping that a little disclosure, a sense of my vulnerability in this relationship, may invite her to a place she experiences as more equally balanced in terms of vulnerability. For our work, as Fewster (2001) has said, involves stepping into the unknown, risking self in the service of other. "It wasn't because I was wanting to," I continue. "I think it was because I was always thinking about other stuff at the time."

I am not really caring if Sharon will understand what I just said, but I am hoping that she will experience my openness, my fragility, for this is an area I don't talk about a lot, and so in raising it here I feel exposed. Young people often pick up on what we are feeling, even though we might not express it or may even try to hide it (Fox, 1995). Just ask any Child and Youth Care worker who has tried to pretend she is having a good day when she is not. I am also hoping that if Sharon experiences my dropped boundaries of protectiveness she will sense that I am willing to risk in this relationship. And maybe that will encourage her to move towards a balance herself.

"I just want to go home," she blurts out.

My heart breaks a little and I tumble willingly into the in-between through the passageway she has opened with her pain. I cannot hear this and stand safely distant. This is the cry of a lost, disconnected child, wanting comfort. I have no choice if I believe in Relational Child and Youth Care practice but to allow my self, with all my fear and hesitation, to step clearly into the in-between, unadorned (Fewster, 2001). For it is only there in the in-between, unhampered by all my preconceptions, intentions, and mandates, that I might encounter the real child who is here. In some senses I must let go of the self I protect in my everyday encounters and expose my self to the experience of the other to truly connect in relationship (Garfat, 2007). It is only, I believe, when I let go of my "intention to be helpful" that we can, together, create a healthy and helpful experience of the in-between. Perhaps only in letting go of my drive to engage can we connect effectively.

All my previous Child and Youth Care training falls to the side as I open myself to encounter this child, this person, in all her pain and uniqueness. I know in that moment that if I am committed to Relational Child and Youth Care practice I must, in spite of my fear of the unknown, give my self to this moment of real "self-to-self" encounter. And then, hopefully, we might "make it together" (Steckley, 2006) and find our way back to wherever we are going.

Well, I could go on, but hopefully that is enough. Attending to the in-between between us, the relational, is different than attending to the content, or even the process, of relationship development. It involves attending to the experience of self and other in connectedness. It involves giving one's self to the experience of encounter and, in that encounter, finding connectedness.

Interestingly, I feel vulnerable here, in this writing, exposing myself and what I believe and do in the hope that it will draw the reader closer, encourage an openness. I sense how I have, with that last writing, moved to a more exposed place with the reader than I demonstrated when I opened this writing with the academic, objective statement "Relational CYC practice exists in the in-between," sounding as though I were sure of myself and what I was to say. I experience my self as anxiously available now, and that is, perhaps, the most I can bring, at this moment, to our fledgling relationship.

Possibly as you, the reader, moved through this chapter (I say, hoping you actually reached this point), you may have noticed my early struggles around "how to be" and "how to be with you" to the point of, finally, becoming "I" present. In some ways, this struggle parallels that of Relational Child and Youth Care practice: the struggle with how to be; the opening of self; the taking of risks; the movement towards the personal *I* and arriving, finally, at the place where both self and other know there is only what is in the in-between. Whatever this chapter turns out to be, it will be that because of the relationship between writer and reader, between you and I. Together we have created the experience you are having of this writing. Not me, not you, but us. It is, in essence, our writing, for you have given to it the meaning you have, as have I, and together we have co-created whatever it now is. We have co-constructed this reality.

Gannon (2003) has said that a relational approach offers "a prototype for special and personal relationships the youngster will establish and live through with other people in the future" (p. 7). Fewster (1991), talking about the importance of relationships, has said that in the context of relationships, young people "come to experience their separateness, their uniqueness and, ultimately, their relatedness" (p. 1). In these two statements, written by authors separated by half the globe, we find the essence of the importance of attending to the relational, the in-between between us. For if we find our Selves, and in doing so learn a way of being in the world through relationship, surely it is our job, as effective CYC workers, to attend to the relational.

Relational CYC practice offers us this: the opportunity to be with others as they experience and re-create their lives and as we re-create our own. Each of us, as participants in the creation of the in-between between us, finds ourselves challenged, stimulated, and changed. If it is true, as Fewster (1991, 2001) and others have observed, that we are created and re-created in the context of our relationships, then the gift of Relational CYC practice is the gift of constant growth for self and other. And for that we may be grateful. As Fewster (2005) states, "For me, relational child and youth care practice …is not only a very different perspective; it is a different pathway, across very different terrain, in search of a very different destination" (p. 4).

Let me end, then, with a thought (a definition?) that comes to mind at this point:

> Relational Child and Youth Care practice is a form of helping that, while being true to the characteristics of contemporary Child and Youth Care practice, attends to the co-constructed in-between of self and other.

REFERENCES

Beedell, C. (1970). *Residential life with children.* London: Routledge & Kegan Paul.

Brendtro, L. (1969). Establishing relationship beachheads. In A. Trieschman, J. K. Whittaker, & L. K. Brendtro (Eds.), *The other 23 hours: Child-care work with emotionally disturbed children in a therapeutic milieu* (pp. 54–56). New York: Aldine.

Brendtro L. (2004). *From coercive to strength-based intervention: Responding to the needs of children in pain.* Retrieved from http://www.cyc-net.org/features/ ft-strenghtbased.html.

Brendtro, L., Brokenleg, M., & Van Bockern, S. (2002). *Reclaiming youth at risk: Our hope for the future* (Rev. ed.). Bloomington, IL: National Educational Service.

Burmeister, E. (1960). *The professional houseparent.* New York: Columbia University Press.

Burns, M. (1983). Rapport and relationships. *Journal of Child Care, 2*(2), 47–57.

Cavaliere, G. (2006). Welcome to the second day. *CYC-OnLine, 90.* Retrieved from http:// www.cyc-net.org/cyc-online/cycol-0607-cavaliere.html

Charles, G., & Garfat, T. (in press). A history of child and youth care. In P. Share & K. Lavor (Eds.), Social Care. Dublin, Ireland.

Fewster, G. (1990). *Being in child care: A journey into self.* New York: Haworth.

Fewster, G. (1991). The paradoxical journey: Some thoughts on relating to children. *Journal of Child and Youth Care, 6*(4), 85–92.

Fewster, G. (1999). Editorial: A new light in old darkness. *Journal of Child and Youth Care, 13*(4), iii–v.

Fewster, G. (2001). Going there from being here. *CYC-OnLine, 25.* Retrieved from http:// www.cyc-net.org/cyc-online/cycol-0201-fewster.html

Fewster, G. (2004). Editorial. *Relational Child and Youth Care Practice, 17*(3), 3–5.

Fewster. G. (2005). I don't like kids. *Relational Child and Youth Care Practice, 18*(3), 3–5.

Fletcher, J. (1998). Relational practice: A feminist reconstruction of work. *Journal of Management Inquiry, 7,* 163–186.

Fulcher, L. (2004). Programmes and praxis: A Review of taken-for-granted knowledge. *Scottish Journal of Residential Child Care, 3*(2), 34–44.

Gannon, B. (2001). Engagement: Making it happen. *CYC-OnLine*, 33. Retrieved from http://www.cyc-net.org/cyc-online/cycol-1001-engaging.html

Gannon, B. (2003). The improbable relationship. *Relational Child and Youth Care Practice, 16*(3), 6–9.

Garfat, T. (1998). The effective child and youth care intervention: A phenomenological inquiry. *Journal of Child and Youth Care, 12*(1&2), 5–178.

Garfat, T. (2001). New beginnings. *Irish Journal of Applied Social Studies, 2*(3), 31–35.

Garfat, T. (2002). 'But that's not what I meant': Meaning-making in foster care. *Irish Journal of Applied Social Studies, 3*(1), 113–124.

Garfat, T. (2003a). Committed to the relational. *Relational Child and Youth Care Practice, 16*(3), 3–5.

Garfat, T. (2003b). The relational male: Reflections on the role of men in child and youth care practice. In N. McElwee & A. Jackson (Eds.), *Where have all the good men gone?* (pp. 14–19). Athlone, Ireland: Centre for Child and Youth Care Learning.

Garfat, T. (2004). Meaning making and intervention in child and youth care practice. *Scottish Journal of Residential Child Care, 3*(1), 9–16.

Garfat, T. (2007a). My shelled self. *Relational Child and Youth Care Practice, 20*(3), 29–31.

Garfat, T. (2007b). Who are we working with: A short history of child and youth care involvement with families. *CYC-OnLine*, 103. Retrieved from http://www.cyc-net.org/cyc-online/cycol-0708-garfat.html

Garfat, T., & McElwee, N. (2006). *Developing effective interventions with families* (2nd ed.). Cape Town, South Africa: Pretext Publishing.

Glasser, W. (1984). *Control theory.* New York: Harper and Row.

Guttman, E. (1991). Immediacy in residential child and youth care work: The fusion of experience, self-consciousness, and action. In J. Beker & Z. Eisikovits (Eds.), *Knowledge utilization in residential child and youth care practice* (pp. 65–84). Washington, DC: Child Welfare League of America.

Heslop, A. (1992). Qualities of the effective counsellor. *The Child Care Worker, 10*(6), 10–11.

Hoghughi, M. (1988). *Treating problem children: Issues, methods and practice.* London: Sage Publications.

Jones, L. (2007). Articulating a child and youth care approach to family work. *CYC-OnLine*, 104. Retrieved from http://www.cyc-net.org/cyc-online/cycol-0709-jones.html

Kostouros, P., & McLean, S. (2006). The importance of self care. *CYC-OnLine*, 89. Retrieved from http://www.cyc-net.org/cyc-online/cycol-0606-mclean.html

Krueger, M. (1991). Coming from your center, being there, teaming up, meeting them where they're at, interacting together, counseling on the go, creating circles of care, discovering and using self, and caring for one another: Central themes in professional child and youth care. *Journal of Child and Youth Care, 5*(1), 77–87.

Krueger, M. (1994). Rhythm and presence: Connecting with children on the edge. *Journal of Emotional and Behavioral Problems, 3*(1), 49–51.

Krueger, M. (1998). *Interactive youth work practice.* Washington, DC: Child Welfare League of America.

Krueger, M. (2004). Interactive youth and family work. In T. Garfat (Ed.), *A child and youth care approach to working with families* (pp. 55–65). New York: Haworth.

Krueger, M., & Stuart, C. (1999). Context and competence in work with children and youth. *Child & Youth Care Forum, 28*(3), 200–201.

Leaf, S. (1995). The journey from control to connection. *Journal of Child and Youth Care, 10*(1), 15–21.

Maier, H. (1987). Editorial. *Journal of Child Care, 3*(3), v–vi.

Maier, H. (1992). Rhythmicity: A powerful force for experiencing unity and personal connections. *Journal of Child and Youth Care Work, 8,* 7–13.

Mann-Feder, V. R. (1999). You/me/us: Thoughts on boundary management in child and youth care. *Journal of Child and Youth Care, 13*(2), 93–98.

Molepo, L. (2004). Your pain or mine? *Relational Child and Youth Care Practice, 17*(2), 16–18.

Peterson, R. (1988). The collaborative metaphor technique. *Journal of Child Care, 3*(4), 11–28.

Peterson, R. W. (1993). Exploring the application of systematic thinking in child and youth care practice: A shift in paradigm. *Journal of Child and Youth Care, 8*(2), 35–54.

Pringle, M. K. (1975). *The needs of children.* London: Hutchinson & Co.

Redl, F. (1959). Strategy and technique of the life-space interview. *American Journal of Orthopsychiatry, 29,* 1–18.

Ricks, F. (1989). Self-awareness model for training and application in child and youth care. *Journal of Child and Youth Care, 4*(1) 33–41.

Ricks, F. (1993). Therapeutic education: Personal growth experiences for child and youth care workers. *Journal of Child and Youth Care, 8*(3), 17–33.

Ricks, F. (2001). Without the self there is no other. *CYC-On-Line, 27.* Retrieved from http://www.cyc-net.org/cyc-online/cyco1-0401-ricks.html

Smart, M. (2006). The Carberry project. *CYC-OnLine, 87.* Retrieved from http://www.cyc-net.org/cyc-online/cycol-0406-carberry.html

Smith, M. (2007). Letting go in love. *CYC-OnLine, 99.* Retrieved from http://www.cyc-net.org/cyc-online/cycol-0407-smith.html

Rogers, C. R. (1961). Some hypotheses regarding the facilitation of personal growth. In C. Rogers (Ed.), *On becoming a Person: A Therapist's view of psychotherapy* (pp. 31–57). London: Constable and Company Ltd.

VanderVen, K. (1991). How is child and youth care unique—and different—from other fields? *Journal of Child and Youth Care Work, 5*(1), 15–16.

Watzlawick, P. (1990). *Munchhausen's pigtail: Or psychotherapy and reality.* New York: W. W. Norton.

CHAPTER 2

Relational-Centred Planning

A Turn Toward Creative Potential and Possibilities

Gerard Bellefeuille, PhD, and Donna Jamieson, MEd

ABSTRACT

Our inquiry into relational-centred planning is intended to offer Child and Youth Care practitioners the opportunity to reflect on this important aspect of practice. In the first part of the chapter, we discuss the premises and requisite capabilities underpinning relational practice. Second, we present the view that reality is constructed by each individual based on his or her life experiences and use of theoretical perspectives. Third, we describe relational-centred planning as a co-constructed process of thinking and doing. Finally, we conclude by noting that implied in each aspect of this discussion is the caveat, "think about this."

INTRODUCTION

> *"Relational practice should be more about asking*
> *questions than finding answers."*

—Gerard Bellefeuille

The emphasis on the relational is one of the most visible and defining leitmotif[1] of Child and Youth Care (CYC) practice. CYC scholars, educators, and practitioners consistently acknowledge the relational core of professional practice in child and youth care (Fewster, 1990; Garfat, 2003; Krueger, 1991, 2004; Maier, 1991, 1994; Ricks & Charlesworth, 2003; VanderVen, 1999). In this chapter we explore the complexity of assessment and planning from a "relational-centred" perspective. Assessment and planning involve an interactive process of determining and assigning value and meaning to what is known about the lives of those we serve while, simultaneously, formulating and determining the methods by which something is done to improve their circumstances. In CYC practice, life-space (known also as therapeutic milieu) interventions are selected to generate favoured results, outcomes, or goals, whatever one chooses to call them. They are intentional and purposeful, and are based on values that are considered important and useful for enhancing the growth and development of children, youth, and families.

When considering assessment and planning in any context, let alone a relational context, some practitioners take a dim view of case-planning approaches, systems, models, or frameworks that prescribe explicit methods of thinking and doing. If this is true for you, note that all frameworks have both benefits and limitations with regard to planning. In the benefits column, frameworks can achieve the following:

- guide thinking and provide a focus for inquiry and reflection
- provide an overview of the issue or problem, including different aspects or parts under consideration
- provide categories to organize information
- establish a shared understanding amongst people working with a particular approach, including those we serve
- make planning more deliberate and intentional

---

1   A *leitmotif* is a recurring musical theme, within a larger piece of music, associated with a particular person, place, or idea. The word is also used, by extension, to mean any sort of recurring theme, whether in music, literature, politics, or elsewhere.

Standing on the Precipice

In order to be intentionally relational in planning, those involved require a framework, or way of thinking, about critical aspects of planning and how each aspect works, or unfolds, in relation to the others. Different aspects of planning serve to identify and define the focus of inquiry and change (i.e., basic premises, behaviour-change frameworks, and process models). They can then be used to organize the essence or fundamental nature of the conversations with children, youth, and families, and our thinking about and planning of what to do within each critical aspect of the planning process. Ultimately, our frames of reference affect how we do what we do.

The benefits of interpretive frameworks, like those identified above, diminish when frameworks are applied in a reductive or simplistic manner that addresses the components but which causes the CYC worker to lose sight of the whole. A framework for assessment also loses its efficacy if it is poorly defined and enables disparate or inconsistent application because it can be interpreted in a variety of ways; on the other hand, if a framework is brought to bear in a prescriptive manner, such that the practitioner believes that "this is how it must be done," and no flexibility in application is permitted, this will minimize the usefulness of an otherwise productive model. Finally, the mechanical and unthinking application of a framework cannot stand in for competence; the step-by-step deployment of a set program of activities does not ensure that the job is done well or thoughtfully, nor does it necessarily serve those the CYC worker seeks to assist.

In seeking to understand the lives and circumstances of children, youth, and families, the use of a singular and narrowly focused assessment and planning frameworks can fragment, reduce, and isolate parts such that the integrity of the whole is lost. However, a framework's bare and essential bones can be useful for suggesting ways to see the essence of what is needed and wanted. *Assessment and planning frameworks should not be assumed to represent all there is to know and understand about aspects of a person's life, nor do they dictate what steps to follow or what formulations will be required.* They are simply tools to work with, or not, depending on one's practice philosophy.

Our inquiry into relational-centred planning is intended to prompt thinking and offer a focus for reflection. Implied in each aspect of the discussion is this caveat: *Think about this.* We discuss the premises and requisite capabilities underpinning relational practice, present the view that reality is constructed by each individual based on his or her life experiences and use of theoretical perspectives, and describe relational-centred planning as a co-constructed process of thinking and doing. Our intention is to promote a discussion about how best to foster interactive participation, learning, staying informed about options, and the co-creation of life changes within the relational-centred planning process.

RELATIONAL-CENTRED PRACTICE

Relational-centred practice is a dynamic, rich, flexible, and continually evolving process of co-constructed inquiry. In this type of inquiry, meaning emerges within the "space between" the individual, family, or community (see Garfat, 2008). This practice model is complex and demands a high degree of ingenuity, creativity, and openness on the part of the CYC worker with respect to others. It requires "being with" and "being in the moment" with others and provides a way of understanding and listening to others that reassures them of their special place in the world.

Relational pedagogy[2] is based on the premise that human growth occurs through authentic, mutually empathetic relationships, and it emphasizes the roles of connection, interdependence, and collectivity (Fletcher, 1998; Jordan et al., 1991; Miller, 1986; Nodding, 2002). At the core of relational-centred practice is the belief that all psychological growth occurs in relationships because it identifies the need for relationships as requisite to growth and adaptation. When we operate from a relational stance, the focus is not on "what we do" (i.e., methods of practice) but, rather, on "who we are" as practitioners.

UNDERLYING PREMISES OF RELATIONAL-CENTRED PLANNING

There are several important premises that underlie the practice of relational-centred planning. These include a non-individualistic construal of selfhood, the necessity of being in the moment, the view that relational-centred practice is inherently a creative process, a belief in the resourcefulness of people, a dynamic view of diversity that extends beyond issues of

---

2   Although pedagogy is sometimes considered a nebulous concept, it is essentially the combination of knowledge and skills required to provide effective teaching. The relational pedagogy approach identifies and values relationships as the foundation of good practice.

difference, critical consciousness of social justice issues, and a conviction that relationally centred practice is a personally transforming endeavour.

Premise # 1: A Non-Individualistic Construal of Selfhood

Relational-centred planning builds upon a relatively new idea: a non-individualistic construal of selfhood. This view represents the flip side of the more traditional narrative of self in contemporary Western culture, which is characterized as the autonomous, separate, ego based individual (Gergen, 1999; Markus & Kitayama, 1991; McGoldrick & Carter, 1999; Weingarten, 1994). Since the early eighties, this relational view of self has emerged within developmental literature. For example, the work of Daniel Stern (1985, 2004), which looks at developmental research and issues from a psychoanalytic perspective, suggests that infants differentiate themselves almost from birth, so that our main task as infants, therefore, is to connect. Stern describes the infant as coming into the world as having already achieved self/other differentiation. This relational view of development as one that shifts from symbiosis to separation reverberates throughout contemporary literature on human growth and development (Dunn, 1993; Stern, 2002). In the field of Child and Youth Care, most of us would agree that the children, youth, and adults who present with the most serious behavioural and emotional issues are those that have never achieved secure attachment and who, as a result, do not have healthy relational skills. From a relational centred perspective, attachment and connection are as important, and perhaps more important, than autonomy to success as a functional human being.

The narrative of the autonomous self is also called into question by social constructivists, who take the position that identity is socially constructed and not located within the mind (Backhurst & Sypnowich, 1995; Gergen, 1994). As Anderson and Goolishian (1992, p. 28) posit, "we live in and through the narrative identities that we develop in conversation with one another." In other words, self-conception occurs within the discourse that occurs between people and is not something that exists, from inception, inside an individual.

According to the non-individualistic narrative of self, knowledge is inherently relational. It is constructed through relationships that are, themselves, embedded in a cultural, socioeconomic, and sociopolitical context (Gergen, 1999). According to Archbishop Desmond Tutu, this non-individualistic view of self can be traced to the theology of *ubuntu*, an African concept of "humanity towards others" (Battle, 1997). *Ubuntu* has generally been described as a world-view enshrined in the Zulu maxim *umuntu ngumuntu ngabantu*—that is, "a person is a person through other persons" (Shutte, 1993, p. 46). This premise combines with the understanding that it's impossible to isolate persons from community (Mokgoro, 1998). Tutu explains *ubuntu* this way:

> A self-sufficient human being is subhuman. I have gifts that you do not have, so consequently, I am unique—you have gifts that I do not have, so you are unique. God has made us so that we will need each other. We are made for a delicate network of interdependence. (Battle, 1997, p. 35)

In a recent interview about the meaning of "self" (McLeod, 2006), Buddhist monk, author, and teacher Thich Nhat Hanh talked about the illusion of the isolated individual. In his view, "true self is non-self." This formulation is based on the teaching that there is no separation between self and other and that everything is connected. Thich Nhat Hanh explains that once you are aware of this,

> you are no longer caught in the idea that you are a separate entity…your happiness and suffering depends on the happiness and suffering of others…you see the nature of interconnectedness and you know that to protect yourself is to protect the humans around you. (p. 52)

This perspective promotes and leads to an understanding of "us" as persons—not as "I," but as a "you and I." Embracing a relational-centred perspective when planning requires the CYC practitioner to enter a space that is shared with others—a relational space in which knowledge, understanding, and multiple perspectives are shared and co-created. Relational-centred planning also requires readiness on the part of the practitioner to be moved by the other, willingness to remain connected through conflict, a desire to be heard and to hear the voice of the other, and a genuineness that allows us to express divergent views.

Premise # 2: Being in the Moment

Second, relational-centred planning requires a focus on the uniqueness of the moment in which coming together with another is fully experienced within the relational dynamic of being in that moment while remaining open to new possibilities. For many of us, being in the moment is first experienced when we become intensely involved in an experience. For example, when we experience the self becoming "a part of" the larger world as we sit by the ocean or on a mountain top. As one of the predominant theorists and advocates of the existential-humanistic therapy movement, James Bugental (1965) points out that being in the moment involves "an opening of awareness beyond the boundaries of our heavily conditioned, daily perceptual limits" (p. 231). Fostering this kind of openness requires a great deal of courage and a willingness to be vulnerable; it also requires a commitment and devotion to be with the other to the fullest extent possible.

Being in the moment shifts the practitioner–client relationship from that of a comparatively fixed entity to an active, ongoing, relationship-building process (i.e., listening, sharing, co-creating meaning). A critical aspect of being in the moment is the self-reflective capacity that is required to monitor one's positioning in relation to the other. Consider, for instance, those occasions when the relationship appears to be in conflict or entangled in a power struggle; in such situations, a reflective inquiry response might involve asking oneself, "How am I contributing to this dynamic?"

We think that in regard to relational-centred planning there is an important distinction to be made here between reflective practice and reflective inquiry. Reflective practice is concerned with looking back and learning through experience, while reflective inquiry is concerned with understanding in the moment. As such, reflective inquiry extends beyond engaging in conventional forms of professional development, which tend to focus on the acquisition of knowledge. Reflective inquiry requires insight about the ground on which one stands (i.e., awareness of one's life position) and about the way one occupies or stands on that ground (i.e., the capacity to think beyond the confines of one's life position). As a result, reflective inquiry entails asking penetrating questions, challenging assumptions, and carefully examining the implications of actions and choices. Reflective inquiry requires a range of beliefs, strategies, and ways of behaving that involve asking questions, maintaining a sense of curiosity, and paying attention to how one's life-positioning "stories" constrain new understandings. From this perspective, "practice" is viewed as a living process, constantly changing, constantly developing.

Reflective inquiry that challenges existing traditions of knowledge also advances issues of social justice. In their interdisciplinary work on relational ethics, Carse and Nelson (1996) assert that practitioners must be conscious of their role in efforts to change the social, economic, and political conditions of the people they serve. This idea that "the personal is political" was first expressed by the ancient Greeks. The Greek notion of the personal as political recognized that personal lives are inextricably linked to and determined by social, cultural, political, and economic relationships. Given today's highly complex, ever-changing, and diverse practice environment, "the personal is political" is a key principle of relational-centred practice.

Premise # 3: A Creative Process

Third, relational-centred planning is a creative process rooted in imaginative thought and occurs by making connections between ideas and, or, experiences that were previously thought of as unrelated. As poet and scholar John O'Donohue put it, "The imagination in its loyalty to possibility often takes the curved path rather than the linear way" (Robinson, 2001, p. 111). Creativity involves originality of thought. This is an important observation, particularly in contrast to the fact that most of the time we humans live our lives in what phenomenologists call the natural attitude.[3] The natural attitude refers to humans being immersed and absorbed in the activity of their everyday business in their accustomed world (Stewart & Mickunas, 1990). The consequences of this natural attitude are that humans remain absorbed by and in the familiar and thus neglect to think creatively—beyond the familiar.

Ellen Langer, a psychology professor and author of *Mindful Learning* (1997), suggests that creativity entails a break with habitual patterns of thought, which requires holding oneself open courageously in order to move beyond the constraints of the natural attitude. She writes, for example,

> a mindful approach to any activity has three characteristics: the continuous creation of new categories; openness to new information; and an implicit awareness of more than one perspective. Mindlessness, in contrast, is categorized by entrapment in old categories; by automatic behaviour that precludes attending to new signals; and by action that operates from a single perspective. (p. 4)

---

3   The natural attitude is hidden to itself. Husserl uses the term *natural* to indicate what is original, naïve, and exists prior to critical or theoretical reflection (van Manen, 1990). The primary feature of this natural attitude is that it is not concerned with critical inquiry into the basis of the world of experience.

Therefore, at its core, the creative dimension of relational-centred planning necessitates that CYC practitioners engage themselves in critical self-reflection of their "lifeworld,"[4] or what is referred to in CYC work as one's life position. This engagement can be challenging because normally we are unaware of our life positions. Hence, CYC practitioners must continually strive to identify and examine their life positions, which evolve out of their past experiences and socialization. As Thom Garfat (1993, p. iv) writes, "it's only through the investigation of our selves, our perceptions, beliefs, biases, philosophies, and ways of knowing that we will learn where our blind and blank spots lie."

Critical self-reflection is not just the search for the best interpretation of what is; it is a dynamic, creative, and collaborative merging of multiple perspectives. Creativity of thought emanates from a reflexive immersion in conversation by paying close attention to one's biases, or "old mental files," and sharing them explicitly with others. This opens up new possibilities for rethinking biases and old files, which, in turn, allows for the generation of new perspectives.

Premise # 4: Belief in the Resourcefulness of People

Fourth, the belief in the resourcefulness of people is central to relational-centred planning. Relational-centred planning embodies a holistic respect for human potential and possibility by recognizing the interconnectedness of the various aspects of a person's well-being. This entails a focus on people's strengths and resources that fosters a climate of hope for seeing beyond current conditions, because when people begin to hope in relationship with one another, they are presented with previously unrecognized opportunities to discover unexplored possibilities. The CYC practitioner's own sense of hope is a vital element of relational-centred planning. Corrina, a 13-year-old student in an inner city junior high school, provides an illustration of the value of seeing resourcefulness.

---

4   A person's lifeworld, or life position, includes the cultural elements that surround a person from birth and the knowledge and norms that are handed down, presenting ways of understanding the world. In our opinion, all understanding is connected to one's lifeworld, which cannot be eliminated. One therefore needs to become conscious of these interpretive influences in order to account for them and challenge them when appropriate.

Case Scenario: Corrina

Upon entering junior high school, Corrina was immediately identified as a "high-risk" student. She was brought to the attention of the student counsellor and the special education assessment team by her teachers, who expressed their dim view of her with the following observations: Corrina is disruptive in class, frequently calling out and making inappropriate remarks. All of her academic skills are two to three years below grade level. Her school record does not indicate a home address or the name of her father. Her mother, who was a teenager when Corrina was born, is addicted to crack cocaine. Corrina is frequently absent from or late arriving to school. Notes sent home about her absences, her behaviour, and her poor academic work remain unanswered.

This presentation of "facts" is provided to support the identified issues from which conclusions are typically drawn; the presentation gives the impression that Corrina is a teenager who is well on the way to repeating her mother's life history. The "facts" predict that because Corrina is academically deficient, and behaviourally and emotionally impaired, she is more likely than not to drop out of school. With few skills and little idea of an academic work ethic or the rules of the marketplace, Corrina will likely be pushed to the margins of society. Little in her past gives a reason to be hopeful about her future.

Not by denying these "facts," but by looking at another part of the picture—that is, Corrina's social and emotional intelligence—one gets a different view. For instance, at home Corrina takes care of both her mother and her brother. Because her mother resists treatment, Corrina escorts her to the drug treatment centre and often waits many hours for her to be seen. She also goes along to the supermarket to be sure that her mother buys food and does not get sidetracked and spend her money on drugs.

Corrina cooks and prepares meals for her brother. When there is not sufficient food to go around, she cuts down on her own portion so that he will not be hungry. She insists that he attend school, even when she does not. Corrina has woven a safety net for herself by cultivating a relationship with her aunt, Edith. It is to Edith's house that she goes with her brother whenever her mother disappears or brings home a man who is unpredictable and frightening.

Acknowledging these "facts" in addition to Corrina's school records and psychological and educational assessments poses more possibilities. Corrina has inherent strengths and the capacity to direct her future. Specifically, she is a mature individual—even wise beyond her years. She has a sense of what is healthy and safe; she is self-sufficient and has considerable common sense.

Premise # 5: Discoveries in Diversity

Fifth, relational-centred planning considers diversity beyond the usual issues of difference (i.e., colour, gender, religion, disability, age, and politics) by taking an inward turn. Exploring and understanding difference has to do with experiencing ourselves and others from each other's perspective. To benefit from the discoveries of difference, CYC practitioners will need to look deeper into who they are and use an open mind to question and examine their own fears around issues of difference. As Canadian-born Jean Vanier (1985, p. 85) put it, simply but eloquently, "Humanity is one. We are all part of the same human race. However different we may be through culture, race, or disabilities, we are all human beings." By exploring the differences in being human, we can discover aspects of self and other that have been unknown and unavailable for understanding.

The following poem, entitled "Other," raises issues of diversity by addressing the characteristics of difference; it was written by a grade-five student who sees opportunity in difference.

Other

Other, an exception
Other, you don't follow the rule
Other, a simple word so cruel
Other, different from the rest
Other, you're either worst or best
Other, you aren't like me
Other, you don't see what I see
Other, you just don't fit in
Other, when will the discrimination end
Other, you don't think the right way
Other, you don't say what I say
Other, you don't look how I look

Other, you don't get the same feeling
From the same holy book
Other, other is you
Other, other is me, too
We are different from one another
We depend on each other
We look at the same world
In just a different way
We breathe the same air
We all have something important to say
We all live on one Earth
We all have one life to live
Better make it worthwhile
Better give.

Caroline Francis, Grant Elementary, 5th Grade,
Essays and Poems by Columbia Public School Students
Columbia Values Diversity Celebration, 17 January 2002

Premise # 6: A Critical Consciousness about Issues of Social Justice

Sixth, relational-centred planning calls upon CYC practitioners to recognize their moral obligation to use their knowledge and skills to consider how social injustices, such as those based on class, race, ethnicity, gender, and sexual orientation, have an impact on human disconnection and suffering. Social justice cannot be ignored in relational-centred practice. It is an important lens through which to view the complex "lived" realities of people's lives within the larger social, economic, and political contexts in which they occur. In order for the aims and goals of relational-centred planning to be realized, the linkages between the restrictive and alienating conditions that often surround the families of children and youth brought into care, and the systems that produce and sustain those systems, must be understood and considered within the planning process. CYC practitioners must also consider the sociopolitical power relations that impact children, youth, and families.

In the following example, the author *begins* to think about how she could shift her focus from client investigation to examining the life conditions in which her client, "Karen," lives.

Case Scenario: Karen

Karen is a lone-parent mother with two children, living
in a subsidized two bedroom apartment. Social assistance
is Karen's only source of income, which in most months
is barely sufficient to provide for her family's basic needs.
In my role as a public health nurse I encountered Karen and
many mothers like her who live in materialistic poverty.
It was my mandate as the "competent" health professional
to conduct home visits to ascertain existing or potential
health needs and to plan appropriate interventions. My
agenda included comprehensive assessment, which entailed
observation and structured interviews to complete complex
family inventories; the development of a problem list;
client teaching and recommendations; referrals; and finally,
lengthy documentation. On all counts I was thorough,
or was I? I certainly "dealt with" Karen and her family
in scrupulous fashion, but did I adequately "dwell with"
Karen? That is, did I understand her experience as a lone
parent enduring on the margins of society due to poverty?
Marginalization and any one of several other phenomena
associated with poverty, such as social isolation, social
exclusion, poor-bashing, demoralization, and helplessness,
may well have been my preconceptions of Karen's existence,
yet I had never sought to validate my assumptions. Rather,
I had reduced Karen's life world to an object of inquiry, to
an entity under investigation. I was "stuck in thinking only
one way."

—Porr, 2005, pp. 190–191

Premise # 7: A Personally Transforming Endeavour

It is not sufficient to merely endorse philosophically the concepts of
relational-centred practice; relational-centred practice is a way of life.
CYC practitioners who want to practice the relational-centred approach
as a basis for planning can expect to see exciting changes in the character of
their practice and in the nature of their relationships with children, youth,
and families. Relational-centred practitioners hold a different attitude, one
that is characterized by a willingness to face the uncomfortable, an attitude
of openness that promotes the exploration of and engagement with the
world in a new way—an attitude of courage to challenge *what is* while
creating *what might be*. This may be threatening for some because it calls

for far-reaching changes in how we see and present ourselves personally and professionally. One might encounter danger, disapproval, rejection, and invalidation while navigating large systems that have prescribed rules and standard practices.

RELATIONAL CAPABILITIES

> *"I believe we can change the world if we start listening to one another again. Simple, honest, human conversation. Not mediation, negotiation, problem solving, debate, or public meetings. Simple, truthful conversation where we each feel heard, and we each listen well. This is how great changes begin, when people begin talking to each other about their experiences, hopes, and fears."*

— Margaret Wheatley, 2002, p. 3

To be a relational-centred planner requires certain capabilities and skills (see relational-centred capabilities framework, Figure 1). They include the capacity for being in the moment, maintaining an attitude of openness, enhanced curiosity, authenticity, social justice, interpersonal collaboration, improvisation, listening relationally, and achieving. It is important to emphasize that while this framework incorporates many of the current concepts and ideas in the field of CYC, this discussion demonstrates their relational-centred potential. While it is not our intention to provide an in-depth look at each of the capabilities outlined in Figure 1, their essence will be made clear through a description of each and discussion of their relevance in regard to assessment and planning.

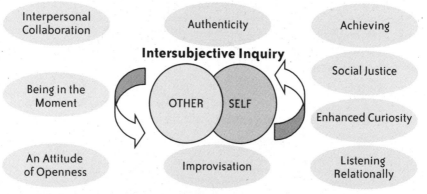

Figure 1. Relational-centred capabilities framework

The Capacity for "Being in the Moment"

Being in the moment means being mindfully aware of what is going on in the present. It is a special way of being with people because it involves listening to, being open and attentive to each other's experiences, honouring each other's uniqueness, and being with each other without distraction. Krueger (2004), Fewster (1990), and Garfat (1998), among others, suggest that being in the moment is an invisible connection, that it is something we feel that exceeds the limits of understanding.

The notion of being in the present resonates with Trungpa's (1991, pp. 18–19) notion of "being in the now" and "sitting on the edge of a razor blade," a state of being that asks one to keep an attentive focus and immediate presence. Levinas (1998) relates being in the moment with "being with others," which he describes as an ethical space where one's ethical responsibility toward the other is enacted. For Levinas, we are ethically responsible in the face of the other to bear witness to the truth of the other person's life. The ethics of responsibility for Levinas suggest that turning away from the other equates to an act of violence. As such, being in the moment is a giving of self that is conveyed through being available and at the disposal of the other person within the state of unknowing. To know is to be aware and to be informed. Ricks and Bellefeuille (2003) note the following:

> Usually we take what we know as representing what is true, and in light of that truth we generate solutions to problems or reactions to previous actions. To not know is to not have information and will likely result in seeking and acquiring information in order to be informed or to learn that which is unknown. (p. 123)

This is not to suggest that not-knowing is a passive concept; rather, it is a powerful way of being that requires the willingness to be involved and to make space internally for the other person.

For a CYC practitioner, being in the moment requires acceptance of the situation as it is, letting go of personal agendas or views about what others ought to do, and resisting the inclination to blame or retreat when difficulties arise. At times, this means resisting the urge to disengage when faced with emotional responses such as anger, sadness, indifference, and other threatening emotional states. To be fully in the moment is the intervention; it is about presence and being fully available and open to all aspects of the client's experiences.

Maintaining an Attitude of Openness

An attitude of openness is characterized as being amenable to new ideas, changes in worldviews, and the unexpected, along with a willingness to grow and even to be radically changed. It requires CYC practitioners to look at differing views and diverse lifestyles as an invitation to discover opportunities for new understanding and creative growth for the self and the other. Such an attitude brings fresh depth to Viktor Frankl's classic work, *Man's Search for Meaning* (1984), which chronicles his experiences as a concentration camp inmate. Frankl maintained that the key to finding meaning in life is choosing one's attitude in response to unavoidable suffering and loss.

The opposite, a closed mind, is a state of rigidity in which one adheres to a single perspective and acts automatically. For example, the practice of Zen teaches us that it is impossible to add anything more to a cup that is already full. If you pour in more tea, it simply spills over and is wasted. The same is true of the mind. An attitude that says "I already know" is one that is immobilized by a rigid mindset and is oblivious to context and perspective, which in turn pigeonholes experiences, behaviours, objects, and other people into rigid categories. A closed-minded attitude is governed by rules, routines, and previously constructed categories (Langer, 1997). An attitude of openness, on the other hand, is an attitude that uses and celebrates the power of exploration, imagination, and discovery. It is an attitude of knowing that you don't know. It is grounded in the mystery of not knowing and recognizes the value of not knowing as simply being the first step toward truth (Palmer, 1993).

Below is an exercise designed to dissolve our usual sense of knowing so that we can open up to new learning possibilities. While looking in a mirror, say the following in a supportive and curious tone of voice.

> I don't know who I really am.
> There is much that I see that I do not understand.
> There is much that I hear that I do not understand.
> There is much that I feel that I do not understand.
> I don't know exactly where my life is leading me.
> I don't know many things that I would like to know.
> I don't know what I don't know.
> I don't know what I do know.

The point of the exercise is to become comfortable with not knowing and to learn to appreciate that "not fully understanding" is an essential part of the human condition. You might consider doing this exercise when you are feeling upset, confused, or despondent. Give yourself time to think about how you can achieve a sense of calmness amidst the ongoing changes in life that you do not fully understand. Avoid rushing to action or an answer; take a moment to breathe and appreciate yourself in the moment.

Enhanced Curiosity

When we shift our attention to the way meanings are constructed relationally within the assessment and planning process, we in turn shift our stance from *knowing* to *curiosity*. When we engage in curiosity our search for understanding is vastly enhanced. "Curiosity leads to exploration and invention of alternative views and moves, and different moves and views breed curiosity" (Cecchin, 1987, p. 406). Curiosity is the dynamic of the mind that provokes the questions that release creativity. For CYC practitioners, having an attitude of enhanced curiosity means asking questions as a way to stay close to the client's unfolding story. It means taking the initiative, staying interested, engaging in experimentation, and shifting from preconceptions to wonderment. Curiosity shifts the focus from judgments and reactivity to seeing each experience as an opportunity to learn.

Transforming Negative Judgments

1. Instead of regretting a past experience, ask what you can learn from it.

2. Listen for negative self-judgment about what you should or should not have done. Judgment blocks learning. You waste precious time and energy beating up on yourself. Take a deep breath and let go of judgment.

3. Be curious; seek to learn. If the judgment won't go away, be curious about it. Who or what does it sound like? Who or what does it look like?

The Capacity for Authenticity

The virtues of expressing oneself *authentically* have been extolled since ancient times (Harbus, 2002). Authenticity is a multifaceted concept that includes being genuine, owning one's personal experiences (values, thoughts, emotions, and beliefs), showing consistency between values and actions, and relating to others in such a way as to encourage (Erickson, 1995; Harter, 2002; Kernis, 2003a; Maslow, 1970; Rogers, 1951; Seligman, 2002). The opposite of authenticity includes being in a state of mindlessness and ignorance; engaging in superficial, arms-length conversations; oversimplifying or generalizing complex phenomena; and practicing in a repetitive and ritualistic manner. The literature suggests that authentic relationships between children and adults in service programs are more important than the specific techniques employed. The authentic relationship is what holds the opportunities to learn.

According to Heidegger (1962/2004), authenticity is a state of being that is active, congruent, contemplative, dynamic, and teleological (Guignon, 1984, 1993). For Heidegger, awareness of our ultimate freedom to act any way we choose, our ultimate ownership of our actions, and our ultimate responsibility even for who we are is so terrifying to us that we are drawn to "root ourselves" in restricted and ever-repeating forms of relationship and behaviour as we seek to contrive the experiences of certainty and control at the expense of being authentic. As a result, authentic existence can only come into being when an individual arrives at the realization of who he or she is and grasps the fact that each human being is a distinct entity.

The humanist tradition, as exemplified by Maslow (1968), suggests that authenticity occurs when individuals discover their true inner nature by sufficiently satisfying higher-order psychological needs. Contemporary discourse is split regarding whether authenticity is more appropriately conceptualized as an individual-differences variable (i.e., an internal structure representing the core, real self) or as a relational construct (i.e., a unique experience of self with a particular "other"). Regarding the latter view, Kernis (2003b) suggests

> relational authenticity involves endorsing the importance
> for close others to see the real you, good and bad. Toward
> that end, authentic relations involve a selective process of
> self-disclosure and the development of mutual intimacy and
> trust. In short, relational authenticity means being genuine
> and not "fake" in one's relationships with others. (p. 15)

Kernis concludes that the deepest sense of authentic self is continuously formed in connection with others and is inextricably tied to growth within the relational context. Like Kernis's relational orientation to authenticity, Jarvis (1992) proposed that becoming authentic is a journey, not a destination. Thus, it is unlikely that a person will awaken one morning and announce, "Today, I will become an authentic person." Rather, it is a process linked with reflective learning that occurs over time and requires self-discovery, self-improvement, and self-reflection.

We also suggest that authenticity necessitates critical participation in life. By this we mean questioning how we are different from the broader community and living accordingly; we neither do something just because it is the way others behave nor believe what others believe without considering whether or not it is true for us. Freire (1970/2005) argued that authenticity comes through having a critical knowledge of the context within which we work and from seeing the principal contradictions of our society, which leads nicely into the next relational capacity: the pedagogical praxis of social justice.

Social Justice Praxis

The term *praxis* originates from the Greek word *prasso*, meaning "doing" and "acting" (Audi, 1995). Praxis for social justice combines learning and doing for the purpose of encouraging critical consciousness, ethical reasoning, and socially responsible behaviour. It is a cycle of action, reflection, and transfer wherein cultural differences are understood and valued; wherein human dignity, the earth, and future generations are respected; and all are encouraged to participate in bringing about a more equitable and compassionate world.

Globalization over the past few decades has profoundly affected the lives of children, youth, and families. The gap between the "haves" and the "have-nots" has widened, leading to increased poverty (Campaign 2000, 2006), which is the main determinant of social problems (National Collaborative Centre for Determinants of Health, 2007). Yet the promotion of social justice within the practice of child and youth care has been hampered by professional and political barriers, because true social justice threatens the interests of those invested in protecting their territory and resources. For example, service agencies are often resistant to challenging government policy because they fear losing their government funded contracts.

Practice is always shaped by the needs of the times and the resulting problems. We believe that our times desperately require an infusion of social justice interventions. As members of a profession, we must find ways to address the social and economic conditions that contribute to the negative, unfortunate, and limiting life histories of the children, youth, and families that we serve. For this to happen, CYC practitioners need to understand the issues of oppression, exclusion, and marginalization within their communities. New approaches are desperately needed and wanted in several areas, including housing for the homeless, subsidized housing for marginal wage earners, education to prevent early pregnancies and unwanted or unhealthy babies, education and employment opportunities in the trades and service sectors, and life skills education for those who have been marginalized in the school system, to mention a few.

Interpersonal Collaboration

Relational-centred planning is a collaborative endeavour that calls for CYC practitioners to work together with others in an open and respectful manner. *Collaboration* has its expression in a mutually responsive and inter-active dialogue between CYC practitioners and those with whom they work. Having no prescriptive planning agenda, the CYC practitioner embraces whatever emerges and goes with this conversational flow as new meaning unfolds. Within the collaborative process, the CYC practitioner and the child, youth, family member(s), and significant others become united in their efforts to make sense of what is. Everything that is said has relevance; nothing is "right" or "wrong," "good" or "bad." There is neither need for nor purpose in a judgment of fault, problems, or inadequacies because the focus is on understanding what is possible.

Interpersonal collaborative conversations primarily take the form of questions posed by the CYC practitioner rather than statements or information. Questions help people see other perspectives or consider other ideas, and questions enable conversations that are different from those they might otherwise have had about their situation. Questions that invite reflection have an impact that differs from that generated by advice or information offered by the CYC practitioner. Questions not only provide the CYC practitioner with information to help him or her make sense of the client's world, they also help people make sense of themselves and to entertain other possibilities. Building from these conversations, co-created plans can be written or framed to fit the agency's "planning forms" while not sacrificing the needs and wants of clients and the overall relational-centred planning context.

Improvisation

Improvisation is defined in *Webster's Dictionary* as "a composition; a course pursued in accordance with no previously devised plan, policy, or consideration" (Gove, 1996, p. 1138). Two Latin verbs closely related to this contemporary definition are *improvisus*, "the unforeseen or unexpected" (Gove, p. 1138), and *providere*, "to forsee" or "to see beforehand, to prepare, or to provide for" (Flexner, 1995, p. 876). Taking into consideration the ideas of "the unforeseen," and to see or prepare beforehand, the art of improvisation involves the capability to sift important information, selectively combine relevant information, and draw comparisons and form analogies. The ability to see things in a fresh way is vital to the improvisation process.

In the theatre arts, Belt and Stockley (1989) explain that performance-based improvisation generates a "unique narrative landscape" among the performers through which their actions on the environment, materials, and each other become the catalyst and context for action. For Belt and Stockley, the deep level of attentiveness, listening, and involvement of the performers during improvisation echo a mutuality and simultaneity of experience. Within the context of CYC, improvisation manifests through the CYC practitioner's ability to perform many functions simultaneously with fluency, immediacy, and creativity. Mark Krueger (2000) uses the metaphor of modern dance to illustrate the intuitive and improvisational competencies of CYC practitioners:

> CYC work is like modern dance. Workers bring themselves
> to the moment, practice, plan (choreograph), listen to the
> tempos of daily living, improvise, and adjust to and/or
> change the contexts within which their interactions occur.
> Consider, for example, the worker above. She moves into
> her day the way a skilful dancer moves on the stage. She, the
> worker, has learned her craft and developed her technique.
> As she works, she improvises and moves, informed by her
> instincts and her head. She senses, in other words, as well
> as knows where to be and what to say or not say. She is in
> each moment, sensitive to the needs of the youth and the
> environment in which they are interacting. (p. 1)

Improvisation captures the openness of the relational context. It is expressed through the CYC practitioner's mastery of the relational skills and competencies noted above and below.

Listening Relationally

Listening relationally requires a number of related attitudes and behaviours and, in fact, probably requires some degree of natural giftedness. From a relational understanding of listening, nothing happens without the client's participation. Listening relationally is about listening from within the conversation rather than from outside the conversation. It is a kind of listening that believes in the human ability to co-create new realities in the process of talking about old ones. Listening relationally means letting go of power. It asks the professional to be a co-participant in the evolution of new meanings (Boyd, 1998). This approach, which promotes the concept of "not-knowing," encourages the CYC practitioner to remain focused on listening to the ongoing language of the client without assuming the probability of a point at which so-called expert knowledge takes over in the process of solving the client's problems. This listening, far from being passive, draws one into an active, co-creative, constructive, narrative-illuminating, imagination-nurturing dialogue.

Relational listening opens us up to ourselves. After years of counselling others, many helpers realize that they, themselves, benefit most from listening to their clients. As people deal with their disappointment, grief, anger, or fear, their helpers learn to deal with their own. By allowing themselves to venture into the realities of others, they are exposed to their own reality. Listening—and how it touches the practitioner—offers opportunities to experience "the story" in ways that may open up new meaning and understanding for the practitioner. It is both a humbling and transforming interaction, because it requires the practitioner to know and not know at the same time: the practitioner must know when and how to inquire and to be with, without knowing where it (i.e., the process) is going and what might be. The practitioner must know different perspectives and offer different opportunities without knowing which ones will be negotiated in this situation. The practitioner uses his or her expertise without being the expert. It is a paradox of having knowledge and not knowing!

Achieving

Achieving comes out of learning theory, which contends that human growth occurs through authentic, mutually empathetic relationships (Fletcher, 1999). It means using one's relational skills to enhance one's own professional growth and capabilities, and it involves attending to one's thoughts and feelings. The requisite relational skills include asking for help—where such asking is not seen as a sign of weakness; paying attention to the emotional overlay of a situation and repairing the potential of, or perceived breaks in, working relationships; staying with contradictory information; blending thinking and feeling in coming to a decision; and paying attention to process.

For Fletcher, achieving is guided by experiential questions rather than conceptual ones. In practical terms, this means that CYC practitioners experience and work with children, youth, and families, and listen to and consult with other CYC practitioners and other professionals, while living a perpetual inquiry into their own knowing and practice. As part of this inquiry, CYC practitioners assess the congruence and/or incongruence of what is being said and experienced while considering the impact of their actions on children, youth, and families.

REALITY AS APPEARANCE

> *"Truth is not what we discover, but what we create."*
>
> —Antoine de Saint-Exupéry

Relational-centred planning involves appreciating and understanding that we bring our own perspectives into our practice. In this spirit, what we perceive as reality is an individual phenomena based on perception (i.e., reality is an appearance and an appearance is reality) (Nietzsche, 1967). Given that appearance is a matter of perception and perspective, we need to be able to step back and understand what we think we "know" to be true. Consider the parable of Plato's cave.[5]

---

5   "The Allegory of the Cave" is an allegory used by the Greek philosopher Plato in his work *The Republic*. The allegory of the cave is told and then interpreted by the character Socrates at the beginning of Book 7 (514a–520a).

Parable of Plato's Cave

The parable of the cave is about the distinction between appearance and reality. Some prisoners were being held fast in a deep cave, with their heads bound so that all they can see are the shadows of things cast on the wall before them, shadows cast by "human images and shapes of animals wrought in stone and wood and every material" carried in front of a fire burning some distance behind the prisoners' heads. The bearers of the objects are hidden behind the wall and so cast no shadows; but occasionally they speak, and the echoes of their words reach the prisoners and seem to come from the shadows. The prisoners are, in Plato's view, removed from truth or reality, although they do not realize this and would object if the suggestion were made to them. If they were freed and made to turn around towards the firelight, the prisoners would be dazzled and unable to make out the objects that cast the shadows on the wall. If they were compelled to look directly at the fire, it would hurt their eyes, and they would probably prefer to go back to the comfortable and familiar darkness of their prison. If they were forced out of the cave entirely, out into the sunlight, it would be even more painful, and objects outside the cave would be even harder for them to make out.

Central to Plato's parable of the cave is the idea that reality, our everyday experiences of the world (like the experiences of those being held in the cave), is a mental event and must be understood before it can be controlled. There are two influential lenses that shape the way we view ourselves, others, and the world in general: the theoretical perspective lens (i.e., the theoretical change frameworks that we are taught in CYC), and the life-position perspective lens (i.e., our own constructed life stories).

Theoretical Change Frameworks that Underpin CYC Practice

The theoretical change frameworks, which are among the foundational elements of professional knowledge, reflect our beliefs about people, and they influence how we construct our interpretations of troublesome behaviour and potential for change (Ricks & Charlesworth, 2003). Calling into question the assumptions about human development and change inherent in theoretical frameworks brings to bear a level of analysis and reflection essential to competent relational-centred practice. It is important to understand that the theoretical frameworks we are taught and use as CYC practitioners affect not only the way we explore the lives of those we serve, they also impact how we approach the issue of change. The frameworks shape the questions we ask, the assessments we make, and, ultimately, the interventions we choose.

Theoretical Change Frameworks

Theories should not be seen as competing entities but, rather, like the shifting, disparately coloured lenses of a kaleidoscope through which we undertake assessment and planning. They can be used singly or in combination; using multiple theories can illuminate different aspects of the person(s) and perhaps offer new and unexpected colours for the imagination.

It is also important to consider the change theory of those we serve. While most people may not have "formal" knowledge of change theories, they certainly have ideas and explanations of how and if one can change behaviour. While we never have a complete view of another person's reality, we can generate multiple perspectives of different aspects of a person's life by using different theoretical perspectives. Below, we present brief summaries of a few selected theories to make explicit the different points of view about behaviour and behaviour change.

Ecological and system theories. This group of theories is based on the idea that human systems are intricately connected to one another; each piece of the system is considered a part of the whole and a whole, in and of itself, at the same time. Beyond human systems, we are also part of the natural order of the world and, beyond that, of the universe. All systems theories affirm that an individual's development is determined by the person's interactions within relationships and circumstances that form his or her environment. For example, Bronfenbrenner's ecological systems theory, which has recently been renamed "*bioecological* systems theory" (Bronfenbrenner & Evans, 2000), defines complex "layers" of the human environment, each of which has an effect on an individual's development. To understand behaviour and development, one must consider the individual and his or her immediate environment, as well as the effects of the larger environment on the person(s). Bronfenbrenner views individuals as developing in four nested systems: the microsystem, the mesosystem, the exosystem, and the macrosystem. (A fifth system, the chronosystem, involves movement across time and history.)

Attachment/developmental theory. Attachment theory has long been recognized as a useful framework for understanding child and youth behaviour. Rather than simply labelling children as bad or emotionally disturbed, among other labels, attachment theory has provided one of the most important conceptual schemes for viewing children's and youth's behaviours as adaptive coping strategies and something to be understood within the context of early socio-emotional development. According to attachment theory, the infant's relationship with the parent develops in a series of sequential stages. Human attachment seems to involve a sensitive period, rather than a strictly critical period—that is, a time at which it is optimal for certain capacities to emerge and during which the individual is especially responsive to environmental influences.

Cognitive-behavioural theory. Cognitive-behavioural theory (CBT) is a blend of two distinct fields: cognitive theory and behavioural theory. Behaviourism focuses on external behaviours and disregards internal mental processes. The cognitive approach, in contrast, emphasizes the importance of internal thought processes. CBT is based on the assertion that changes in behaviour can occur through the ways in which a person understands and interprets, and can alter the person's thinking in relation to events in his or her life (France & Robson, 1975). CBT is based on the idea that how we think (cognition), how we feel (emotion and affect), and how we act (behaviour) all interact and go together—specifically, that our thoughts influence our feelings and behaviour, our feelings influence our behaviour and thoughts, and behaviour influences our emotions and thoughts. These modalities are therefore interrelated, and change in one modality will in all probability influence one or all of the others. The aim of CBT is to help clients acquire strategies to better manage their behaviours, independent of the need for a therapist. While the therapy generally proceeds from assessment to intervention to closure, problem identification and interventions may be modified throughout the course of the therapy.

Person-centred theory. Person-centred theory is often considered within the framework of humanistic psychology. The person-centred approach places great emphasis on the individual's ability to control his or her own positive change (Barrett-Lennard, 1998). The main tenet of person-centred theory is that people are born with an innate motivational drive, defined by Rogers (1959, p. 196) as the "actualizing tendency."

Practitioners of the theory believe in the competence and trustworthiness of individuals and in their innate ability to move toward self-actualization and health when the proper conditions are in place. Tied to these beliefs is the confidence that individuals also have the inner resources to move themselves in positive directions. Three basic conditions are needed to support an individual's natural inclination for positive growth: a genuine relationship with a relatively congruent individual, acceptance and caring from the counsellor, and an accurate understanding on the part of the counsellor of the client's phenomenological world (Sheldon & Kasser, 2001). Finally, a core concept of the theory states that individuals perceive the world in a unique phenomenological way, so that no two people's perceptions of the world are the same.

> When exploring theories, consider these questions:
>
> 1. What theoretical orientations have influenced your beliefs about people and change?
> 2. Do you have a preference for working with individuals, families, groups, or communities? Explain your preference.
> 3. What areas do you inquire into when exploring someone's life circumstances? Who do you ask?
> 4. What premises do you use to give meaning and significance to the information?
> 5. Is your philosophy congruent with or does it compliment the client's worldview?
> 6. What is your philosophy regarding cultural backgrounds within and outside the dominant culture?
> 7. How does your theoretical lens limit your perspective? (What are you likely to mishear, or not see?)

The Life-Position Perspective Lens

The life-position perspective lens requires being mindful about one's own "life story"—the life experiences that influence how we position ourselves in relation to others. Rand and Fewster (1997) argue that the personal development and professional development of the CYC practitioner cannot be separated. They explain that "in its fullest form this self is more than physical, more than emotional, and more than cognitive. It is the sum total of all our aspects, and more; it exists at the core of our experience" (p. 80).

Figure 2. Adapted from *All Together Now: Creating a Social Capital Mosaic* (Ricks, Charlesworth, Bellefeuille, & Field, 1999).

Accordingly, self-awareness is central to the educational process of CYC practitioners. While we all have some level of awareness, a deeper understanding of the importance of the life-position lens can only encourage us to be more critical and to revisit our basic assumptions about many things. Having an awareness of one's life-position is, therefore, one of the most fundamental lifelong-learning challenges for CYC students, practitioners, and educators alike. Our life-positions reveal the prejudices that operate as filters through which we interpret events and people. These biases become apparent through exposure to different beliefs, such as the opinions of other students or practitioners. Relational-centred practitioners commit to developing a better understanding of their prejudices by engaging in an ongoing process of examining the field of vision in which they conduct their thinking. Like wearing eyeglasses, we do not see our filters; we see through them. The more we use them, the more they become us. We do not realize that they are there. That is why self-awareness is a lifelong strategy. One way to expose our filters is to examine our conversations. Consider, for instance, the contrasting statements in Figure 2. Conversations about practice sound very different from a relational stance.

A CO-CONSTRUCTED PROCESS OF THINKING AND DOING

A relational orientation regards assessment and planning as a dynamic, relational process of meaning-making that points to new possibilities in perspective and opportunities for change. As Dachler and Hosking (1995) explain, meaning has no ultimate origin and can never be finalized, because it is always in the process of being made. Thus, relational-centred planning is best understood as a process of ongoing and flexible inquiry that allows information to "fold in" on itself repeatedly, allowing for validation and clarification (Ricks & Charlesworth, 2003). It is a process of respectful and compassionate inquiry into the other's experiences of what matters and opportunities for change that are jointly negotiated, monitored, and revised. This requires a continuous and changing picture of what is needed and wanted. The two key premises for success in relational-centred planning are these: that success is built on a deep understanding of what people need and want, and that everyone is involved and engaged in the process. From the opening moments of connecting with a client, CYC practitioners use the assessment and planning process to involve everyone in attending to the relational context, listening to and allowing the sharing of stories, opening up new possibilities and perspectives about the self and the world, facilitating engagement in hope and opportunity, and making transparent the child's, youth's, or family's ideas about how they want to experience their lives in the future.

It is important to point out that aspects of assessment are, in fact, interventions, and all interventions result in opportunities to observe and assess what matters and what does not. In relational-centred planning there is no artificial distinction between assessment and planning except that both assist the CYC practitioner to observe and understand the person or persons involved. Remembering that relational-centred planning is the intervention, then intervention planning is synonymous with being on a journey in which people are engaged in meaningful conversations. These meaningful conversations transcend the limits of personal perspectives and take on a quality of inquiry characterized by engagement, listening, and respecting, while unravelling and making feelings and values transparent.

Another basic tenet of this approach is that events, behaviours, and attitudes can only be understood in relation to their context (Ricks & Charlesworth, 2003). By listening to and honouring clients' stories, the CYC practitioner assists others with making meaning of their experiences.

Life stories offer a more holistic view and integrative understanding of personal meaning associated with experiences (Anderson, 1997; Krueger, 2004). By exploring the person's world through story development, the CYC practitioner and youth work collaboratively to reveal, see different perspectives, and re-create life stories. Life story development is a dynamic process that generates new meaning and insights that enable clients to identify themes in their stories. Clients also gain insight into their lives by asking questions about these elements:

- how they feel their current situation or life circumstance developed (i.e., Could you help me understand...?)
- what approaches or practices have been tried to resolve issues (i.e., I am curious about...)
- to what degree have efforts been or not been successful (i.e., In what way...?)
- what clients have considered but haven't tried (i.e., How might it have been helpful to...?)
- what they might consider in future (i.e., How would it make a difference if...?)

This type of inquiry explores the unique meaning that clients assign to their experiences, and this unique meaning can then be considered in planning. In essence, the processes of relational-centred planning shift from fact gathering to exposing and discovering personal truths and meaning, from setting goals for the client to co-creating intended outcomes or success indicators, and from establishing service plans to engaging in conversations and activities that expose opportunities for change that are developmentally enhancing. It is a collaborative approach based in conversations about "preferences" that can make a difference in clients' lives (Walter & Peller, 2000). This collaborative approach is guided by relational questions such as *What do we seem to need at this moment?* or, *What does our conversation require?*

We cannot avoid, nor would we want to avoid, determining where we are headed and what possibilities and opportunities might be pursued. The clear purpose in working with children, youth, and families is to assist them in achieving the developmental level of functioning they want in their lives.

There is also an awkward aspect of assessing and planning that occurs when people do not want to be involved. This poses a challenge: not in terms of whether or not we will identify possibilities and opportunities for change with them, but what it will take to connect, engage, and have conversations with people who do not want to have conversations. High-risk children and youth are known to avoid engaging in conversations about change. These children, youth, and families are simply trying to protect themselves by holding on to whatever safety and stability they have achieved in their lives.

This view is consistent with the work of Prochaska, Norcross, and DiClemente (1994), and more recently Freedman and Dolan (2001), who have researched the therapeutic change process. In their first two stages of the change process, *non-contemplation* and *anti-contemplation*, individuals are unaware of a problem or do not feel a need to change. For Freedman and Dolan, clients who have not considered the need to change are not rejecting or embracing the need for change: they have simply not yet discovered the need for change. It is only during the third stage, *pre-contemplation*, that people perceive their need to change, and it is during the fourth stage, *contemplation*, that they consider how they want to be different or want their circumstances to be different.

Whether the CYC practitioner is working with someone *ready to go* or with someone who has been ordered by the court into care and *does not want to be here* (i.e., group care), the terms for planning and assessment are the same. However, the conversations will be quite different because the stories will be quite different. The ready to go conversation will likely be open to exploring how we got here, what happened, who is involved in the story, what strengths and assets can be brought into play, what possibilities and opportunities abound, who can be relied on for support and care, what changes are appealing, and so on. The conversation for the *person who does not want to be here* will likely create a story of how they do not belong here, do not want to be here, do not know how they got here and do not want to explore it; further, this person will likely see no strengths or assets, and will repeatedly respond with "I don't know" to any question posed. The "I don't want to and you can't make me" stance makes it challenging to connect, to engage, to explore and inquire. For the practitioner and for the client, this condition of resistance and refusal to engage and move forward can all feel very negative and black. Until there is a respectful connection and engagement with each other, longer-term possibilities and opportunities for change are at best unrealistic, and usually are not relevant at this time.

Regardless of the client's readiness, consider the following categories when having conversations about preferences and outcomes.

- **Positive:** direct the focus to activities needed and wanted.

- **Process:** emphasize what the person will be doing differently or how the circumstances for the person will be different. For example, *Thank you for talking to me. Can we meet again? Is there anything I can do to make these conversations more comfortable for you? Would you rather talk to another staff member? What do you need and want from me to support you while you are here? Let's go for a walk.*

- **Present:** encourage the person to stay on task, and not to be dissuaded by the past or distracted by the future. What does the individual want to do right now?

- **Practical:** determine attainable preferences and outcomes that are meaningful enough to be significant and lead to a solution.

- **Specific:** identify preferences. For example, *How will you know when things are different?*

- **Client-control:** place the emphasis on what the client is doing so that he or she owns the solution.

- **Client-language:** allow the client's description of his or her situation to guide the formulation of preferences and outcomes.

Think/Do, Think/Do, Think/Do

The planning process is both a way of thinking and doing. It is incumbent on the CYC worker to understand how he or she works from thinking to doing while also attending to how the client thinks and does. One must avoid giving answers or telling people what to do but, at the same time, provide a map or blueprint for hearing the individual's story, use the unfolding facts from the story, determine what the client needs and wants, help the client decide what success will look like, take actions that will support the client's success, and allow that individual to celebrate his or her achievements with you.

The think/do process occurs at three levels in our minds: what is happening at this moment? what was happening in this session? and what is happening overall for the person(s) being served. It is necessary for the CYC practitioner to monitor these three levels of functioning for him- or herself and for all others involved in the assessment and planning process—including the *think/do* of other practitioners. The assessment and planning is a complex process of relating through the acquisition of story and meaning making to determine success indicators and move forward on a path that is still under construction.

After those involved in the planning are satisfied with the plan, it is often written out and submitted to the record keeping system. It is important to understand ahead of time what is required by the record keeping system, while recognizing that the steps and ways of thinking are guidelines for planning, not the law! The process moves forward, and then backtracks, moves forward, then stalls, and moves forward again, until the planners are ready to put the plan on paper and submit it. The steps and ways of thinking are not intended to dictate exactly what must be done but, rather, to suggest: *Hey, think about this!* or *Are the goals or outcomes realistic and relevant?* or, *Did we come up with an evaluation plan?*

OWNING ONE'S PRACTICE

Finally, to talk about assessment and intervention planning as relational requires CYC "workers" to function more as conscious "practitioners." This is particularly important in view of the fact that CYC practice is often situated within bureaucratic structures of the human services system and manifested across various institutional settings, including group homes, institutions, schools, non-profit agencies, and government services. These settings are regulated by long-standing cultures steeped in administrative requirements that can run counter to relational-centred practice. If CYC practitioners do not have a clear sense of effective relational practice, they may acquiesce to the bureaucratic culture, which can lead to feelings of frustration, resentment, and "burnout."

CONCLUSION

Our intention in this chapter has been to explore the creative potential of relational-centred practice as a frame for assessment and intervention planning. The discussion has been offered as an opportunity for CYC practitioners to critically reflect on how they undertake assessment and planning within the context of a relational-centred practice and what they might do differently.

REFERENCES

Anderson, H., & Goolishian, H. (1992). The client is the expert: A not-knowing approach to therapy. In S. McNamee & K. J. Gergen (Eds.), *Therapy as social construction* (pp. 25–39). London: Sage Publications.

Audi, R. E. G. (1995). *The Cambridge dictionary of philosophy.* Cambridge, UK: Cambridge University Press.

Backhurst, D., & Sypnowich, C. (Eds.) (1995). *The social self.* New York and London: Sage Publications.

Barrett-Lennard, G. T. (1998). *Carl Rogers' helping system: Journey and substance.* London: Sage.

Battle, M. (1997). *Reconciliation: The ubuntu theology of Desmond Tutu.* Cleveland, OH: Pilgrim Press.

Belt, L., & Stockley, R. (1989). *Improvisation through theatre sports: A curriculum to improve acting skills.* Seattle, WA: Thespis Productions.

Boyd, G. (1998). Pastoral conversation: A postmodern view of expertise. *Pastoral Psychology, 46*(5), 307–321.

Bronfenbrenner, U., & Evans, G. W. (2000). Developmental science in the 21st century: Emerging questions, theoretical models, research designs and empirical findings. *Social Development, 9*(1), 115–125.

Bugental, J. F. T. (1965). *The search for authenticity: An existential-analytic approach to psychotherapy.* New York: Holt, Rinehart, and Winston, Inc.

Campaign 2000. (2006). Reducing child poverty to increase productivity: A human capital strategy. Retrieved January 16, 2007, from http://www.campaign2000.ca/res/briefs/ReducingChildPovertyToIncreaseProductiivity.pdf

Carse, A., & Nelson, H. L. (1996). Rehabilitating care. *Kennedy Institute of Ethics Journal, 6*(1), 19–35.

Cecchin, G. (1987). Hypothesizing, circularity, and neutrality revisited: An invitation to curiosity. *Family Process, 26*(4), 405–413.

Dachler, H. P., & Hosking, D. M. (1995). The primacy of relations in socially constructing organizational realities. In D. M. Hosking, H. P. Dachler, & K. J. Gergen (Eds.), *Management and organization: Relational alternatives to individualism* (pp. 1–28). Aldershot: Avebury.

Dunn, J. (1993). *Young children's close relationships.* London: Sage.

Erickson, R. (1995). The importance of authenticity for self and society. *Symbolic Interaction, 18*(2), 121–144.

Fewster, G. (1990). *Being in child care: A journey into self.* New York: The Haworth Press, Inc.

Fletcher, J. (1998). Relational practice: A feminist reconstruction of work. *Journal of Management Inquiry, 7*(2), 163–186.

Fletcher, J. (1999). *Disappearing acts: Gender, power and relational practice at work.* Cambridge, MA: MIT Press.

Flexner, S. B. (Ed.). (1995). *The Random House dictionary of the English language, unabridged* (2nd ed.). New York: Random House.

France, R., & Robson, M. (1975). *Cognitive behavioural therapy in primary care: A practical guide.* London: Jessica Kingsley.

Frankl, V. (1984). *Man's search for meaning.* New York: Pocket Books.

Freeman, A., & Dolan, M. (2001). Revising Prochaska and DiClemete's stages of change theory: An expansion and specifications to aid in treatment planning and outcome evaluation. *Cognitive and Behavior Practice, 8*(3), 224–234.

Freire, P. (1970/2005). *Pedagogy of the oppressed.* (New rev. 20th anniversary ed.). New York: Continuum.

Garfat, T. (1993). On blind spots and blank spots. *Journal of Child and Youth Care, 8*(4), iii–iv.

Garfat, T. (1998). The effective child and youth care intervention. *Journal of Child and Youth Care, 12*(1), 1–178.

Garfat, T. (2003). Committed to the relational. *Relational Child and Youth Care Practice, 16*(3), 3–5.

Gergen, K. J. (1994). *Realities and relationships: Soundings in social construction.* Cambridge, MA: Harvard University Press.

Gergen, K. J. (1999). *An invitation to social construction.* London: Sage.

Gove, P. B. (Ed.). (1996). *Webster's third new international dictionary of the English language, unabridged.* Springfield, MA: Merriam-Webster.

Guignon, C. (1984). Heidegger's "authenticity" revisited. *Review of Metaphysics, 38*, 321–339.

Guignon, C. (1993). Authenticity, moral values, and psychotherapy. *Cambridge companion to Heidegger.* (pp. 215–239) Cambridge: Cambridge University Press.

Harbus, A. (2002). The medieval concept of the self in Anglo-Saxon England. *Self and Identity, 1*, 77–97.

Harter, S. (2002). Authenticity. In C. R. Snyder & S. Lopez (Eds.), *Handbook of positive psychology* (pp. 382–394). London, UK: Oxford University Press.

Heidegger, M. (2004). *Being and time* (J. Macquarrie & E. Robinson, Trans.). Oxford: Blackwell. (Original work published 1962)

Jarvis, P. (1992). *Paradoxes of learning: On becoming an individual in society.* San Francisco: Jossey-Bass.

Jordan, J. V., Kaplan, A. G., Miller, J. B., Stiver, I. P., & Surrey, J. L. (1991). *Women's growth in connection: Writings from the Stone Center.* New York: Guilford Press.

Kernis, M. (2003a). Optimal self-esteem and authenticity: Separating fantasy from reality. *Psychological Inquiry, 14*(1), 83–89.

Kernis, M. (2003b). Toward a conceptualization of optimal self-esteem. *Psychological Inquiry, 14*(1), 1–26.

Krueger, M. A. (1991). Coming from the center, being there, meeting them where they're at, interacting together, counselling on the go, creating circles of caring, discovering and using self, and caring for one another: Central themes in professional child and youth care. *Journal of Child and Youth Care, 5*(1), 77–87.

Krueger, M. A. (2000). Child and youth care as dance. *CYC-Online, 13*(4).

Krueger, M. A. (Ed.). (2004). *Themes and stories in youthwork practice.* New York: The Haworth Press.

Langer, E. (1997). *The power of mindful learning.* Menlo Park, CA: Addison-Wesley Publishing Co., Inc.

Levinas, E. (1998). *Entre nous: On thinking-of-the-other* (M. B. Smith & B. Harshav, Trans.). New York: Columbia University Press.

Maier, H. W. (1991). Exploring the substance of care practice. *Child and Youth Care Forum, 20*(6), 393–411.

Markus, H., & Kitayama, S. (1991). Culture and the self: Implications for cognition, emotion, and motivation. *Psychological Review, 98*(2), 224–252.

Maslow, A. H. (1968). *Toward a psychology of being* (2nd ed.). New York: Van Nostrand Reinhold.

Maslow, A. H. (1970). *Motivation and personality* (2nd ed.). New York: Harper & Row.

McGoldrick, M., & Carter, B. (1999). Self in context: The individual life cycle in systemic perspective. In B. Carter & M. McGoldrick (Eds.), *The expanded family life cycle: Individual, family, and social perspectives* (3rd ed., pp. 27–46). Boston: Allyn and Bacon.

McLeod, M. (2006, March). This is the buddha's love. *Shambhala Sun,* 50–57.

Miller, J. B. (1986). *Toward a new psychology of women* (2nd ed.). Boston: Beacon.

Mokgoro, J. (1998). *Ubuntu and the law in South Africa.* Retrieved February 5, 2005, from http://epf.ecoport.org/appendix3.html

National Collaborative Centre for Determinants of Health. (2007). Web Site, http://www.nccdh.ca/index.html

Nietzsche, F. (1967). *Basic writing of Nietzsche* (W. Kaufmann, Ed. & Trans.). New York: Modern Library.

Nodding, N. (2002). *Educating moral people: A caring alternative to moral education.* New York: Teachers College Press.

Palmer, P. (1987, September/October). Community, conflict, and ways of knowing. *Change*, 20–25.

Porr, C. (2005). Shifting from preconceptions to pure wonderment. *Nursing Philosophy, 6*(3), 189–195.

Prochaska, J. O., Norcross, J. C., & DiClemente, C. C. (1994). *Changing for good.* New York: Avon Books.

Rand, M., & Fewster, J. (1997). Self, boundaries and containment: Integrative body psychotherapy. In C. Caldwell (Ed.), *Getting in touch: The guide to new body-centered therapies* (pp. 71–89). Illinois: Quest Books.

Ricks, F., & Bellefeuille, G. (2003). Knowing: The critical error of ethics in family work. *Child and Youth Services, 25*(1/2), 117–130.

Ricks, F., & Charlesworth, J. (2003). *Emergent practice planning.* New York: Kluwer Academic/Plenum Publishers.

Ricks, F., Charlesworth, J., Bellefeuille, G., & Field, A. (1999). *All together now: Creating a social capital mosaic.* Ottawa, ON: Vanier Institute of the Family.

Robinson, K. (2001). *Out of our minds: Learning to be creative.* Oxford, UK: Capstone.

Rogers, C. R. (1951). *Client-centered therapy: Its current practice, implications, and theory.* Boston: Houghton Mifflin.

Rogers, C. R. (1959). A theory of therapy, personality and interpersonal relationships, as developed in the client-centered framework. In S. Koch (Ed.), *Psychology: A study of science* (pp. 184–256). NewYork: McGraw Hill.

Seligman, M. E. P. (2002). *Authentic happiness: Using the new positive psychology to realize your potential for lasting fulfillment.* New York: Free Press/Simon and Schuster.

Sheldon, K. M., & Kasser, T. (2001). Goals, congruence, and positive wellbeing: New empirical support for humanistic theories. *Journal of Humanistic Psychology, 41*(1), 30–50.

Shutte, A. (1993). *Philosophy for Africa.* Rondebosch, SA: UCT Press.

Stewart, D., & Mickunas, A. (1990). *Exploring phenomenology: A guide to the field and its literature* (2nd ed.). Ohio: Ohio University Press.

Stern, D. N. (1985). *The interpersonal world of the infant.* New York: Basic Books.

Stern, D. N. (2004). *The present moment in psychotherapy and everyday life.* New York: W. W. Norton.

Stern, M. B. (2002). *Child-friendly therapy: Biopsychosocial innovations for children and families.* New York: W. W. Norton.

Trungpa, C. (1991). *Orderly chaos: The mandala principle* (S. Chodzin, Ed.). Boston: Shambhala.

Vanier, J. (1985). *Community and growth.* New York: Paulist Press.

VanderVen, K. (1999). You are what you do and become what you've done: The role of activity in the development of self. *Journal of Child and Youth Care, 13*(2), 133–147.

van Manen, M. (1990). *Researching lived experience: Human science for an action sensitive pedagogy.* Albany, NY: State University of New York Press.

Walter, J., & Peller, J. (2000). *Recreating brief therapy: Preferences and possibilities.* New York: Norton.

Weingarten, K. (1994). *The mother's voice: Strengthening intimacy in families.* New York: Harcourt-Brace.

Wheatley, M. J. (2002). *Turning to one another: Simple conversations to restore hope to the future* (1st ed.). San Francisco: Berrett-Koehler Publishers, Inc.

CHAPTER 3

Building Developmental Capacities

A Developmentally Responsive Approach to Child and Youth Care Intervention

Jack Phelan, MS

ABSTRACT

Child and Youth Care (CYC) work is described as a relational process with a developmental focus. While relational approaches and developmental theory are fundamental aspects of CYC education, practice often does not reflect the use of developmental approaches. In fact, many CYC strategies are focused on creating responsible behaviour, not responsible people, which actually blocks developmental progress. This chapter will describe the value of working developmentally, presents a model of developmentally responsive practice, and describes the difficulties CYC practitioners often experience when trying to implement a developmentally responsive program model.

INTRODUCTION

This chapter will describe the developmental issues and "stuckness" of the people we serve, the professional stages of Child and Youth Care (CYC) practitioner development, and the critical developmental *Line in the Sand* that needs to be crossed to be successful in managing life challenges.

Why is Developmental Theory Useful?

All developmental theories organize human growth and capability in a series of stages that occur in a predetermined pattern. A person moves through these stages by mastering the tasks or competencies of each stage in a predictable order. The usefulness of knowing about developmental stages is that it assists you as the helper to focus support where the person being helped is most capable of learning and growing. By understanding the behaviours and beliefs prevalent during any stage, you can determine what stage the other person is in and how to create learning and support for growth into the next stage. For example, a person who is struggling with personal safety needs to feel safe and secure before any other growth can occur. Using Erikson's formats (Berk, 2006), the focus after feeling safe is to struggle with personal power. Instead of directing our efforts to create, in general, some ideal or problem-free person, we are able to support growth in manageable steps. Developmental theory can also assist you, as a continually growing professional, to manage your own attempts at helping by enabling you to accurately determine your own constantly evolving competencies. A final use for developmental approaches is that they can create a *Line in the Sand*—a goal or target for your overall helping efforts, a critical point of developmental growth—that will determine future self-directed success.

The Youth and Families are Often Stuck

The developmental issues we often see in our youth and families start with the belief that people have only two options: either you are a victimizer or a victim. This eat or be eaten world view usually creates troublesome behaviours. Low attachment ability and a belief that no one is willing to help you are also combined with this ego-centric, unsafe point of view. Consequently, our youth and families live in a world where the only people who seem to be willing to help them are also, apparently, trying to take advantage of them in some fashion. There appears to be no particular reason for anyone to be kind to them without expecting something in return. In essence, then, most of the youth and families referred for CYC interventions do not have the developmental capacity to understand the demonstrations of generosity and caring that they receive, except as some form of paid task that CYC staff members are required to provide. The concepts of caring for and nurturing children are beyond the experiential and cognitive ability of many of our youth and parents to grasp.

Often the youths do not understand why they are being punished or rewarded by the adults around them, except in a very ego-centric manner. They believe that everyone acts entirely out of self-interest (which is logical to them); thus, when an adult punishes them, it is because it gives the adult some satisfaction, even joy. CYC practitioners often look satisfied in the youth's eyes when delivering some "logical consequence" to teach a lesson, and the only logic available to the youth is that the worker enjoys punishing kids. Many youth are stuck in a distorted reality that is limited by their emotional, social, cognitive, and sometimes physical development.

The profound level of this *developmental stuckness* is neither identified nor appreciated by many helpers. Often we expect that the developmental stage–logic available to us is shared by our charges. When the response to our good intentions is suspicion or resentment, we have a hard time understanding that the other person is being developmentally appropriate in that moment, given their developmental stage. It is only through creating safe relationships in the youth's life-space, and truly understanding the world from the youth's developmental perspective, that strengths and skills become visible. The intrinsic values and strengths of a youth who happens to be functioning at the level of primary developmental stages only become apparent after connecting with this stuckness. Interestingly, as soon as we are able to join in the youth's logic, many new approaches, strategies, and opportunities emerge. Once we break through this barrier to understanding the world view of the youth, we will see myriad life-space strategies to support change.

The combination of the two dynamics just discussed—survival fears and an inability to reach out for help—dooms people to be stuck fairly permanently and tragically in the lowest developmental stages. Unless they can move forward, slowly approaching the critical line in the sand, they will continue to need intervention and support in their lives. Because we are able to join people where they live developmentally, we can create this growth and change opportunity. The focus on behaviour moves into the background and becomes the landscape that frames the environment. Developmental issues and stages become the highlighted area of attention.

Stuck on an Island

The metaphor of a person stuck on a desert island—barely surviving, living day to day, and feeling powerless to create any change—is a useful model for consideration. The developmental logic and physical needs of that person are significantly different because of where he is, and he will continue to be stuck using lower-stage forms of coping until the situation changes. If you were to attempt to help him by advising him to use better table manners, use socially acceptable speech, go to school, get a job, or establish regulated bedtimes, he would probably resist, perhaps fairly loudly, saying that this isn't what he needs.

Perhaps you are able to recognize the youth's situation more accurately but don't have any resources to help, merely agreeing that he/she is stuck. The person in need clearly requires a person who can join him and who also has the tools and skills to support him to move to a better place. What is needed is a helper who can join with the youth in this difficult place and then journey to a better place with him, where that individual can let go of the behaviours and beliefs that currently limit his opportunities for change. Once the person is free of the conditions that are keeping him stuck, he can begin to move ahead developmentally.

To be effective, we must be willing to enter the other person's world view and belief system, and this is very demanding. Working with some youth and families can be as daunting as performing a rescue mission. The interesting part is that once you are able to see the world through the other person's developmental lens, a multitude of possible helping strategies emerge and, more importantly, there is also a clarity about what is not needed.

When working in a large children's agency many years ago, I asked children and youth a list of time- and space-orientation questions. Examples of these questions are how old are you, when is you birthday, what year is it, how far do you have to go to get to school, where do your brothers and sisters live, what is your phone number, and so on. The children were all between 8 and 13 years old. The youth who had been identified by the CYC staff as the most difficult scored significantly lower on time and space orientation. These children did not know where they were. Literally, they could have been on a desert island.

Building Developmental Capacities

Effective CYC practitioners see behaviour as a manifestation of developmental stages, not as a separate phenomenon or indicator for meaningful analysis. The social logic utilized by the youth and families we serve often makes their behaviour appear to be self-defeating and chaotic, when it is really a self-protective, practical response to the world as they experience it. Understanding a person's developmental stages is the key to creating useful growth and change. For example, the developmental stuckness most frequently displayed is a lack of personal power and an inability to cause many personally favourable results, which severely impedes any higher-level developmental successes. For Erikson, the issue of autonomy can also be understood as a lack of belief in having an internal locus of control, a victim stance, an ego-centric and uncaring point of view that is sometimes labelled oppositional and even sociopathic. The epitome of autonomy expression is the "terrible two-year-old" shouting NO to every request. Somehow, even though parents label this behaviour terrible, they are still able to support the toddler to feel strong and move ahead. This very primitive developmental stage creates an interesting counter-response in helpers, especially new, unsafe people. The reaction to this developmental need for more pure power and self-determination is to deliver threats of reprisal and counter-aggression, which keeps the youth feeling powerless.

Children and youth with low attachment ability and/or have suffered many disappointments and traumas, and who generally have good reasons to lose hope for the future, can quite often get stuck in the Autonomy stage of development. The only powerful response obviously available to them is to resist external control, and the resulting emotion is anger, which grows out of shame. One of the usual responses from us to this resistance to control, when we lack awareness of the developmental approach, is to demand compliance with our view of what is needed. Thus, we often create unsuccessful people who do not learn how to solve their own problems. We manage to subvert our own intentions to be helpful and effectively keep these people stuck in a helpless, powerless, and hopeless state. Unfortunately, our treatment for this unfocussed resistance to being controlled by us is to regularly reinforce them for compliance.

Developmental Dynamics

There are many examples of behaviours we experience in CYC work that are puzzling and frustrating until interpreted developmentally. As described more fully on pages 84–88, Level 1 workers (Phelan, 1990) tend to evaluate behaviours from a personal reference viewpoint and do not consider a more ego-centric, primary level of development. The challenge is to learn to view behaviour empathically and to shift one's perspective from this "common sense" logic. Some examples may help:

> Youth who challenge our authority at every opportunity, especially in the presence of other youth, can be seen as trying to be strong and powerful, needing to win recognition.

> A youth who appears to be particularly inconsiderate— playing music too loudly, not sharing space, equipment, or the CYC staff's attention with others—is ready to struggle with self-control and empathy. This is the five-year-old's task. Her selfishness can be valued by CYC staff as a move forward rather than viewed as an immature response.

> Youth who engage in bullying or refuse to attend school can be seen as people who are struggling to be strong and independent rather than antisocial and problematic. They need practice with being strong rather than requiring external control.

CYC Family Support Workers face similar issues:

> Parents who are unable to clean their homes, get to the food bank, fill out needed forms, and so forth can be seen as lacking agency, autonomy, and hopefulness, rather than being uncooperative. Parents who neglect or abuse their children and seem to be resentful, even angry, about having to worry about someone else's neediness can be seen as having low attachment ability, stuck in feeling alone and powerless, with little ability to display nurturing behaviour, and having no personal experience or models to draw upon. Attempts to engage them in parenting classes, without focussing on the developmental stuckness, will just create more frustration, shame, and resentment.

Modlin (2003) describes a powerful example of running a group for parents that shifted dramatically as the CYC workers became more developmentally aligned with the parents, many of whom never felt that anyone even knew they existed:

> What was most striking about this group, for both facilitators, was the level of neediness and isolation experienced by these parents. Although we were aware of this going into the group, it was still an eye-opener to grasp the reality of these parents' situations. They were dealing with all the same issues as their children and, in some ways, were in much worse shape. In many cases, parents had a lot of information about appropriate parenting practices, absorbed through years of child welfare intervention, but were unable or unwilling to translate this knowledge into action. Until the parents' own needs could be met, it was impossible for them to look after the needs of their children. (p. 183)

Karen VanderVen (2003) has coined the term *Oxygen Principle* for working with parents:

> On airplanes, we have all experienced the instruction that should pressure decrease and oxygen masks be [deployed], parents should put their own masks on themselves before helping their children. Of course, this is counter-intuitive. Would we not want to help our children before ourselves? However, there is an important lesson here for our work with parents: *Before parents can truly accept and apply more nurturant and sensitive methods of parenting, they must first feel more nurtured and cared for themselves.* (p. 137)

Nurturing the parent is an important part of the helping process. Treatment strategies that assume the parents are already developmentally capable of creating a nurturing environment are fundamentally flawed. Cognitive awareness and behavioural training methods do not have a significant impact on these parents.

Living In the Moment

We encounter situations with youths in which they seem to have no ability to reflect on the past or anticipate future issues. They get into difficulty regularly and often display very poor judgement. Developmentally, I would like to suggest that these youths are trapped in the moment, not able to think about the past or future. Youths who have lived in alcoholic families often do not plan ahead because they have been unable to anticipate whether or not what was promised would actually occur. Some of our youths have been even more seriously damaged and have lost the ability to see cause and effect, or to use timeframes in their life situations.

> An example of this is a 16-year-old boy who asked me, his CYC worker, to lend him money on a Thursday, promising to pay me on Friday when he got his allowance. I lent him the money, and he disappeared Friday without paying me. On Saturday the same boy asked me to lend him money until the following Friday. When I incredulously refused, citing the Thursday promise, he became very angry and asked me why I was always bringing up the past! It took me several weeks of carefully observing this youth to realize that he was being very genuine, and that he lived moment to moment. It explained a great deal about his behaviour, and I was gradually able to support him to function more effectively after I stopped using my logic with him.

PROFESSIONAL DEVELOPMENT STAGES

Building Capacity to Work Developmentally

The capacity to be relationally present and developmentally congruent is a skill that constantly increases during your professional career. A parallel process occurs as your professional developmental capacity increases: you are more able to build developmental capacity in others in increasingly challenging situations. The question facing us is how can this capacity to join people in these fearful places be effectively developed in CYC practitioners? Typically, what stands in our way is that we are inclined to listen to the behavioural messages more than the developmental information communicated in day-to-day interactions.

Some examples may help:

> Level 1 workers regularly wonder how to handle a youth who refuses to follow directions—won't do homework, clean up, go to bed, and so on—without a major battle. The usual unsuccessful response of the worker is to overpower the youth with punishments or threats so that she complies. This power response to the youth's need for power keeps the youth stuck in a cycle of shame, doubt, and resultant anger and aggression that goes nowhere. Typically, the

power demands of the youth trigger competence fears in the Level 1 worker, who immediately becomes a parallel two-year-old pushing back and shouting "No."

A youth with a small physical build who sometimes acts aggressively to protect himself from possible attack by others often challenges CYC staff, who will not retaliate. Helping him feel powerful would reduce this behaviour. If we treat this youth as if he were a larger, more powerful youth, he would not need to be so aggressive. Likewise, a bigger youth who relies on intimidation to feel powerful can be supported to discover other talents and interests that enable him to feel strong and capable; this is preferable to treating him as an aggressive threat.

When we are able to work developmentally, our response is to look for as many opportunities as possible in the life-space for youth to feel powerful and strong and to avoid overpowering them in the battle for compliance. This requires us to be strategic and thoughtful workers who are not threatened by "two-year-old" behaviour. Our fight/flight reaction has to be mastered so that we may calmly interact with a demanding, intimidating youth.

The real work is to join people at their developmental level and journey with them to a higher functioning level. CYC practice involves meeting people at the place they are stuck and trying to see the world from that point of view. This does not happen in a comfortable office but, rather, in the life-space (Phelan, 2007, p. 4). Charlie Appelstein (1998) says it well in his chapter on developmental considerations in his insightful book *No Such Thing As a Bad Kid*:

> Children who have difficulty relating to others are often displaying unmet needs. At such times, the message behind their misbehaviour is: "I'm stuck at an earlier developmental stage and need help moving through it. Give me now what I should have received *then*." The better we are at recognizing the developmental messages behind misconduct, the more effective our response will be. (p. 29)

Appelstein suggests that adult care givers need to become "fillers, not talkers," to create effective change (p. 41). He goes on to describe developmental filling as providing experiential, activity based interventions rather than counselling conversations.

In Appelstein's (1994) earlier work, *The Gus Chronicles*, his young protagonist describes the task:

> What a child care worker does is *parent two-year-old behavior*. I'm clear about this. Acting-out, obstinacy, tantrumming—all normal two-year-old behaviors—appear everyday in a residential center. When kids improve and display three-, four-, and five-year-old behavior, they're discharged and a new two comes in. Like clockwork. (p. 16)

The real question is, can you think like a delinquent youth, a sexually irresponsible young person, an apparently neglectful mother, a depressed child? What exactly does this require? For Level 1 workers, this is accomplished by means of a surface connection, not a deeper relationship. Occasionally some staff will have a background similar to that of the person they are helping and can see the developmentally different logic more clearly. Taking on the less sophisticated logic of a primitive and ego-centric (developmentally stuck) person requires knowing your own developmental process and how it can be used to support what is missing for the one being helped. Consider these examples:

> It can be helpful to support a male teen be sexually responsible by getting him to understand that if he wears a condom more girls will want to have sex with him. Our tendency is to recoil at this rationale, yet it can be a useful starting place to compare developmental logic.

> Persuading a teenage girl to worry about pregnancy by appealing to her need to look good, and describing how fat and unattractive she will become when pregnant, is not generally the argument proffered by adults seeking to promote safe sex practices, but it is the most sensible one to motivate some youths.

We tend to use arguments that are developmentally logical to us, but our logic will have no impact on a person who is developmentally less mature. Using the developmentally sound logic of an adult to encourage a youth who lives and thinks on a day-to-day basis to go to school, because it will significantly influence future success, is likely to be ineffective. There actually are many good reasons, day-to-day, to attend school. If we do not identify and understand the different reasons that children and youth attend school, we will probably not be able to tap into what might prove motivating in a particular situation.

Professional Development is a Parallel Process

Another important dynamic is the personal developmental stage of the CYC practitioner, illustrated in the inset on pages 84–88 (Phelan, 1990). Each CYC practitioner progresses through stages of professional competence that are influenced by experience and supervision. Educational preparation does not shorten the process, although it strongly influences eventual professional capability. CYC practitioners need to realize that their classroom education is the starting place, the foundation for a series of professional development stages that are always evolving.

During the first year of practice, CYC professionals struggle with physical safety concerns as well as competence anxiety (Phelan, 1990). Developmentally, you are functioning at Level 1 in the model, mastering the skills of providing safety and managing behaviour. The focus for the Level 1 worker is on creating external control and safety, both for the youths and for the worker him- or herself. During your first year of practice, your main goal is to master your fight/flight reaction as you encounter conflict and resistance. Experience and good supervision gradually support the Level 1 worker to develop competence and confidence, which is the foundation that enables one to move to the next stage.

As a Level 2 worker, you are now able to implement a developmentally responsive approach. You are personally safe and grounded in your practice, so relationships and developmental strategies are now your focus. Conflicts and challenging behaviour are met with curiosity, not anxiety. Your ability to see skills and resiliencies has greatly expanded, and your need for punishments and external control has diminished. The Level 3 worker exercises further expansion of professional competency; now you are able to establish Nexus relationships (Krueger, 1995) and use the life-space in creative, complex ways.

The Personal Challenge

There are some good reasons for this real inability to connect developmentally with youth and families. When we engage with people at a lower developmental level, there are some clear challenges. The major challenge for us becomes one of developing our capacity to be curious about developmental differences and be willing to join the other person at a developmentally lower place. This fundamental shift in perspective is more than a skill set or a theoretical technique, although it does require a firm grounding in theory and a variety of in-the-moment skills. We each have a basic ego-centric point of view that informs all our thinking and sensing as we engage in life events with others. Because of the ego-centric nature of "knowing," we generally assume that a great deal of our "meaning-making" is shared by the other. Yet the social logic that we use is often quite different than it is for people who are in a developmentally different place.

Level 1 CYC practitioners struggle with physical safety concerns as well as competence anxiety, which dominate the first year of practice. Using a developmental approach is very challenging for them, and external control remains a major focus because it reduces the worker's anxiety. It is worth noting that some mature practitioners also struggle with developmental approaches. As workers becomes better able to join people in developmentally different places, because they have mastered the ability to form safe relationships, these workers begin to appreciate the emotional and spiritual risks of connecting and joining at these dark and helpless places and prefer to avoid such challenges (Phelan, 2002, p. 52).

The term *nexus* (Krueger, 1995) has been used to describe this connection, which is a comprehensive joining with the other, not just a point of contact. To see the world from a developmentally different point of view and appreciate the logic and behaviour that emerges from it is to challenge your own beliefs and principles for conduct. An effective CYC practitioner must be physically, emotionally, and spiritually grounded. Anything less and the practitioner will either need to argue with the other person's mental framework or be tempted to join them.

The stages of CYC practitioner development, which are more elaborately detailed in an article on CYC supervision (Phelan, 1990), are described below.

Level 1 – The Capable CareGiver

The basic dynamic that drives this stage is the issue of Safety. This is a fundamental step in professional development that lasts for 12 to 18 months for the new worker.

The tasks for the Level 1 worker include these:

- creating a safe environment
- establishing external control where and when needed
- using rules and routines to develop predictability

- establishing oneself as a competent and trustworthy "caregiver"
- handling aggressive threats and interactions with youth
- handling aggression between youth
- removing aggression as a dynamic in the environment
- creating strategies to establish one's authority as an adult
- avoiding the use of threats or coercion to control behaviour

The internal process for the new worker includes these components:

- feeling unsafe, overwhelmed, outside of one's personal comfort zone
- looking outside oneself for techniques and models to imitate
- having frequent fight or flight reactions to situations
- looking for safe youth to connect with

Level 1 supervisory strategies include the following:

- needing to be seen as trustworthy and safe by the worker
- modelling the safety and trust that the worker can achieve
- being congruent, and not being a "Monday morning quarterback"
- minimizing power struggles with and coercion of the worker
- focusing on how to feel safe

Level 2 – The Treatment Planner and Change Agent

The challenge of this stage is for the worker to let go of the comfortable skill set that has been so useful in dealing with youth and to learn a new set of skills that will transfer control to the youth. The use of external control to create safety will be reduced and perhaps, in some cases, eliminated so that the youth can begin to develop the self-control needed to be successful.

The tasks for the Level 2 worker include these:

- creating opportunities for youth to be independent
- relaxing external control, and eliminating punishments and consequences
- developing comfort with uncertainty and confusion when youths refuse to be responsible for themselves and try to get adults to take over and make decisions for them
- encouraging experiments with choices, and providing the freedom to succeed or fail
- being able to trust one's judgement and trusting a youth to make good decisions
- understanding how to use the environment creatively to challenge youth
- using recreation and daily living experiences in a strategic and educational way
- using theoretical knowledge and assessment concepts to create learning opportunities for youth
- reducing the focus on negative behaviours
- becoming capable of doing things differently when existing strategies aren't working
- fine tuning the program for each youth, and not expecting the same ideas to work for everyone
- as a team member, supporting other workers' creative ideas and experiments
- planning treatment and individual programming
- becoming a key worker and creating relationships with youth

Level 2 supervisory strategies include the following:

- encouraging creative thinking, focussing on letting go of rules and consequences
- developing strength-based approaches that focus on the worker's strengths and the youth's strengths
- establishing a new level of learning and discouraging reliance on external control techniques

- supporting a differential view of the group by acknowledging the need for unique approaches to youth and group change over time
- evaluating the amount of self-control being transferred to the youth as an indicator of success generated by the work being done
- supporting risks with the program rules and routines without criticizing failed experiments

Level 3 — The Creative, Free-Thinking Professional

The worker at this stage has mastered the basic safety and caring skills and has developed the ability to use relationships and the youth's internal motivation to create a focus on self-control.

Capacities for the Level 3 worker include these:

- Strategic use of life-space interviews, experiential learning, and development of competence are embedded in all of the worker's interactions.
- This worker is articulate about the treatment that is happening and can design plans for both individuals and the group.
- The new challenge at this stage is to be able to develop innovative treatment strategies and to modify the program where needed to fit individual youth.
- This worker can use the experience gained with prior youth to fit new behaviour into a context that isn't formulaic but builds on this knowledge.
- This worker is convinced of the importance of self-awareness and discusses his/her own issues as often as the youth's when creating ways to support change.

Level 3 supervisory strategies include the following:

- treating the Level 3 worker as a colleague who may want to learn supervision skills
- assigning the job of mentoring newer workers

- expecting the Level 3 worker to evaluate existing program ideas and suggest changes
- creating a training workshop or writing about a CYC skills
- re-designing a recreational program to fit youths' needs

Professional Development Levels

A central issue for CYC staff is that we cannot function at a higher developmental stage professionally than we have achieved personally, which is why the newer Level 1 worker, who is stuck focussing on personal safety and personal power, has great difficulty letting go of the need to exert control over upsetting behaviour. The Level 1 worker describes being challenged or tested by youth. Another way to understand this is that the worker's developmental struggles with safety create an energy that triggers the youth's developmental fears, and he or she responds accordingly.

Level 1 family support workers who are functioning in a less mature Family Life Cycle stage than some of their case family members may need particularly sensitive supervision. Newer family support workers often report being challenged by family members who ask them if they have children of their own. This rarely comes up after they have been practicing for a few years and believe in their own competence. Effective workers have moved through the professional development stages of mastering concerns about safety and competence and have acquired a belief in their own ability to create growth and change, and they are significantly more advanced in their practice.

Good supervision and supportive colleagues help new workers to develop self-awareness and, through this process, to access resiliencies and developmental strengths acquired through life experiences. This use of the "observing ego" can support the worker to grow and mature. Schon (1983) has accurately described the skills of personal reflection that benefit helpers, and this type of self-consciousness is very useful for CYC professionals.

Recent CYC graduates often find that the theories that were so clearly understood in the classroom are not easily applied in the life-space. There is a clear difference between experienced, less-academically qualified staff on the one hand, and, on the other, new graduates who are still Level 1 workers. Social services agencies have always valued older, more mature workers in their hiring practices, although perhaps not fully cognizant of why this is, other than an intuitive recognition of the greater complexity that more developmentally experienced people bring to the table. Our field is one of the few professions that values older people at both the educational admission and hiring points. I would suggest it is because age innately includes the possibility of developmental complexity.

THE DEVELOPMENTALLY RESPONSIVE APPROACH

The Functioning Club

The goal of every theory of helping is to create more members of The Functioning Club, a metaphorical, imaginary place that expels people who do not behave well enough. We try to enrol our charges in this club and hope that they remain capable members after we stop supporting them. For the youth or family to gain entry into the club and remain as socially functioning members, there is a clear developmental line in the sand that must be crossed. I suggest our primary role is to support the youth or family's developmental progress to this critical point, after which their developmental energy and maturity will sustain them and enable them to move forward independently.

The two basic developmental skills required for continuing club membership are self-control and empathy. Both of these are built on a foundation of autonomy, personal agency, and power. Self-control is not necessary or even possible until a person believes that he or she is able to initiate action voluntarily. The social contract, often referred to as the Golden Rule, is neither logical nor practical until one can take other people's needs into account. Empathy, simple consideration for others, is a basic motivator for self-control. Once a person has progressed developmentally to this level of awareness, he or she will have the ability to manage life challenges without our support. This should be the target of all our developmental efforts.

The Developmental Line in the Sand

The developmental journey that must be completed can be explained with various theories that are familiar to CYC practitioners at every level of professional practice. The stuckness experienced by each individual may be unique, but the pathway to developmental progress is similar in that development is progressive, and progress in one area of development generally supports progress in other areas.

Children, youth, and families need to feel safe and that they are able to have a predictable environment before progressing developmentally, so chaos and poor management have no place in a developmentally responsive program. Self-direction and personal agency are the foundations that self-control is built upon. Moral reasoning and thinking ability, particularly in relation to cause-and-effect beliefs, have to be a focus, as does creating attachment and connection through relational practice. Resiliency and strengths must be supported, and social control may have to be sacrificed in the short run. All behaviour, even self-defeating and hard to manage behaviour, has to be nested within and seen as part of the developmental journey.

Figure 1.

Erickson	Piaget	Kohlberg	Attachment Ability	Grief and Loss
Trust Safety Power	Pre-operational magical one-dimensional Concrete	Pre-conventional	Insecurely attached Anger	Denial Bargaining
The Functioning Club		The Line In The Sand		
Self-Control Competence Identity	Logical Formal abstract	Conventional Post-conventional	Securely attached	Sadness Acceptance

THE COMPLEXITY OF WORKING DEVELOPMENTALLY

Complexity Inside Simplicity

In order to understand this approach, let's first examine the complexity of working developmentally. CYC practice is very complex, though done with seemingly simple tools in everyday settings. To the outsider it can look fairly easy and straightforward, but that is an illusion. The ability to let go of your own "common sense" point of view and join another in a difficult place is a major personal challenge. The added ability to support the other person to get unstuck and move ahead requires understanding and preparation in terms of growth and development and how to support this shift. The people with whom we work tend to resist simple and straightforward helping strategies because these behavioural strategies typically do not address the complexity of their lives. Such strategies tend to focus on specific behavioural changes rather than address the person's belief in the need for change.

Dynamic Connections

Working developmentally is a bit like playing three-dimensional chess: all the components exist in a complex and dynamic relationship. The more angles you can bring into conscious focus to reveal the situation, the better you and those you work with can see what is needed. Every aspect or the theory of development affects other developmental issues. Each aspect of functioning (social, emotional, physical) affects the youth's total developmental growth; therefore, increasing capacity in one area often affects other areas of functioning. In developmental work it is important to consider attachment dynamics, which are not, strictly speaking, considered developmental, but they, too, influence and potentially block developmental progress. Trauma experiences and loss issues must also be considered, although the main focus is developmental stuckness and ego-centric thinking.

Our focus shifts to creating support for people, especially youth in care, to enable them to move forward through the various developmental struggles that keep them stuck in immature and ego-centric behaviours. The goal of developmental programming is to develop responsible people who know how to exercise responsible behaviour.

A recent discussion with a CYC team about a 17-year-old male who is developmentally stuck in autonomy and displays quite immature behaviour may help to illustrate.

> The youth is the oldest and longest-standing member of the group home, but he is very childish and is often a scapegoat. He has joined a Tae-Kwon-Do club to help him develop a sense of personal strength as well as connect him to other community youth. He comes to breakfast one school-day morning wearing his Tae-Kwon-Do outfit, and the CYC practitioner is concerned that this is inappropriate to wear to the local high school and will probably result in the youth's being laughed at and possibly bullied by other youth. Developmentally, this youth needs to feel strong and capable, but his wearing of these clothes will probably create the opposite result. The CYC worker described how prior to adopting a developmental approach he would have refused to let the youth wear this outfit and would have indicated to the youth that his behaviour was childish. Instead, he admired the youth's choice of clothes, but then commented that he was concerned that some other teens at

school might laugh at his outfit and create the possibility of a fight erupting, in which case this youth would most certainly have to hurt someone. The youth was advised that because he was so powerful in martial arts, it was probably not a good idea to create unsafe conditions for other students. The youth decided to change his clothes based on being strong, not on being immature.

Good developmental CYC practice does not ignore behaviour: it simply does not focus on behaviour as the fulcrum for growth. CYC practitioners in a developmentally focussed program have more energy, feel less fatigue, and use more positive emotions. They are willing to risk being engaged and open, and to think beyond the obvious, surface-level of behaviour.

This approach is particularly appealing to CYC practitioners who understand the emotional and physical weariness that gradually pervades a behaviour control program. Staff, youth, and families can become jaded by the daily focus on trivial behaviour changes that everyone expects might not last longer than the amount of time that the controls are in place. One comes to appreciate that the more intently that those involved focus on specific behaviours, the easier it is to miss completely what is really going on.

Illustrations from the CYC Literature

There are many descriptions of developmental practice and its challenges in the CYC literature. Krueger (2008) describes the work this way:

> Two themes emerged...Relationships and human development. Without an understanding of relationships and human development and their multiple applications in the lived experience (interactions between workers and youth), we do not have child and youth care. Everything seems to move forward and back from these two ideas/phenomena, at least for me and many others, at least the ones I read and talk to. (n.p.)

Fewster (1990) has described the discussion that effective CYC practitioners engage in when describing the challenges of working developmentally. This scenario is drawn from a staff meeting discussion about who will be the best "key worker" for a particular youth:

> Doreen, the most experienced worker on the shift, described the "seductiveness" of moving toward the isolated world of a "detached" child.... [For Marlene, the] prospect of

working with Anna Marie brought up a number of issues around her own competence. As a child care worker, she continued to attribute a youngster's lack of response to her own lack of skills. She explained her sense of confusion whenever some "unknown" factor interrupts the flow of routine communication and behaviour. Beneath it all was the possibility of "being discovered." (pp. 82–83)

Kagan (1996) describes the difficulty of connecting with a chaotic family:

Visiting the Williams family was like sailing into a storm. Whatever direction we had was quickly lost. Our own balance and safety was precarious at best. After all, when things are flying through the air, anyone can be hit. (p. xii)

Krueger (2004) identifies the risks experienced by a family support worker (Amy Evans) in his recent book:

I am about to voluntarily encounter a potentially tense situation. It is currently my job, and I am getting paid for it and, spiritually, it feels like my journey at this time, but sometimes I would like to avoid it. This is how I often feel prior to arriving at many sessions with individuals and families, because what will be encountered is unpredictable. (p. 65)

Anglin (2002) has written about the pain experienced by virtually all youth in care and the reluctance of many CYC practitioners to connect with the youth at this difficult place. He writes eloquently about our tendency to create control rather than to create connection because it is too challenging for staff to go to this painful location. "The manner and degree to which this pain is responded to is one of the key indicators of the quality of care in a residence as experienced by the youth." (p. 111)

Ward and McMahon (1998) have written extensively about the difficulty of connecting with youth and how we often expect CYC workers to use some magical form of "intuition" rather than good developmental frameworks. In discussing assessment in a later work, Ward (2007) makes this statement:

It can be argued that assessment is the main means by which workers 'make sense', both in the sense of understanding the complexities of their task, and in the sense of helping their clients to understand and resolve the complex issues facing them. In the group care context, making sense of one's own task as a worker and helping the client make sense of her own life and its challenges often amount to the same thing, and it may be especially important for the worker to recognize that both activities are taking place at one and the same time. (pp. 125–126)

The emotional courage and maturity essential to competent CYC practice is noted by other authors (Hardwick & Woodhead, 1999):

Young people need adults who are brave enough to become aware and own that the adolescent problems they are working with are their own problems repeated, externalized in the young people. (p. 354)

Articulating Our Approach

The challenge for CYC treatment programs and CYC practitioners is to support people to be responsible, not just support responsible behaviour. In order to do this we must articulate our developmental methodology to other professional groups that expect us to deal with behaviour and continue to reinforce us for shaping the behaviour of youth and families into the required standards. When our overall approach to helping people who function in immature, unsophisticated (anti-social) ways is to create external control and demand adherence (compliance) to our more acceptable logic about behaviour, we violate our professional integrity.

The use of relationship to create this connection, potentially a nexus, where strengths and skills emerge, and developmentally different logic can be explored, is what we do better than other helping professions. The use of the life-space by a fully engaged CYC practitioner, who is present, skilled, and knowledgeable, enables people who have been beyond the reach of other, less intimate and less intense approaches, to move forward and be successful members of the Functioning Club.

The following case provides an example:

A CYC practitioner who worked in a small town in Alberta as a community youth liaison worker, under an FCSS grant, had a social worker as her supervisor and, in many ways, was perceived as an authority who would keep the adults in the community informed about youth issues—a sort of infiltrator of the youth sub-culture. She asked for a larger

Standing on the Precipice

office area because she wanted to run some groups, but this was refused because the other helping professionals didn't want groups of youth in the office area, which was a professional space.

This worker had many years of experience and knew what she wanted to create, so fortunately she didn't need supervision. She worked on establishing relationships with individual youth and families and quickly connected with the people that the court and school considered troublemakers.

As she created safe relationships, she gradually helped youth create relationships with each other: she supported older youth to work as reading mentors with younger, daycare-age children, and organized them to help out with the seniors home. She took her group rock climbing, which required youth to trust each other to provide safety (under the supervision of a trained professional), and they each grew in feeling safe, connected, and strong in many ways. She worked with some youths on Life Books, which helped them picture both a past and a future constructed from their own focus. She described herself as doing Relational CYC Work, and through this focus on growth she created behavioural influence.

One young man called her to ask if she would accompany him to court on a particular afternoon and she agreed. On the way to court he explained that he had not done the community hours of restitution ordered by the judge, and this was a hearing to deal with his breach of the conditions of the court order. He asked her if she would help him to accomplish the court ordered conditions, and she agreed to help him. When they arrived at the court, the young man was asked to explain his lack of compliance with the judge's order. Everyone expected him to mumble and express some form of "I don't know why." Instead, he was very polite and clear as he apologized to the judge and declared his intention to complete the required hours if the judge would approve of this, based on the support he expected to receive from his CYC worker. The judge, visibly surprised and obviously pleased, agreed to this. After the hearing, the judge approached the CYC worker and congratulated her for getting this youth to behave so well in court. The CYC worker looked surprised and stated that she had nothing

> to do with his court behaviour, and she had no need for him to behave one way or the other. The social worker and probation officer, also present in court, received similar responses when they also congratulated her for the youth's appropriate behaviour.
>
> Over the next few days, the CYC worker had coffee with the judge, the social worker, and the probation officer to explain that her work involves creating safe relationships that gradually extend to connecting youth to the community in a variety of ways. She did not try to create responsible behaviour; instead, she created the developmental shifts that eventually resulted in responsible people, a much more complex task.

The result of the expanded of awareness of her role, on the part of the other authorities involved in the legal and youth care system, was the creation of a group work area in the office, a raise in pay, and approval of a request for tuition to support her return to college to get a BA in CYC. This CYC practitioner's ability to resist the justice and care systems' agenda to create a social control program by reframing their goals and tasks, and the effective use of CYC approaches, demonstrated her developmental maturity. If we are willing to be told what and how to do our work by others, then we need to be aware of the low level of our own professional development.

The developmentally responsive practitioner is a confident, mature CYC professional who has mastered the praxis of his or her craft. Our future as a method of professional practice is critically connected to our capacity to set the bar high for ourselves and others. Truly helping "difficult to serve" people will require those of us who claim the CYC title to move away from safe and simple interventions and superficial explanations of what we do.

The strategic use of the life-space to create experiences that build strength and competence is our unique CYC agenda. The use of nexus relationships to join people in dark and difficult places, and moving forward with them without coercion, is a far more intimate connection than we often describe in our treatment plans.

As CYC professionals we must be more articulate about what we do, and we must set our own agenda. A developmentally responsive CYC professional displays creativity and energy for life-long learning. CYC educational programs initiate the first developmental stage of a multi-phased series of growth steps that continues throughout one's professional lifetime. Our developmental journey is no less challenging than the one we prescribe for others.

Advocacy and Articulate Rationales

We have to comprehensively describe our work to other professionals to advocate effectively for the families we serve. Obvious approaches, or professional boundaries that do not appreciate life-space work, do not serve us or our families.

Family support workers confront many situations that seem simple, yet are quite complex. A young mother abandons her child to go out and have some fun. The treatment plan is to get her to become more responsible and motherly. Typical approaches often include some form of cognitive training in parenting skills paired with threats of apprehending the child. If the helper is unable to see any strengths or skills in the mother's behaviour, even as she walks out on her child, this is unfortunate. The worker's fears about the safety of the child, as well as the worker's developmental logic that blinds her to the mother's stuckness, keeps both the mother and the worker far apart.

One developmental possibility here is that the mother has very low attachment ability—a basic dearth of experiences of being cared for—and thus has little appreciation for the need to care for others. Typically, children whose parents have low attachment ability grow up to replicate the experience with their own children. This inability to nurture others, based on never having been nurtured, is a complex problem that can't be solved by the training provided in a parenting skills workshop. Perhaps a developmentally complex explanation would address the young mother's frustration with her child's neediness, and as she tries to deal with these demands, she finds herself becoming angry because no one ever took care of her when she was small and needy. The unconscious cause of becoming more angry, and her connection with her own neediness, makes the mother's anger escalate, and she leaves the house to take care of her own neediness (have fun) rather than become abusive to her child. Can a skilled worker, after creating a safe connection, see the basis of a good decision here, rather than the behaviour of an irresponsible mother? Will this developmentally astute worker simply recommend parenting skills training and resort to threats of apprehension as legitimate treatment goals?

Skilful workers realize that mothers with little experience of being nurtured need a developmentally sensitive approach. This worker may bring toys, like a colouring book, for the mother to use with her children and, instead of merely dropping it off, will actually colour some pictures with the mother. The experience of enjoying the connection, and feeling special, will enable the mother to repeat this with her child. Experienced CYC family support workers describe the need to "join before you jar" when helping parents.

MAKING THE SHIFT TO CREATING A DEVELOPMENTALLY RESPONSIVE PROGRAM

Control and Trust

There is resistance to using a developmentally responsive approach because it requires a loosening of the controls on behaviour, and it may, for a period of time, seem chaotic and out of control to the untrained eye. It takes maturity and a practical understanding of developmental theory to operate within this chaos and see the developmental issues that are being expressed. Level 1 workers will experience being "out-of-control" and will likely project this onto the youth or family. Program managers need to be in partnership with frontline staff, have confidence in the CYC staff, and have respect for the developmental approach. Everyone involved needs to maintain a focus on the line in the sand rather than on day-to-day tidiness and order. We must focus on the big picture rather than become panicked by the obvious but superficial loss of external control and good order while the youth or family reassess the living environment and choose to use self-control. Families also appear to increase their distress when you refuse to tell them how to behave. Case managers and supervisors need to be supportive, rather than critical, as CYC practitioners consciously create this tension that will eventually enable people to move ahead developmentally.

Responsible People Focus

Sometimes we child and youth care practitioners create situations in which we hinder developmental progress, even though this is not our intention. This can occur in residential programs, hospitals, schools, and even community settings—anywhere that practice is wrongly focused on creating responsible behaviour, which is represented by behaviour that is orderly and compliant rather than focused on developmental progress. CYC family support workers can also end up enforcing behavioural mandates created by others in the social service system, rather than helping families discover ways to move ahead developmentally. I have regularly witnessed agencies and individual practitioners maintain a focus on specific behavioural changes even when this behaviour management approach regularly failed to produce the intended result of personal development.

Staff Meetings

Shifting the program focus requires valuing each member of the team for developmental differences. Treatment discussions and staff meetings must move workers' focus from behavioural issues and reinforcement strategies to developmental dynamics and the limited social logic that is prevalent. Staff members might have different perspectives, based on each practitioner's own professional developmental stage, and all of the workers, whether they are Level 1, 2, or 3 (Phelan, 1990), will have contributions to make. Level 3 workers can discuss their own challenges and developmental struggles as they create a nexus relationship; Level 2 workers will describe their ability to engage in the developmental logic of the youth or family and discover the strengths and abilities amid the stuckness; and Level 1 workers can describe their increasing ability to create a safe interaction with the youth or family and their own awareness of fight and flight reactions to challenging behaviour, particularly in regard to boundary issues and power struggles. The increasing ability of the team to develop a multitude of life-space interventions to support "developmental filling" (Appelstein, 1998) will indicate the accuracy of their developmental picture and the capacity of their assessment skills.

Preparing Yourself

So how do CYC practitioners prepare themselves to be developmentally focussed practitioners? One suggestion is to have each team member analyze behaviour from the distinct developmental stage that each member occupies and propose developmentally logical explanations for the behaviour being discussed. The case examples that make the most sense to new workers are often based in the moment—we want a response that will solve the immediate issue; more experienced workers will see a bigger picture. The youth and families whom we work with also think day to day, ignoring the long-term view. Examples that illustrate the logic of a person at a developmentally disparate level can be linked in a mirroring process that exposes the limited viewpoints of people at several developmental stages, including the workers. Questions posed in the following manner— "What would you suggest I do in a situation like this…?"—can provide opportunities to explore developmentally different logic.

Theory in Action

The CYC treatment team discussion uses behaviour as a background issue, a place to create developmental filling. The focus is to create learning challenges that will enable workers to achieve mastery of the various developmental tasks that each of us encounter as we grow into well-functioning people. Leon Fulcher (2004) connects the concept of *praxis*, theory into action, with developmental approaches:

> While each child strives to achieve developmental
> milestones, they are still different, each in their own special
> ways. Such differences shape the core of child and youth
> care praxis. (p. 35)

Later, Fulcher (2004) writes:

> Regardless of developmental milestones, the unique
> character of each child or young person receiving care
> requires ongoing attention, focusing on individual rhythms
> and opportunity events through sensitive engagement in
> caring relationships that promote personal development
> and social maturation through interactions that are, in many
> ways, auto-therapeutic. (p. 36)

Henry Maier (1987) wrote these words twenty years ago:

> The worker thus gains an understanding of the individual's
> pattern of coping—an invaluable basis for discerning what
> the next developmental task should be. Caring work means
> helping to meet an individual's developmental requirements
> rather than a focus on working to undo or to correct
> unwanted behaviours. (p. 15)

> Once a person feels assured that dependency needs will
> be met, self-mastery ("me-do-it") becomes alive as a
> developmental issue. In residential situations, this frequently

occurs after the individual has seemingly "fit-in so well." Youngsters will suddenly rebel, such as by rejecting well-meant suggestions although these were earlier accepted. They act not unlike the two-year-old who insists on self-feeding. (p. 21)

CYC programs that believe responsible behaviour is the ultimate objective of treatment will not absorb this shift from compliant, safe behaviour into loud, power-seeking behaviour. Yet, in developmental terms, there will be no exercise of self-control until a person transitions through a stage of loud, powerful behaviour.

Developmental Complexity Expands

The more complex developmental stuckness of a person with very limited attachment ability or serious trauma that creates developmental gaps can be beyond the scope of most workers, but we can develop an appreciation for the practitioner maturity required to be effective in these situations. The ability to value connection over control (Leaf, 1995) and to respond to developmental needs rather than behaviour is not easy to achieve. Level 2 and 3 practitioners have this ability, and when the program structure supports them, great changes can occur.

Most CYC programs want every worker, experienced or not, to act as though they are totally prepared for all the tasks they will face; this frustrates newer staff and keeps more experienced staff from developing developmental complexity. Developmentally responsive programs always function at many levels simultaneously, and our job is to highlight the *line in the sand* metaphor by comparing the emerging capability of youth and families with our own journey. Newer workers can appreciate that they have acquired just enough skill and maturity to begin their own journey, with a lifetime of enriching experiences yet to discover and absorb. The ability to function as a developmentally mature Level 3 practitioner is still many years ahead.

Thinking Differently

Our challenge is to think and act with a developmental purpose. Diagnostic categories and behavioural intervention plans are less important than this and can serve as background, not foreground, frameworks. In almost every situation—how we conduct staff meetings, how we format reports and highlight issues, how supervisory sessions occur, and how we learn to interact with youth and families—we need to be congruent with a developmental perspective. Empathy and meaning-making discussions can be framed developmentally. We can become aware of the developmental issues in our own lives that keep us from openly examining a different, perhaps personally challenging, social logic because of a more ego-centric and rigid world view.

An example of "developmental filling" may help:

> Many of the youth we deal with have little ability to form positive relationships, even with well-intentioned and skilled CYC professionals. They have been described as "relationally resistant," and require a CYC worker to establish "relationship beachheads" (Brendtro as cited in Treischman, Brendtro, & Whittaker, 1969). Developmentally hampered by low attachment ability, a youth would not be able to see any logical reason for one person to care for another, except out of self-interest. Creating an opportunity for this youth to own a plant, or care for a pet, would begin to establish a new idea: sometimes you care for someone else because they rely on you, and this can be satisfying.

Often a focus on responsible behaviour can subvert this process:

> Unfortunately, when a discouraged CYC staff member complains about having to do some of the "extras" for a demanding youth that occur in the life-space, he is acting in accordance with the logic of this particular youth (or family, for example), and in many ways is subverting the healing process that CYC practitioners try so hard to initiate. When a youth calls at an inconvenient time to be picked up after running away, and gets an angry, frustrated response, she believes that no one cares. Parents and youth generally ask us to tend to their needs when we are busy doing other, important things, and this is deliberate because they want us to refuse so they can maintain their existing belief about how the world works.

A FINAL NOTE

Developmentally Responsive Theory Frontiers: Group Work and Family Support Work

One area of developmental learning that shows promise is the conscious use of group processes and tapping the innate strengths of youth in groups to create developmental change. There has been some initial study of how a group of young people can support developmental movement with skilful guidance. A Scottish researcher lived with a group of young people in care for several months as an observer. Her goal was to determine whether or not group living was a necessarily negative process, as was described in a long-standing CYC classic study, *Cottage Six* (Polsky, 1962). Rather than finding a delinquent sub-culture, she found enormous potential and positive developmental support that existed in the group's dynamics. Emond (2002) wrote:

> There are beginnings of an awareness of the role of peers in child development more generally and a move within social work practice to the importance of maintaining positive friendships for young people (this push to consider the role of friendships and peer relationships when planning care for children has much to do with the acceptance of resilience models of practice). However, this has yet to be translated in any comprehensive way to the residential setting. (p. 32)

There is much to discover about how to connect good group theory and individual developmental progress. Our work is generally done in groups, while relational work is one to one, and the better our theoretical maps can help to guide practitioner efforts, the more effective we will be. Emond had the opportunity to connect developmentally with each of the members of this group of youth and, as a result, saw a multitude of strengths and resiliencies. One important area for further study is that of how to use the members of the living group to support developmental growth in "stuck" members.

A developmentally responsive approach in group work would not focus on modelling responsible behaviours but on providing opportunities for youth to demonstrate strength through humour, creativity, lived experience, and acquired skills. CYC staff could step back and let the group struggle collectively with developmental challenges. Youth who know how to navigate the public transit system, or how to survive in the outdoors, or how to use humour to defuse a situation, can support each other to grow and mature. Programs that have youth meetings that focus on rule making and chore decisions don't accomplish this.

Family support work programs that support the developmental needs of parents in addition to the children have a clearer focus on nurturing and caring for the adults until they reach a point where they can move forward developmentally. Nurturing parents so that they can understand the logic of wanting to care for another is not a simple task, and the usual professional boundaries would have to be renegotiated. The need for self-consciousness and developmental self-awareness is paramount for CYC practitioners in these programs.

CONCLUSION

Our work is complex because of the people we are trying to help. Using a developmental lens changes our judgments about the value of the strategies our youth and families use to create success in their lives.

The capacity building that we attempt is also connected to our evolving competence and professional readiness to engage in relational, developmentally responsive work. There is an ongoing obligation to nurture our own development and to support the developmental journey of others on our team.

We are targeting a developmental milestone, metaphorically named the *Line in the Sand,* as a framework for treatment planning. Programming developmentally is a challenging process that requires partnerships between supervisors and practitioners, and a willingness to let go of safe, controlling interventions where appropriate.

While there is general consensus that CYC practice is relational and developmental, the complexity of actually behaving this way needs further study. Life-space work requires a pragmatic, everyday style in which theory is embedded and energetic. This chapter has attempted to set out a professional pathway for moving forward, a theoretical map for viewing people in the life-space, and a description of the extraordinary journey we choose to take.

REFERENCES

Anglin, J. (2002). *Pain, normality, and the struggle for congruence.* New York: Haworth.

Appelstein, C. (1994). *The Gus chronicles: Reflections from an abused kid.* Needham, MA: A.E. Treischman Center.

Appelstein, C. (1998). *No such thing as a bad kid: Understanding and responding to the challenging behavior of troubled children and youth.* Weston, MA: The Gifford School.

Berk, L. (2006). *Development through the lifespan* (4th ed.). New York: Allyn & Bacon.

Emond, R. (2002). Understanding the resident group. *Scottish Journal of Residential Child Care, 1*(August–September), 30–40.

Fewster, G. (1990). *Being in child care.* New York: Haworth.

Fulcher, L. (2004). Programmes & praxis: A review of taken-for-granted knowledge. *Scottish Journal of Residential Child Care, 3*(2), 33–45.

Hardwick, A., & Woodhead, W. (1999). *Loving, hating and survival: A handbook for all who work with troubled children and young people.* Aldershot, UK: Ashgate Publishing.

Kagan, R. (1996). *Turmoil to turning points.* New York: Norton.

Krueger, M. (1995). *Nexus: A book about youth work.* Milwaukee, WI: University Outreach Press.

Krueger, M. (Ed.). (2004). *Themes and stories in youthwork practice.* New York: Haworth.

Krueger, M. (2008). Mark Krueger on child and youth care libraries. *CYC On-Line,* 108 (February). Retrieved February 20, 2008, from http://www.cyc-net.org

Leaf, S. (1995). The journey from control to connection. *Journal of Child and Youth Care, 10*(1), 15–21.

Maier, H. (1987). *Developmental group care of children and youth: Concepts and practices.* New York: Haworth.

Modlin, H. (2003). The development of a parent support group as a means of initiating family involvement in a residential program. In T. Garfat (Ed.), *A child and youth care approach to working with families* (pp. 169–189). New York: Haworth.

Phelan, J. (1990). Child care supervision: The neglected skill of evaluation. In J. Anglin, C. Denholm, R. Ferguson, & A. Pence (Eds.), *Perspectives in professional child and youth care* (pp. 131–141). New York: Haworth.

Phelan, J. (2002). The relationship boundaries that control programming. *Relational Child and Youth Care Practice, 16*(1), 51–55.

Phelan, J. (2007). An attempt to be articulate about child and youth care work. *Child and Youth Care Work, 25*(1), 4.

Polsky, II. (1962). *Cottage six.* Huntington, NY: Krieger Publishing.

Schon, D. (1983). *The reflective practitioner.* New York: Basic Books.

Treischman, A., Brendtro, L., & Whittaker, J. (1969). *The other 23 hours.* Hawthorne, NY: Aldine Publishing.

VanderVen, K. (2003). Activity-oriented family-focused child and youth care work in group care: Integrating streams of thought into a river of progress. In T. Garfat (Ed.), *A child and youth care approach to working with families* (pp. 131–147). New York: Haworth.

Ward, A. (2007). *Working in group care: Social work and social care in residential and day care settings.* Bristol, UK: Policy Press.

Ward, A., & McMahon, L. (1998). *Intuition is not enough: Matching learning with practice in therapeutic child care.* London: Rutledge.

Understanding Critical Aspects of Relational Practice

Part Two introduces the concepts of praxis, boundaries, and ethics, which are important features of relational Child and Youth Care practice. The nature of relational practice requires increased attention from and increased intention on the part of Child and Youth Care practitioners regarding praxis, boundaries, and ethics, and to other aspects of the relational context.

CHAPTER 4

The Knowing, Doing and Being in Context

A Praxis-Oriented Approach to Child and Youth Care

Jennifer White, PhD

ABSTRACT

Engaging with youth and families in collaborative and respectful ways; taking practical actions to create the conditions for young people to experience meaning, worth and connection; supporting them to imagine hopeful futures for themselves; and bringing oneself fully to the therapeutic relationship are all hallmark characteristics of child and youth care (CYC) practice. Those who do this work and those who prepare practitioners for the field recognize the need for conceptual frameworks that can adequately represent the complexities of everyday CYC practice. By taking up the notion of praxis as knowing, doing and being in context, I hope to plant some fresh seeds to animate and extend current conceptualizations of everyday CYC practice.

INTRODUCTION

Like many of the other human caring professions, everyday child and youth care (CYC) practice is complex, unpredictable, and value-laden. It is also highly relational work that is deeply embedded within very specific local contexts. Engaging with children, youth, families and communities in collaborative and respectful ways; taking practical actions to create the conditions for young people to experience meaning, worth and connection; supporting them to imagine hopeful futures for themselves; and bringing oneself fully to the therapeutic relationship are all hallmark characteristics of CYC practice. Those who do this work and those who prepare practitioners for the field recognize the need for dynamic conceptual frameworks that can adequately represent the complexities of everyday CYC practice, while also offering a practical tool for critical reflection and analysis.

Building on the work of others who have highlighted the thoroughly interpretive and ethical dimensions of CYC practice (Garfat, 2004; Nakkula & Ravitch, 1997; Ricks & Bellefeuille, 2003; Stacey, 2001) and drawing from other strands of postmodernism, including social constructionism (Gergen, 2000), pragmatism (Fishman, 1999), hermeneutics (Schwandt, 2002; VanderVen, in press) and narrative approaches (Freedman & Combs, 1996; Pendlebury, 1995; White & Epston, 1990), I hope to plant some fresh seeds to animate and extend current conceptualizations of everyday CYC practice. To begin I introduce the concept of praxis. It is defined here as ethical, self-aware, responsive and accountable action, which reflects dimensions of knowing, doing and being. Next, as a way to contextualize my contribution I provide a very brief history of the field of CYC. This includes a brief consideration of other related postmodern perspectives as well as a critique of some of the conceptualizations of CYC practice that have recently been advanced. The final section, representing the main contribution, includes a series of tables that explicate various ways of knowing, doing and being. A graphic illustration of some of the specific contexts and ecological influences that give shape and meaning to everyday CYC practice is also included. By outlining some of the conceptual underpinnings of the field and by locating them within a postmodern, non-linear perspective, my hope is to offer a potentially useful resource for guiding, advancing, analyzing and researching everyday CYC practice.

PRAXIS

The concept of praxis has enjoyed a resurgence of late and has been enthusiastically taken up by theorists and practitioners working across a diverse range of academic disciplines. The notion of praxis occupies a central place in the professional literature of many of the human caring professions, including teaching, nursing, health care and social work (Carr, 1987; Dorazio-Migliore, Migliore & Anderson, 2005; Nelson, Poland, Murray & Maticka-Tyndale, 2004; Tarlier, 2005). In many people's minds, the term praxis refers to the integration of knowledge and action (theory and practice), which is indeed a core feature of the concept. It is however much more than that. Briefly, praxis is a concept that finds it origins in Greek philosophy, particularly the teachings of Aristotle. For Aristotle, praxis was "guided by a moral disposition to act truly and rightly; a concern to further human well being and the good life" (Smith, 1999). Friere (1970) also wrote extensively about the place of praxis in emancipatory education, highlighting the role of values, respect, dialogue, and action in the effort to "make a difference in the world." Schwandt (2002), following from Habermas, suggests that *Praxis* does not require knowledge of how to make something, but knowledge of how to be a particular kind of person; it is 'action-oriented self-understanding'" (p. 49).

While the term praxis roughly corresponds with contemporary under-standings of practice, there are a few unique and important features that distinguish praxis from commonsense understandings of practice. Specifically, theory and practice are integrated and one does not precede nor hold greater value than the other (Carr, 1987). Praxis is creative, "other-seeking" and dialogic (Smith, 1999). It is the place where words and actions, discourses and experience merge (Stacey, 2001). Praxis includes conscious reflection both on and in practice (Tarlier, 2005). Praxis is expressed in particular contexts and thus can never be proceduralized or specified in advance (Schwandt, 2002). Finally, praxis is guided by practical wisdom (Schwandt) and is expressed through committed moral action (Carr) and practices of accountability (Stacey, 2001).

Picking up on some of the core features of praxis identified by these theorists, for the purposes here I am defining praxis as ethical, self-aware, responsive and accountable action. In other words, praxis involves knowing, doing and being. The use of verbs is deliberate and signals the active and dynamic character of praxis. Within the field of CYC, there are diverse ways of knowing, doing and being and these actions always get expressed within specific historical, sociocultural, political and institutional contexts. Language, context, values, situated meanings, dialogue, relationships and multiple interpretations all play a role in the approach I develop here, revealing its decidedly postmodern character (Bohman, Hiley & Shusterman, 1991; Fishman, 1999; Gergen, 2000). Many of these ideas will be taken up in a later section.

First however, I need to situate this particular contribution within a rich theoretical and practice tradition that has been actively shaped by the contributions of many gifted CYC educators, practitioners and scholars[1] (Anglin, 1992; Beker, 2001; Denholm, 1990; Fewster; 1990; Garfat, 2003; Krueger; 2004; Maier, 2001; Mattingly, 1995; Nakkula & Ravitch, 1998; Pence, 1987; Ricks, 1989; VanderVen, 1991). Their diverse contributions have laid the groundwork for the emergence of a distinct, multi-vocal community of practice which, to take but one contemporary example, is regularly made visible through the lively, diverse and thoughtful discussions currently underway on the CYC-Net (http://www.cyc-net. org/network.html). By building on this rich foundation, I am engaging in a form of theorizing that could best be described as "imaginative reflection on possible modifications of practice" (Bohman et al., 1991).

One other point of clarification is in order. I am writing this from the perspective of a relative newcomer, that is, someone who is joining a scholarly discussion that is already in-progress—a position which can be both risky and (hopefully) facilitative. I am carrying with me my own intellectual traditions and disciplinary training (psychology, counselling, education), practice experiences (residential child and youth care, child and youth mental health, prevention and health promotion, community development) and personal life history and social location (white, hetero-sexual, middle-class, 4th generation Canadian) as I embark on this task.

It is my hope that by critically and respectfully engaging with a diverse range of resources and intellectual traditions that I will be able to offer

---

1   The number of individuals who have made a significant contribution to the CYC field are too numerous to mention and inevitably this is an incomplete list. My apologies for the omissions.

a perspective that is creative, generative and useful to the CYC field. As others have noted,

> Changing circumstances and encounters with other practices can nourish the imagination; and since no practice is defined for all possible situations, there is always need for imaginative projections and creative decisions in pursuing a practice. (Bohman, Hiley & Shusterman, 1991, p. 13)

LOCATING THE CHILD AND YOUTH CARE FIELD

CYC is an active and diverse, relatively new field of professional practice that is broadly concerned with promoting and supporting the optimal development and well-being of infants, children, youth and families in specific contexts through approaches that focus on individuals and their social circumstances and environments. CYC work is deeply rooted in a strong set of values and principles, including: holistic, strengths-based, context sensitive, developmentally-informed, collaborative, and committed to social justice and diversity (Association of Child and Youth Care Practice, 2001; Corney, 2004; School of Child and Youth Care, 2005).

Of considerable interest here is the ongoing dialogue regarding the nature of CYC work, which includes various attempts to explicate and legitimize the field's existence and activities. As early as 1982, following the Conference-Research Sequence in Child Care Education, a series of principles and guidelines were developed to guide those involved in the planning and delivery of child and youth care education (Peters & Kelly, 1982). Later, a Code of Ethics was developed to signify the field's status as a formal profession (Mattingly, 1995). Several authors have tried to define the essence of CYC work (Anglin, 1992; Ferguson & Anglin, 1985; VanderVen, 1991), which has occasionally included attempts to distinguish the CYC profession from other related fields of practice like social work (Anglin, 1999; Bates, 2005) or counseling (Phelan, 2005). Others have described a distinctly CYC approach to working with families (Garfat, 2003; Ricks & Bellefeuille, 2003).

The Rise of Postmodernism

Paralleling developments in other professional fields and consistent with the emergence of postmodern ideas within the social and human sciences generally (Fishman, 1999; Polkinghorne, 1988), many CYC practitioners and scholars have articulated some of the limits of positivist epistemologies and have expressed concern over the encroachment of overly mechanistic models and proceduralized approaches into CYC practice. For example, some have suggested that CYC work might be more appropriately conceptualized as a craft based on its distinctively practical and emergent character (Eisikovits & Beker, 2001). Such a conceptualization of CYC work has clear implications for professional development.

> Such work cannot be effectively standardized...because
> its success is a function of the practitioner's interpersonal
> sensitivity in applying the requisite knowledge and skills
> contextually in situations where the need is determined in
> part by the dynamic and often unpredictable responses of all
> those involved. (p. 418)

Others have expressed concern with the limitations of rule-based formulations and so-called "value-neutral" approaches to practice and have called or more personal, embodied, narratively informed and situationally immersed understandings of practice (Corney, 2004; Krueger, 1997; Ricks & Bellefeuille, 2003). Constructivist and hermeneutic (interpretive) approaches to CYC work, which highlight the role of self-understanding, language, dialogue and context have also been well-articulated (Fewster, 1990; Garfat, 2004; Hoskins, 1996; Nakkula & Ravitch, 1998; Ungar, 2004, VanderVen, in press). These approaches recognize that CYC work, with its emphasis on self-reflection and mutual transformation, are thoroughly ethical endeavours (Nakkula & Ravitch, 1998). More critical perspectives, which illuminate the political and sociocultural forces that serve to perpetuate inequities among marginalized groups, including many youth and families, have also been advanced (Skott-Myhre, 2003).

Clearly there is no one singular or final view of CYC practice and it is the embrace of multiple perspectives, openness to critique, and serious, respectful engagement with each others' ideas that lends the field its richness. In an effort to keep pace with the field's growing diversity, various models for preparing CYC practitioners have been developed, including the generative curriculum model used in early childhood education (Dahlberg, Moss & Pence, 1999) and the Knowledge, Skills and Self (KSS) model (described below). It is out of this rich history that several different ways of thinking about, describing, and teaching CYC practice have been advanced. It is to some of these models and conceptualizations of CYC practice that I now turn my attention.

Conceptualizations of CYC Practice

Various models and descriptions of CYC practice have been developed over the years, including the umbrella model (Denholm, Ferguson & Pence, 1983), the cube model (Ferguson, 1991), and the ecological onion model (Ferguson, 1991). Each new image and metaphor appears to reflect an increasing appreciation for the complexity and ecological character of CYC practice. These models—which incidentally have been defined as "curriculum models" as opposed to models of practice—have done a good job of mapping the scope of the field. They are largely descriptive in nature (i.e., they name the settings where the work typically occurs, the target audiences, and the types of interventions used) and testify to the field's growth over time. Two specific conceptualizations of CYC practice will be briefly reviewed below: the Knowledge, Skills and Self (KSS) model and the more recent North American Certification Project: Competencies for Professional Child and Youth Work Practitioners.

Knowledge, skills and self (KSS)

The KSS model, which has occupied a central place in the School of Child and Youth Care (SCYC), University of Victoria curricula for many years, offers students and practitioners new to the field an efficient and easy-to-grasp understanding of the unique character of CYC practice.[2] What began as a conceptual tool for guiding curricula development in the applied tradition of a professional school (Ferguson, personal communication, 2007), soon became a primary pedagogical resource for helping CYC students understand the unique character of CYC work. It was an approach that explicitly recognized the practitioner's values, beliefs and experiences in making meaning of the social world (Ricks, 1989). It was this notable emphasis on the "Self" that served to signal the field's distinctive commitment to developing and valuing qualities of reflexivity and critical self-awareness among CYC practitioners (Fewster, 1990).

North American certification project

More recent efforts have been undertaken through the North American Certification Project to articulate the specific competencies required of CYC practitioners across a number of broad domains including:

---

2   A more recently developed model expands on KSS by making explicit links between the CYC field, the post-secondary curriculum and client outcomes (Stuart & Ray, 2006).

professionalism, applied human diversity, applied human development, communication and relationship, and developmental practice (ACYP, 2001).[3] In addition to identifying specific foundational knowledge and associated competencies within each of these broad domains, there is also an explicit statement of nine foundational attitudes that underlie all professional CYC work. The focus on knowledge, competencies and attitudes is consistent with the categories of knowing, doing and being that I am advancing here and yet there are some important distinctions in the way these ideas are being conceptualized which I will discuss in a later section. For now, it is important to acknowledge that the North American Certification Project reflects a high level of collaboration, careful thought, rigorous analysis and adds much needed clarity to directing the future growth of our field.

Critical Commentary

Despite the considerable strengths of both the KSS model and the North American Certification Project, each of them in their own way implicitly conveys a rather flat view of practice whereby knowledge is *acquired*, skills are *mastered*, attitudes are *adopted*, self-awareness is *gained* and then these *things* are applied to children, youth, families and communities. Such a conceptualization of practice (and pedagogy) is consistent with the technical rational paradigm that is currently favoured by funders and policy-makers across a wide range of health, education and social care fields (McKee Sellick, Delaney & Brownlee, 2002; Usher, Bryant & Johnston, 1997). Guided by an instrumental view of practice, this approach is centrally concerned with the development of results-oriented goals, clear measures of success, and the demonstration of tangible, measurable outcomes. Such a narrow and mechanistic approach to characterizing practice is often taken for granted. Program logic models, which are increasingly demanded by funders, are but one expression of this. At one level, we are comforted by the clarity and certainty that these unproblematic conceptions of practice seem to promise,

> Increasing scrutiny and pressure from agency administrators, insurance providers, and consumers to prove that we know

---

3   Based on consultation with faculty and staff in the School of Child and Youth Care, University of Victoria, these domains have been extended to include community capacity building and social policy.

what we are doing and that what we are doing really works, makes us susceptible to the clarion call of the empirical practice and evidence-based practice movements. Their certainty is seductive, an answer to our desire for real competence. (McKee Sellick et al., 2002, p. 493)

Without question, it is important for CYC practitioners to be able to articulate what they are doing and why and to what effect. My intent is not to reject or replace a competency-based approach, but rather to expand the possibilities for thinking about CYC practice in a way that explicitly recognizes its social, moral and political character (Schwandt, 2002). Helping practitioners to practice wisely by helping them to cultivate a respect for principles and an attunement to particulars is a stance that Pendlebury (1995), who borrows from Nussbaum, describes as "perceptive equilibrium," a concept that has much in common with the notion of praxis being developed here.

As a starting place, we need to recognize that a narrowly defined, technical rational view of practice that is based on the assumption that the complexity of practice—and professional development—can be adequately conceptualized and measured by discrete "outputs" like knowledge, skills and attitudes can be highly problematic. This is because "practice situations are not only unique, they are also characterised by a complexity and uncertainty which resist routinization" (Usher, Bryant & Johnston, 2001, p. 127). As Schon (1983) famously said,

> In the varied topography of professional practice, there is a high, hard ground where practitioners can make effective use of research-based theory and technique, and there is a swampy lowland where situations are confusing 'messes' incapable of technical solutions. (p. 42)

I contend that a more contextually rich, theoretically informed, explicitly moral, and dynamic view of CYC practice is needed. In the next section I will describe a praxis-oriented approach for understanding and analyzing CYC practice that attempts to respond to the diverse and emerging needs of the field.

Figure 1. Praxis as Knowing, Doing and Being

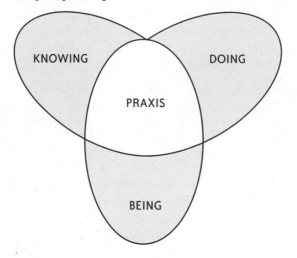

PRAXIS AS KNOWING, DOING AND BEING

Praxis, which is ethical, self-aware, responsive and accountable action involves the reciprocal integration of knowing, doing and being. Consistent with the thinking of others calling for a re-imagined view of professional development in the human services field (VanderVen, in press) the perspective on praxis being presented here also attempts to collapse the sharp—rather unhelpful, yet historically entrenched—distinction between theory and practice. Praxis is thus seen as the active integration of knowing, doing and being and is visually depicted in Figure 1. The use of verbs is deliberate since taken together, these actions respond to the question, "what is to be done?" *the* question that remains at the heart of any practice (Usher, et al., 1997). In many respects, with these linguistic moves one could say that I am "verbing" the world of practice.

Clearly there are multiple ways of knowing, doing and being that contribute to self-aware, ethical, responsive and accountable practice in the CYC field. What follows is a description of some common ways of conceptualizing knowing, doing and being in CYC. This is not intended to be an exhaustive description of everything a CYC practitioner will ever need to know, do or be in order to become a competent and caring CYC practitioner. Instead, it is offered as one entry point to a community of practice and a tradition of working that is firmly rooted in a solid foundation. I have also made every attempt to make this model compatible with the material included in the North American Certification Project (ACYP, 2001). In the sections that follow, I will further unpack each of these contributions to praxis with the understanding that this is but one potential view for thinking about and engaging in CYC practice as opposed to the final word.

Knowing

There are multiple ways of thinking about knowing and types of knowledge that guide CYC practitioners in their everyday work. Indeed, it is the development of a specialized body of knowledge that typically defines a profession (Eisikovits & Beker, 2001; Hoyle & John, 1995; Usher et al., 1997). Given the complexity and holistic character of CYC work however, it would be unreasonable to assume that a single form of knowledge (e.g., experiential or empirical) could reliably guide practitioners in every practice encounter, an observation that has convincingly been made by others in the human caring professions. For example Tarlier (2005) writing about the need for multiple ways of knowing in nursing writes, "praxis demands epistemologies that are sufficiently broad to support all of its complexities" (p. 129).

Many very useful attempts have already been made by others to categorize different ways, types and patterns of knowing that are relevant to CYC practice. For example, Artz (1994) suggests that our feelings serve as important ways of knowing. Feminist scholars (Goldberger, Tarule, Clinchy & Belenky, 1996) have challenged conventional understandings of what it means to know, leading to new epistemological orientations inspired by women's ways of knowing. Much earlier, Aristotle theorized about three different forms of knowledge: *episteme* (theoretical, contemplative knowledge), *techne* (action-oriented, pragmatic and productive knowledge) and *phronesis* (practical and context-dependent deliberation about values or "wise judgement" (Greenwood & Levin, 2005; Schwandt, 2001).

While it is not the intent here to provide a systematic review of the diverse epistemologies informing CYC practice, it is important to declare my own orientation which is grounded in a postmodern, social constructionist, hermeneutic perspective that locates and understands knowledge-making in particular relationships, communities and traditions (Gergen, 2000; Schwandt, 2002; Taylor & White, 2000). Five assumptions about knowledge/knowing are guiding this work (Greenwood & Levin, 2005; Tarlier, 2005):

1. Knowledge/knowing is inherently social and collective.
2. Knowledge/knowing is always highly contextual.
3. Singular forms of knowledge/knowing (e.g., empirical or experiential) are insufficient for informing complex, holistic practices like CYC.
4. Different knowledges/ways of knowing are equally valid in particular contexts.
5. Knowledge is made, not discovered.

One way to assist CYC students and practitioners start thinking about the diverse ways and types of knowing that are relevant to CYC practice is to name them. Of course the danger of such an exercise is to inadvertently leave an impression that there is such a thing as a fixed or final way of thinking about knowing in CYC practice. This is not the message I want to convey. Instead, with Table 1, what I am offering is one potential approach to considering the diverse ways of understanding and thinking about knowing in the CYC field as part of an overall praxis orientation. Such a conceptualization is designed to challenge taken-for-granted ideas about knowledge, call attention to the social process of knowledge-making, and heighten practitioner reflexivity (Taylor & White, 2000). I fully expect that this will evolve over time as others engage with it.

It is important to remember that the distinctions being made between various ways of thinking about knowing are not this sharp in reality. This artificial way of categorizing knowing is designed as a tool to aid teaching and support analyses of practice. The questions are included as a way to invite further reflection and to remind students and practitioners of the value of drawing from and critically examining multiple ways of knowing when trying to make sense of the social world and their place in it. While a key strength and a unique aspect of CYC work is the profession's explicit valuing of multiple ways and forms of knowing, Table 1 is not meant to be a grocery list from which practitioners can pick-and-choose their favourite "way of knowing" as a way of justifying their own idiosyncratic and unexamined approach to practice.

By proposing a tentative language and a set of questions for thinking about various ways of knowing, the hope is that CYC practitioners can begin appreciating the possibility for multiple ways of reading and seeing

Table 1. Some Ways of Thinking About *Knowing* in Child and Youth Care

Knowing	Key Questions	Common Characteristics	Example(s)
Self understanding • Values, beliefs, feelings • Assumptions • Biases/prejudices • Relational identities	• Who am I? What might I become? • Where do I come from? • What do I stand for? • How does my social location influence how and what I can know and who I can be?	• Rooted in relationships and communities of meaning • Always incomplete/partial • Determined/limited by available language • Sharpened through critical reflection and engagement with others	• Recognition and articulation of personal values, feelings and experiences • Locating understanding of self and others within social, cultural and historical traditions • Ability to reflect upon one's own impact on others • Reflexivity
Practical/ Experiential • Tacit/craft knowledge • Narrative knowing • Routines/habits • Subjective "lived experience"	• How is this situation like or unlike others I have encountered? • What is the story here? • What does my experience tell me? • How should I act in this moment? • What is my gut telling me?	• Individual/private • Usually unarticulated and uncritically accepted • Action-oriented • Contextualized • Often felt in the body	• Practical wisdom • Clinical judgment • Trial and error knowledge • "Speaking from the heart" • "Common sense" • Practice stories
Professional • Professional knowledge, values and ethics	• What does my profession tell me is the right way to proceed? • What professional resources are available to guide me?	• Public • Codified/ Sanctioned • Rooted in specific intellectual traditions and communities of practice	• History of the profession • Professional values statements • Codes of ethics • Pre-service curricula/ professional development
Creative/Artistic • Intuitive • Aesthetic • Improvisational	• What metaphors might apply here? • Which of my senses are activated? • What rhythms am I noticing? • What possibilities can I imagine?	• Expressed in multiple forms • Open to multiple interpretations • Unpredictable • Symbolic meanings	• Art/Poetry • Play • Imagination • Beauty

(Continued)

Table 1. (Continued)

Knowing	Key Questions	Common Characteristics	Example(s)
Theoretical/ Empirical • Research • Theory	• What does the scholarly literature say? • How can these resources help me? • Are these claims plausible/viable/ credible? • How do I judge the worthiness of these ideas?	• Public/Open to scrutiny • Systematic • Often text-based • Advancing truth claims • Rooted in specific intellectual traditions	• Research findings/ evidence • Theories (e.g. applied human development, change, learning) • Perspectives and paradigms (e.g. critical, feminist, postmodern)
Communal/Dialogic • Co-constructed knowledge • Local knowledge(s) • Community wisdom • Knowledge-making	• What interpretations are we making together? • What are the implications of these ways of listening/ talking? • What cultural/ traditional stories might have relevance?	• Constructed with others • Developed in dialogue • Collective • Sedimented	• Co-generated local knowledge(s) • Cultural stories and rituals • Communities of practice • Intellectual traditions
Critical • Exposes relations of power • Locates knowledge in social, cultural, political and historical contexts • Questions the "givenness" of social facts and reality	• Whose interests are being served? • What social, cultural, historical, and political forces have contributed to the emergence of this issue? • Whose voices have been silenced?	• Committed to social justice • Questions the givens or status quo • Exposes asymmetrical relations of power	• Critical analysis of practice discourses • Articulation of social group membership/ location • Recognition of systemic forms of oppression and privilege
Philosophical/ Epistemological/ Ethical • Understandings of human nature/ reality • Nature of knowledge • Understandings of right and wrong	• What is human nature/reality? • What counts as knowledge? • Whose knowledge counts? • What is the good and right thing to do?	• Concerned with truth, reason, knowledge • Rooted in specific intellectual and historical traditions	• Assumptions about the nature of knowledge (e.g. objectivity, subjectivity) • Worldview • Ethical deliberation

the world. Deftly navigating between general principles and concrete particulars to respond to the situation at hand, being able to rely on intellectual traditions and imagination to respond freshly and creatively when faced with the novel or the unknown, having an emotional investment in how things turn out—these are the characteristics of a wise and discerning practitioner according to Nussbaum (1990). Describing this quality as a special form of perception, she writes, "Perception, we might say, is a process of loving conversation between rules and concrete responses, general conceptions and unique cases, in which the general articulates the particular and is in turn further articulated by it" (p. 95). By challenging CYC practitioners to articulate what and how they know, and by supporting them to begin clarifying their own epistemological stance based on self-understanding, practical wisdom and experience, theoretical, artistic, empirical, philosophical, constructivist and critical theories and ideas, a richer, more open—and importantly a more problematic—view of everyday practice is possible.

Doing

In addition to the multiple types and ways of knowing in CYC work, there are a number of specific skills (ways of doing) that contribute to ethical, self-aware, responsive and accountable practice. Table 2 summarizes some of these skills and competencies. Even though knowing, doing and being are being analyzed separately for the purposes of explicating this framework, it is important to remember that there is a great deal of overlap and praxis is the enactment of all three.

The upper half of Table 2 describes the specialized skills and competencies that are understood to be foundational for competent practice in CYC as identified by the North American Certification Project (ACYP, 2001). CYC work involves intervening with individual children, youth and families and their social environments. This requires skills in professionalism, direct client care, program planning, social justice advocacy, plus an ability to strengthen social environments and analyze social policies.

In addition to developing specific competencies in each of these content areas, CYC practitioners also need to be especially skilled in their critical thinking, reflection and analytical skills. Thus the skills of noticing/attending, interpreting/making meaning, collaborating/deliberating, acting/self-reflecting, and articulating/justifying have been separated out

Table 2. Some Ways of Thinking About *Doing* in Child and Youth Care

Specialized Professional CYC Skills

Domain	CYC Competency[4]	Example
Professional Identity and Conduct	• Professionalism	• Professional/ethical conduct and work habits • Professional boundaries • Facilitation of others' learning • Ability to give and receive feedback
Direct Client Care and Engagement	• Applied Human Development • Communication and Relationship • Developmental Practice	• Needs assessment • Client engagement and communication • Therapeutic change skills • Group facilitation • Family support
Program Planning, Implementation and Evaluation	• Developmental Practice • Community-Capacity Building	• Program design • Identification of indicators of progress • Program evaluation
Social Justice Advocacy	• Applied Human Diversity	• Diversity competency • Identifying systemic barriers and forms of oppression • Inclusive practices
Strengthening Social Environments and Social Policies	• Community-Capacity Building • Social Policy	• Community-capacity building • Social support enhancement • Policy analysis/critique

for particular attention and are described in the lower half of Table 2. Many of these critical thinking skills overlap with the different forms of knowing introduced earlier.

Being

Much has been written about the special and unique personal and relational qualities that distinguish CYC work from other helping and caring professions (Anglin, 1999; Fewster, 1990). Many of these qualities represent the active expression and embodiment of values and virtues as well as ways of being in the world. Often, these values and relational qualities are difficult to teach to new practitioners, in part because these qualities cannot be easily "pinned down" with words. As overall ethical orientations and habits of mind (Eisikovits & Beker, 2001) these "ways of being" are typically not conducive to being counted and measured.

---

4   These CYC Competencies include those developed by the North American Certification Project (NACP) (Mattingly,2002), and those identified by the School of Child and Youth Care. These Competencies continue to be defined and debated in the field and will likely evolve over time.

Table 2. (Continued)

Critical Thinking and Reflection Skills

Domain	Key Questions
Noticing and attending	• What am I noticing? • Where is my attention drawn? • What is my initial account of what is happening?
Interpreting and making meaning	• What are my hunches about what is going on? • What role is my own history and experience playing? • How is my language/description affecting what I see? • What are some of my working truths or tentative conclusions?
Collaborating and deliberating with others	• Who will I talk with/listen to about this? • How can I enlarge my perspective about this? • Am I willing to shift my position in light of new information? • Do I need to revise my account of what is happening? • What sense are we making together?
Acting and self-reflecting	• What choices do I have? • What is my decision/action? • What are the intended and unintended consequences of my actions? • What have I learned for next time?
Articulating and justifying	• What are my reasons for acting this way? • On what grounds (e.g. ethical, legal, empirical, professional) have I taken this action? • How will I articulate my reasons in public? • How will I practice accountability?

Some authors have relied on metaphors to convey the uniqueness of CYC work. For example, Krueger (2004) likens youth work to a modern dance. Others have suggested that being in child care is a "journey into self" (Fewster, 1990). Writing about the need to re-conceptualize practice in the broader field of evaluation, Schwandt (2002) following Rorty, advances the idea of the practitioner as "strong poet," a metaphor that resonates with CYC practice very well:

> The ability to deliberate well rests on the habit of
> attentiveness or interpretive perspicuity by which one
> recognizes what is at stake in a particular situation. This
> is a kind of insight, an awareness of the morally relevant
> features of a situation. This ability might be spoken of as the
> *poetics* of practical reason, for it invokes images of a creative,
> inventive, imaginative mind; one with an ability to decipher
> a situation. (emphasis in original, p. 53)

What he and other writers are suggesting is that wise practice is inextricably linked to qualities of discernment, engagement and imagin-

Table 3. Some Ways of Thinking About *Being* in Child and Youth Care

Orientation	Characteristics	Key Questions
Mindful and Self-Aware	• Active and interpretive • Ongoing self-reflection and monitoring • Recognition of the influence of one's own history on current practice • Acceptance of one's own limits	• What is it about this client that reminds me of my own experience? • What biases am I bringing to this situation? • Do I have some of my own "unfinished business" to attend to? • How do I make sense of my own reactions to this client in this instance? • What other interpretations are possible?
Relational and Collaborative	• Based on trust, presence, connection and mutuality • Actively works to minimize the power differential • Collaborative goal-setting	• How can I join with this child, youth or family? • How can I co-create a climate based on mutuality and trust? • How will I draw from the client's strengths and perspectives? • Who can I talk with/listen to about my reactions?
Curious and Open	• Rooted in a posture of "not knowing" • Honours client knowledge and expertise • Emphasis on understanding	• How does this child, youth or family see and make sense of the world? • How can I stay open to their experience and ways of understanding? • Whose view of reality is being privileged?
Respectful	• Support for the integrity, dignity and self-determination of all clients • Engaging clients as persons, not labels	• How do my actions and words convey my belief in the fundamental dignity of this person? • How can I speak out against the practice of reducing human beings to labels or diagnoses?
Strengths-Orientation	• Each child, youth and family has strengths and resources that can be mobilized • Protective factors exist within individuals and systems/environments	• What specific strengths or unique perspectives/knowledge(s) does this child, youth or family bring to this problem or issue? • How can I work to mobilize/call forth this knowledge? • What are some features in the social environment or community that can further promote client competence and well-being?
Caring and Responsive	• Emotionally invested • "Being with" vs. "doing to" • Human connection • Empathy, warmth and genuineness • Moral engagement	• How am I conveying care and compassion through my presence? • How will I recognize when I am no longer practicing from a place of care? • What specific actions do I need to take?
Holistic	• Sees the "whole child or youth" in context • Concerned with the emotional, physical, spiritual and intellectual growth and development	• Am I seeing the "whole child" or just his/her symptoms or behaviours? • How does my involvement with this child, youth or family affect other areas of their life?

Table 3. (Continued)

Orientation	Characteristics	Key Questions
Inclusive and Participatory	• Supports the emergence of the child/youth voice • Actively works to involve children, youth and families in decision-making	• Whose voices are being heard? • Whose voices are being silenced? • How can I increase youth participation in this decision-making process?
Situationally Immersed	• Recognizes the particularities of place and context • Attuned to local norms	• What is going on in this particular moment? • What are some of the most salient features to attend to? • How is my decision affected by this place or setting?
Social Justice Advocacy and Accountability	• Recognizes systemic barriers to full and equitable participation • Takes responsibility for recognizing and addressing forms of oppression and privilege	• In what ways do I enjoy certain unearned benefits (privilege) as a result of my social group membership (e.g., gender, ethnicity, ability, sexual orientation, class)? • How might these privileges be unwittingly blinding me to certain client realities? • What will I do about this? • How am I practicing accountability?

ative reflection; reflecting an overall stance of "being with" as opposed to "doing to." Thus, the issue of "knowing how to be" is a critically important feature of praxis and figures prominently in becoming an ethical, self-aware, responsive, accountable CYC practitioner. Table 3 summarizes some of the types and ways of being in CYC. Many of these ways of being are the expression of specific moral values, ethical commitments, and orientations to the world.

KNOWING, DOING AND BEING IN CONTEXT

CYC work always takes place within a broad context of intersecting influences, some of which we are directly aware (e.g., agency mandates or client needs) and some of which seem more remote or less directly connected to our everyday work with children, youth and families (e.g., government policies, funding decisions or social and historical forces). Bronfenbrenner's (1979) ecological theory, which highlights the interacting and reciprocal role of multiple influences on children's development, occupies a central place in most conceptions of CYC practice.

Bronfenbrenner's (1979) ecological model can also be adapted and applied to understanding the complexity of CYC practice. It is typically represented through concentric circles. In order to move away from

Figure 2. Knowing, Doing and Being in a Web of Influences

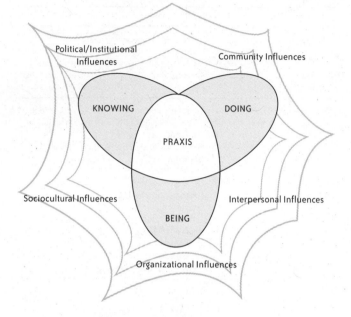

the idea that contextual influences on practice are isolated, discrete dimensions (which is one of the limitations of using the concentric circles model), the metaphor of a web is being introduced here to depict the active, intersecting, embedded, shifting and asymmetrical qualities of everyday practice. Figure 2 illustrates a number of common social forces and institutional influences that, taken together, create the complex and dynamic context for a praxis-based (knowing, doing and being) approach to CYC.

Such a view of CYC work enables us to "see" the number and range of potential influences on our practice (Nutley & Davies, 2002) and the metaphor of the web provides one way of illustrating these multiple, intersecting and reciprocal influences. Community influences include local knowledge, understandings and expectations, the local service delivery context and media influences. Interpersonal influences recognize the relational character of everyday CYC practice, including relationships with and expectations of children, youth and families; relationships with peers, colleagues, mentors and supervisors; and relationships with community members and other service providers. Organizational influences refer to local workplace norms, policies and resources, agency mandates and professional routines. Sociocultural influences include social, cultural and historical factors, including relations of power. Political/institutional influences include government legislation and policies; funding decisions; discourses of professionalism and practice; post-secondary training and professional associations; and regulatory bodies.

Finally, we are all caught in this web together and there is no such thing as standing apart to "see the world as it really is" (McKee Sellick et al. 2002). Ultimately, this conceptualization is designed to highlight the centrality of praxis (knowing, doing and being), while simultaneously recognizing the inter-subjective, contingent, and context dependent character of everyday CYC work.

IMPLICATIONS FOR PROFESSIONAL EDUCATION AND PRACTICE

As an educational resource, this approach offers students a glimpse into the complexity of the work, highlights its active and relational character, activates curiosity and reflexive practice through posing generative questions, and it provides an initial language for discussing and analyzing a variety of practice narratives and encounters. For example, students can be invited to analyze their own experience working with a child, youth or family (or reflect on prepared cases) using the questions in the Tables as a guide for thinking about how and what they know and what the source and history of some of these ways of knowing, doing and being might be.

As an analytical tool, this framework builds on and extends existing conceptualizations of CYC practice. Specifically, it may be of benefit to researchers who are interested in studying everyday CYC practice from a perspective that recognizes the contingent quality and inherent unpredictability of practice and who are interested in studying how practitioners understand and make sense of this complexity in their everyday work. For example, when faced with the dilemmatic aspects of practice, which ideas, theories, actions and values do CYC practitioners favour? What is the history of these ideas? What intellectual traditions are being sustained? What are the consequences of framing and responding to practice challenges and dilemmas in these ways (Gergen, 2000)?

CYC practice, much like nursing, teaching and social work, is characterized by diverse ways of knowing, interpersonal relationships, practical obligations, value-laden decisions and complex ethical challenges, all of which take place within a complex context of sociopolitical, historical, cultural and institutional forces (Nutley & Davies, 2002; Smith & White, 2000; Tarlier, 2005). The conceptual framework being presented here attempts to convey a realistic and lively view of practice; one that challenges traditional "knowledge transfer" views of practice. It is predicated on a belief that by critically reflecting on our intellectual traditions and ways of knowing we are practising an important form of accountability.

> Our accountability to the people we serve will come not
> from efforts to prove the authority of our knowledge,
> nor from efforts to dismantle it and prove it groundless.
> It will come instead from a more reflective and dialogic
> engagement with our knowledge, and with the people
> served through it—an engagement that seeks constantly to
> problematize our knowing, to probe and critique it, to trace
> its origins and assumptions, and explore its implications, to
> open it to inquiry and transformation. (McKee Sellick et al.,
> 2002; p. 493)

Clearly CYC work is more than just learning some theories, adopting some attitudes, and mastering some skills that can be applied in a straightforward, unproblematic manner when the time is right. Instead, CYC practice, like most human caring professions, is characterized by choices and dilemmas, ambiguities, ethical tensions, and competing sets of interests about what constitutes good and right action and our models need to reflect this messiness and complexity, while still providing a constructive way forward (Nutley & Davies, 2002; Schon, 1983; Taylor & White, 2000). We need more approaches and conceptual tools that can accommodate the dilemmas, uncertainties and paradoxes of practice while also supporting the development of reflexive, critically conscious, praxis-oriented practitioners. It is my hope that the ideas presented here offer a step in this direction.

REFERENCES

Anglin, J. (1992). What exactly is child and youth care work? *The International Child and Youth Care Network, 14,* 1–3.

Anglin, J. (1999). The uniqueness of child and youth care: A personal perspective. *Child and Youth Care Forum, 28*(2), 143–150.

Artz, S. (1994). *Feeling as a way of knowing: A practical guide to working with emotional experience.* Toronto, ON: Trifolium Books.

Bates, R. (2005). A search for synergy: The child and youth care educated child protection worker. *Child and Youth Care Forum, 34*(2), 99–110.

Beker, J. (2001). Towards the unification of the child care field as a profession. *Child and Youth Care Forum, 40*(6), 355–362.

Bohman, J., Hiley, D., & Shusterman, R. (1991). The interpretive turn. In D. Hiley, J. Bohman, R. Shusterman (Eds.), *The interpretive turn: Philosophy, science and culture* (pp. 1–14). Ithaca, NY: Cornell University Press.

Bronfenbrenner, U. (1979). *The ecology of human development.* Cambridge, MA: Harvard University Press.

Carr, W. (1987). What is an educational practice? *Journal of Philosophy of Education, 21*(2), 163–175.

Corney, T. (2004). Values versus competencies: Implications for the future of professional youth work education. *Journal of Youth Studies, 7*(4), 513–527.

Dahlberg, G., Moss, P., & Pence, A. (1999). Minority directions in the majority world: Threats and possibilities. In G. Dahlberg, P. Moss, & A. Pence (Eds.), *Beyond quality in early childhood education and care: Postmodern perspectives* (pp. 159–186). London: Falmer Press.

Denholm, C. (1990). Canadian child and youth care 1979–1989. *Youth Studies, 9*(2), p. 51.

Dorazio-Migliore, M., Migliore, S., & Anderson, J. (2005). Crafting a praxis-oriented culture concept in the health disciplines: Conundrums and possibilities. *Health: An Interdisciplinary Journal for the Social Study of Health, Illness and Medicine, 9*(3), 339–360.

Eisikovits, Z., & Beker, J. (2001). Beyond professionalism: The child and youth care worker as craftsman. *Child & Youth Care Forum, 30*(6), 415–434.

Ferguson, R. (1991). Umbrellas to onions: The evolution of an interactive model for child and youth care education. *Journal of Child and Youth Care, 5*(2), 11–23.

Ferguson, R., & Anglin, J. (1985). The child care profession: A vision for the future. *Child Care Quarterly, 14*, 85–102.

Fewster, G. (1990). *Being in child care: A journey into self.* Binghampton, NY: The Haworth Press.

Fishman, D. (1999). *The case for pragmatic psychology.* New York: New York University Press.

Friere, P. (1970). *Pedagogy of the oppressed.* New York, NY: Seabury.

Garfat, T. (2003). Working with families: Developing a child and youth care approach. *Child & Youth Services, 25*(1/2), 7–37.

Garfat, T. (2004). Meaning-making and intervention in child and youth care practice. *Scottish Journal of Residential Child Care, 3*(1), 9–16.

Gergen, K. (2000). *An invitation to social construction.* London: Sage Publications.

Goldberger, N., Tarule, J., Clinchy, B., & Belenky, M. (Eds.). (1996). *Knowledge, difference, and power: Essays inspired by women's ways of knowing.* New York: Basic Books.

Greenwood, D., & Levin, M. (2005). Reform of the social sciences and of universities through action research. In N. Denzin & Y. Lincoln (Eds.), *The sage handbook of qualitative research* (3rd ed., pp. 43–64). Thousand Oaks, CA: Sage.

Hoskins, M. L. (1996). Constructivism and child and youth care practice: Visions for the 21st century. *Journal of Child and Youth Care, 11*(4), 83–93.

Hoyle, E., & John, P. (1995). *Professional knowledge and professional practice.* Cambridge, UK: Cassell.

Krueger, M. (1997). Using self, story and intuition to understand child and youth care work. *Child & Youth Care Forum, 26*(3), 153–161.

Krueger, M. (2004). Youthwork as modern dance. *Child & Youth Services, 26*(1), 3–24.

Maier, H. (2001). Should child and youth care go the craft or professional route? A comment on the preceding article by Zvi Eiskovits and Jerome Beker. *Child and Youth Care Forum, 30*(6), 435–440.

Mattingly, M. (1995). Developing professional ethics for child and youth care work: Assuming responsibility for the quality of care. *Child and Youth Care Forum, 24*(6), 379–391.

Nakkula, M., & Ravitch, S. (1998). *Matters of interpretation: Reciprocal transformation in therapeutic and developmental relationships with youth.* San Francisco: Jossey-Bass Publishers.

Nelson, G., Poland, B., Murray, M., & Maticka-Tyndale, E. (2004). Building capacity in community health action research: Towards a praxis framework for graduate education. *Action Research, 2*(4), 389–408.

Nussbaum. M. (1990). *Love's knowledge: Essays on philosophy and literature.* New York: Oxford University Press.

Nutley, S., & Davies, H. (2002). Making a reality of evidence-based practice. In H. Davies, S. Nutley & P. Smith (Eds.), *What works? Evidence-based policy and practice in public services* (pp. 317–350). Bristol, UK: The Policy Press.

Pence, A. (1987). Child care's family tree: Toward a history of the child and youth care profession in North America. *Child and Youth Care Quarterly, 16*(3), 151–161.

Pendlebury, S. (1995). Reason and story in wise practice. In H. McEwan & K. Egan (Eds.), *Narrative in teaching, learning, and research* (pp. 50–65). New York: Teachers College Press.

Peters, D., & Kelly, C. (1982). Principles and guidelines for child care personnel preparation programs. *Child Care Quarterly, 11*(3).

Phelan, J. (2005). Child and youth care education: The creation of articulate practitioners. *Child & Youth Care Forum, 34*(5), 347–355.

Polkinghorne, D. (1988). *Narrative knowing and the human sciences.* Albany, NY: State University of New York Press.

Ricks, F. (1989) Self-awareness model for training and application in Child and Youth Care. *Journal of Child and Youth Care, 4*(1), 33–41.

Ricks, F., & Bellefeuille, G. (2003). Knowing: The critical error of ethics in family work. *Child & Youth Services, 25*(1/2), 117–130.

School of Child and Youth Care (2005). *Values.* Retrieved January 26, 2007, from http://www.cyc.uvic.ca/about/values.php#values

Schon, D. A. (1983). *The reflective practitioner: How professionals think in action.* New York: Basic Books.

Schwandt, T. (2002). *Evaluation practice reconsidered.* New York: Peter Lang Publishing, Inc.

Skott-Myhre, H. (2003). Radical youthwork: Creating and becoming everyone. In T. Strong & D. Pare (Eds.), *Furthering talk: Advances in the discursive therapies* (pp. 217–232). New York: Kluwer Academic/Plenum Publishers.

Smith, M. (1999). *Praxis: An introduction to the idea plus an annotated notebook.* Retrieved January 25, 2007, from http://www.infed.org/biblio/b-praxis.htm#praxis

Stacey, K. (2001). Achieving praxis in youth partnership accountability. *Journal of Youth Studies, 4*(2), 208–231.

Stuart, C., & Carty, B. (2006). *The role of competence in outcomes for children and youth: An approach for mental health.* Ontario Ministry for Children and Youth Services.

Tarlier, D. (2005). Mediating the meaning of evidence through epistemological diversity. *Nursing Inquiry, 12*(2), 126–134.

Taylor, C., & White, S. (2000). *Practising reflexivity in health and welfare: Making knowledge.* Buckingham, UK: Open University Press.

Ungar, M. (2004). A constructionist discourse on resilience: Multiple contexts, multiple realities among at-risk children and youth. *Youth & Society, 35*(3), 341–365.

Usher, R., Bryant, I., & Johnston, R. (1997). *Adult education and the postmodern challenge: Learning beyond the limits.* London: Routledge.

VanderVen, K. (1991). How is child and youth care work unique—and different—from other fields? *Journal of Child and Youth Care, 5*(1), 15–19.

VanderVen, K. (in press). If theory and practice were the same – then what? A new approach to designing professional education. In S. Ravitch & M. Nakkula (Eds.), *Teaching, learning and doing: Interdisciplinary approaches to educational inquiry and professional development.*

White, M., & Epston, D. (1990). *Narrative means to therapeutic ends.* New York: W. W. Norton and Company.

CHAPTER 5

Shaping the Rules

Child and Youth Care Boundaries in the Context of Relationship. *Bonsai!*

Carol Stuart, PhD

ABSTRACT

This chapter is a deep exploration of the topic of boundaries in Child and Youth Care practice. The metaphor of a fence guided a personal inquiry into the meaning of boundaries and how boundaries are expressed in professional practice. Inquiry is essential to our current and future learning in Child and Youth Care practice and the chapter models my own inquiry process. I explored existing knowledge to answer some questions, which, in turn, raised additional questions that required further exploration. The answers were not always present in the writing of others or even in discussion, though both these elements were valuable during the inquiry process. How one manages the space between self and other is the ultimate focus of boundary setting. This involves maintaining or taming the wild space in the gap between two fences.

INTRODUCTION

Boundaries are the interface of intimate communication
between people within a particular context.

The concept of boundaries fascinates me, and as such demands an inquiry. What are boundaries? How can I explain the concept along with the development and shaping of professional boundaries to new practitioners? This is an exploration of and inquiry into boundaries, in particular the meaning of boundaries in Child and Youth Care practice. The personal and the professional meaning of boundaries and the nature of the space between the boundaries of two (or more) people in a relationship are the foci of practice and the foci of this inquiry.

To begin an inquiry into boundaries, I picture boundaries as fences that mark our personal territory as our own. Should someone climb over my fence without permission and I notice the intrusion, the law allows me to prosecute for trespassing. This metaphor comes to mind quickly and likely, therefore, accurately represents my interpretation of the concept. It is worth further exploration and de-construction.

Prior to exploring the fence metaphor, the inquiry requires the definition of some terms. The next section examines how academics and researchers define the terms that are relevant to boundaries within the context of professional–client relationships.

DEFINING BOUNDARIES

Boundaries

Actual definitions of the concept of boundaries are rare in the literature of the helping professions. Within the social work, nursing, and counselling/psychotherapy literature, I found discussions of the concepts of boundary violations, though they lacked clear definitions of boundaries.

> Boundaries [are] the way in which each one of us organizes
> the distinction between self and others,…. They make
> autonomous functioning possible, and are expressed in
> our needs for privacy and individuality. Boundaries also
> function actively to preserve our sense of identity and
> uniqueness. (Mann-Feder, 1999, p. 93)

Smith and Fitzpatrick (1995) identify a treatment boundary as a therapeutic frame that defines a set of roles for participants. The therapist defines the boundaries, and the client is expected to contribute. "The therapeutic frame includes both the structural elements (e.g., time, place, and money) and the content (what actually transpires between therapist and client) of therapy" (Smith & Fitzpatrick, 1995, p. 499). When the therapist states that she will meet with the client weekly and she will focus on helping the client with a job search, or resolve an underlying depression, a boundary has been set. When the therapist reviews her commitment to confidentiality, a boundary is set. In independent practice, most boundaries are set through discussion with clients. If a therapist is working for an organization, many of the boundaries are set through the mandate and treatment philosophy of the organization and through the organization's policies. Policies address issues such as client contact after "discharge"; meeting with clients outside of work hours; gifts, the exchange of money, and "personal relationships"; and so on.

Therefore, my definition of boundaries—*Boundaries are the interface of intimate communication between people within a particular context*—is quite different from what appears in the academic literature. Indeed, the more traditional definitions focused on restricting communication and helping the therapist and client stay within differentiated and unique roles; these definitions appear to restrict the idea of and practice of intimate communication between people. My definition is simple and makes sense to me in my world. However, as I discovered in reviewing literature in other professions as well as my own, boundaries seem to have a singular ownership; the professional is usually in control of defining boundaries. The traditional definitions I encountered also address therapeutic content and exclude other content, such as friendship and caring. Finally, boundaries define and are defined by specific times and places for "therapy." I am cognizant of the Child and Youth Care literature on relationships that focuses on the depth of relationship and the mutuality of communication, and Child and Youth Care practice is often defined by its LACK of restricted times and places that occur within the milieu. Is it possible to resolve these inconsistencies? *Can boundaries maintain a unique identity, define particular roles, AND encourage or allow the intimate communication needed for personal growth and development?*

Our interactions with family and community teach us about personal boundaries as we grow up and occasionally our personal boundaries are shaped by professional educational experiences. Pre-service educational programs that are designed for helping professionals explicitly teach about professional boundaries. Thus far, there is an implication that these two types of boundaries are not supposed to "touch."

Ethics

We cannot really talk about boundaries without defining ethics. *Ethics* are the rules that we adhere to in terms of our behaviour and the behaviour of those around us (Ricks & Charlesworth, 2003). Ethics are based on morals and values, which are often instilled by family with contributions from peers and community, and these are generally formed by the end of adolescence. Ethics express our boundaries. Professional organizations develop codes of ethics to guide professional behaviour; they are the collective professional community's "group" rules for behaviour. The formation of professional codes is a marker of the development of the profession, because having a professional code of behaviour is a criterion for a legitimate profession. Once a professional code is in place, a person can be charged with a violation and will then be judged "fit" or "unfit" for practice, thereby protecting the public. Ethical codes appear to function to help us distinguish between the personal and the professional boundaries in a helping relationship. Ethical codes set group guidelines and form a basis for ongoing discussion of group norms and standards.

Relationships

Relationships don't need definition do they? Relationships are highly varied and highly valued by most people. Each time we encounter another person in our lives a relationship begins and then evolves. Relationships contain feelings, thoughts, boundaries, ethics, and activities. They produce other relationships. They are complicated and defy a definition. As I undertake this inquiry into boundaries, interpersonal relationships are the context for boundaries. Boundaries define our relationships, and relationships re-define our boundaries. *Through self-exploration and exploration of the other (in relationship), we come to understand and address our issues and our uniqueness, bringing to consciousness our relationship boundaries. For those of us who work within the context of relationship, each new relationship defines a new set of professional boundaries. In our personal and life-long process of inquiry, we are given limited guidance, except through ethical codes of practice, which are of limited assistance because they change, are challenged, and are re-defined by members of the professional community.* I discovered as I explored the nature of boundaries in Child and Youth Care practice that other professions were challenging and re-shaping professional codes of ethics, and these, consequently, were becoming more open. Practitioners were undertaking personal inquiry and sharing their discoveries with others to help us to challenge and refine the professional ethics we bring to bear on boundaries and relationships.

Having inquired briefly into other definitions of boundaries and ethics (and relationships) in the context of the helping professions, I now return my attention to the "fences" that form our boundaries and what can be learned through the construction/de-construction of this metaphor. The definitions above are the basis for what we learn during the professional education process. What follows is an example of an inquiry that I hope all practitioners will create for themselves.

FENCES

Fences come in many forms. They can be very, very tall or they can be invisible, powered with electrifying force. They can be made of material that is slippery and hard to hold. They can be strong to the touch, easy to grab or hold. Footholds, handholds, or prickly barbed wire on the top may characterize them. Fences that surround a potentially unsafe area must meet certain legal requirements defined by community representatives—the town council, for example. They can be opaque, clear glass; blended with the natural surroundings; built of nature (trees and evergreens); or open and easy to slip through. There are removable snow fences and adjustable panels that let some objects in through large gates that appear solid. The Great Wall of China is a fence that marks a boundary intended both to protect and to preserve the territory. The Great Wall is no longer needed for its original purpose, and people are able to walk the entire length for adventure, personal challenge, and conquering (of a different type).

Boundaries in helping relationships are "derived from social, cultural, political, philosophical, clinical, ethical, legal, and theoretical considerations as well as the therapist's own personal limitations and choices. Their purpose is to contain the therapy and do no harm" (Harper & Steadman, 2003, p. 66). Like fences, boundaries are not isolated from the social world. Depending upon how they are constructed (slippery, prickly, easy to grab), both personal and professional boundaries can create isolation. The theoretical orientation of the therapist and the ethical code of his particular profession define the character of the boundaries within the therapeutic relationship.

Freud initiated the discussion of boundaries when he stated that love relationships (and sexual relationships) were counterproductive to the therapeutic alliance and when he defined counter-transference as a therapeutic tool that is different from the love relationship (Smith & Fitzpatrick, 1995). As is the case with many concepts in the world of helping professions, the father of psychotherapy helps us understand the purpose of boundaries. Noting that Freud is part of the history of the concept of boundaries also means that we need to reconsider the relevance of the concept in today's society and, most particularly, in the context of therapy in the Child and Youth Care milieu. First, it is worthwhile to explore the concept of boundaries as it developed out of Freud's initial concerns.

Early in the professional development of the caring professions, there was no discussion or explanation of the character of boundaries. Wrenn (1973) describes the nature of caring as an activity that involves self-respect and acceptance of self. He says nothing about boundaries, only about caring. In this sense, there are no legal requirements for the fence; it has a natural character that is defined by the mutual owners. Boundaries are identified by Wrenn in the context of "knowing the boundary of one's knowledge" or the "limit" of knowledge and how that limit restricts interactions with the client. Caring and knowledge of theory and change go hand in hand to create a fence, a therapeutic framework, that the client can hold onto, with strength, but the therapist must know the nature of the materials and their limitations. Fences can be set back from the line, or boundary, between two properties, resulting in a gap between the fences; alternatively, fences can have a mutually agreed upon character and be set on the actual boundary between two properties. Establishing and maintaining the latter is more challenging and requires discussion and agreement between neighbours. Knowing which type of fence to construct is one of the challenges of each helping profession.

What are fences for?

While not all boundaries are marked with a fence, fences are about marking territory and defining ownership so that those who use or have access to the property are restricted. Fences protect the owner from unknown and unwelcome visitors. Some fence builders choose to "trust" others; there are hiking trails hundreds of kilometres long that wander through farmers' fields and across crown land where each fence that blocks the trail includes a stile that allows the visitor to go over or through the fence and continue on a journey that explores the lands belonging to many different people. These people share the beauty or harshness of their lands with strangers and trust that these strangers will care for the land.

In traditional helping professions, boundaries recognize the separateness of the client and therapist and validate their distinctness. Boundaries foster safety for self-disclosure; determine the context for power, authority, trust, and dependence; and make it possible for the client to express fears, worries, and frustrations while knowing the therapist will not judge the client based on what is said. Like a fence, there are three ways to alter the boundaries established in a helping relationship: boundary crossings, boundary violations, and boundary shifts. According to Smith and Fitzpatrick,

> Boundary crossing is a non-pejorative term that describes departures from commonly accepted clinical practice that may or may not benefit the client. A boundary violation, on the other hand, is a departure from accepted practice that places the client or the therapeutic process at serious risk. (1995, p. 500)

Boundary shifts are purposeful changes that encourage the client to take more responsibility and power in the relationship and have not been the subject of much attention (Harper & Steadman, 2003).

BOUNDARY CROSSING

In essence, boundary crossings involve the therapist constructing a gate or a stile so that the client remains safe within the territory of the therapeutic relationship. If a child discloses suicidal intent, for example, the parent or another caregiver is informed. Confidentiality is broken without consulting the client but is done so to ensure her safety. Another person is invited into the client's territory by way of the therapist's gate.

The urban fence around a home tends to be about privacy, establishing a visual barrier between neighbours. Privacy is in part about protection of self and, in part, about solitude and keeping a space in which you can be yourself, to maintain and express your own identity. Some fences, perhaps more so in urban locations, are about power, prestige, and control. Urban fences surround workplaces, stores, and public spaces according to the needs and designs of the community. Such fences guide the flow of movement and protect the space and the people who use it.

Boundary crossings are purposeful and benefit the client (as in the breach of confidentiality example above). Protocols defined by the professional community guide the therapist's behaviour and protect both clients and professionals. Steps to mitigate the effects of boundary crossings should include the following considerations:

> [First,] any therapist behaviour that might be construed as a boundary violation should be justified by sound clinical reasoning. Second, in the current litigious climate, clinicians must ensure that boundary crossings are well documented. The documentation process is both a protection for the conscientious clinician and a further opportunity to examine the event itself. Finally, boundary crossings present opportunities to examine, discuss [with the client], and understand the counseling process. (Smith & Fitzpatrick, 1995, p. 505)

Changes to the 2005 American Counseling Association (ACA) ethical code indicate a paradigm shift occurring in the area of ethics and boundaries:

> The standards related to boundary issues between counselors and clients and counselors and former clients are evolving. A paradigm shift is currently taking place within the counseling profession and within other mental health organizations when it comes to how professionals view dual or multiple relationships with clients.... recent ethics scholars challenge this notion and say that dual/ multiple relationships, sometimes known as "boundary crossings", are normative and can actually be meaningful in the counseling relationship, particularly in rural or certain cultural communities. (Kocet, 2006, p.231)

BOUNDARY VIOLATIONS

Boundary violations are transgressions that occur when the therapist breaks through into the client's personal territory, moving beyond the usual protective fences established in such a relationship. The personal history of a client may result in the construction of a boundary that is distorted, built of weak material, or it may be broken or damaged by previous relationships. Such boundaries move; they can be slippery and difficult for the therapist to detect. Thus, they are prone to boundary violations that may be purposeful or accidental but are always harmful to the client and to the therapist.

Fences are also about keeping things in—people, property, and animals, for example, that require protection from the dangers beyond the fence. In some cases, the beings that are inside the fence are naïve and innocent and require protection from hurt and injury. In other cases, innocence may have grown to maturity and the fence is merely an artifact; it was solidly built to protect those inside and is not easily removed. In still other cases, the people or animals on the inside are dangerous, and thus the fence protects those in the outside world. Fences have gates for access and egress. Gates can be locked from either side, and are opened with keys that are easily reached or combinations that are more difficult to discover.

Fence Maintenance: The Rules for Looking After Boundaries

In the literature, maintaining, addressing, correcting, and setting boundaries is identified as the therapist's responsibility because of the power differential in the therapist–client relationship. The therapist holds the key. Power is ascribed by society to shamans and healers, and with that power comes the responsibility for addressing boundary issues (Holder & Schenthal, 2007). According to Smith and Fitzpatrick (1995), the principles that underlie boundary guidelines in most ethical codes include these three:

1. **Abstinence**—Therapists will not seek personal gratification and the only acceptable payment is the fee.
2. **Duty to neutrality**—The client's agenda is the primary focus and therefore therapist self-disclosure is limited as is interference outside of the therapy hour.
3. **Client autonomy**—The therapist must strive to enhance autonomy and independence, and boundary violations restrict client freedom to explore and choose.

These principles then describe the character of the fences that define the professional's boundaries with clients in several areas. In each of the following areas, there are limitations or rules that describe the therapist's obligation not to violate boundaries that need to be re-considered:

1. Therapists are discouraged from using self-disclosure. Freud discouraged self-disclosure and instructed therapists to remain "opaque" to the client, for the benefit of the client. Typically, self-

disclosure is a technique that removes the focus from the client's concerns. Research demonstrates that progressive self-disclosure is strongly associated with inappropriate sexual contact with clients (Harper & Steadman, 2003; Holder & Schenthal, 2007). Apparently—in contrast to the research on therapist behaviour— client satisfaction research demonstrates that reciprocity in the helping relationship, as well as love, friendship, and caring, are important to the client's view of effective work (Maidment, 2006).

2. Confidentiality, the guarantee that information disclosed to the counsellor will not be shared with others without permission, is a hallmark of professional–client relationships, and is enshrined in many code of ethics (Harper & Steadman, 2003; Holder & Schenthal, 2007). Confidentiality protects the client from undue harm that others would perpetrate and, in essence, keeps dangers outside of the fence.

3. Many ethical codes contain statements that discourage touch, with some implication that touching leads to sexual contact, which is clearly prohibited. Little research addresses this area or considers the impact of cultural norms (e.g., the French Canadian habit or kissing as a greeting). There is also little theory about how boundaries on touch should be formed in light of the practitioner theory about how to create change (e.g., psychodynamic practitioners believe that touch inhibits the development of transference and counter-transference). There is no research to indicate the effect of touch or other forms of physical contact on therapeutic outcome, yet touch is known to be essential to human development (Harper & Steadman, 2003; Holder & Schenthal, 2007). A contradiction such as this can confuse the practitioner who might be exploring how to set boundaries around touch as an element of his practice. The damaging after effects of therapist– client sexual contact are clearly documented, but there is little that describes the relationship precursors to sexual contact or the risk factors present in either party, or the environment, that might lead to therapist–client sexual relationships (Harper & Steadman, 2003; Holder & Schenthal, 2007). Therefore, clients (and therapists) do not know what danger signs to watch for.

4. Gift giving is another limit addressed by ethical codes and is typically discouraged. Gifts are thought to be a form of payment from clients and, as such, could be presented with the expectation additional service will be provided. In reality, gifts are an expression of gratitude. In some cultures, gifts are expected under certain circumstances. For children, gifts often serve as spontaneous recognition of the importance of adults

in their lives. Ethics and boundaries in the helping professions have shifted away from the common societal norms to create a professional culture that does not include the usual norms. Social etiquette may demand that one bring a gift and, or, acknowledge the special assistance of a friend or neighbour during a difficult time. As noted above, in the professional culture receiving a gift from a client is considered a boundary violation and would not be accepted by the professional. Not accepting the gift could impede the practitioner–client relationship. A more reasonable approach, more consistent with broad social norms, might be that gifts are acceptable unless they are clearly intended as a bribe or are solicited by the professional.

5. Dual relationships, the definition of which varies by theoretical orientation and by profession, is another area that requires further consideration. In comparison to other professions, being engaged in a dual relationship is considered a MORE serious ethical violation by psychotherapists. Dual relationships are unavoidable in small communities and in certain professional circles, including Child and Youth Care, in which one can encounter former clients as a supervisor, employer, and so on. Ethical codes rarely address the conflicts that arise in these circumstances.

The Smith and Fitzpatrick (1995) decision-making model instructs psychologists to make judgments about the original professional relationship (from the perspective of the consumer) based on three dimensions: power, duration, and clarity of termination. According to the model, the risk of harm to the consumer increases when an additional relationship is added, and the increase in risk is greater if power and duration of the original relationship are greater but might be mediated by increased clarity upon termination (Holder & Schenthal, 2007, p. 502).

Boundary violations are rarely isolated, discrete events. They occur in a context and generally result from the "slippage" of boundaries over time. Slippage is often identifiable in hindsight. As in Figure 1, below, the boundary crossing is unidentified by the therapist and is followed by a transgression or more purposeful decision to step over the fence or boundary of appropriate behaviour. Often a boundary transgression is initiated by an event within the social world of the client or therapist that changes the nature of one person's needs within the relationship and creates a catalyst.

THE SLIPPERY SLOPE

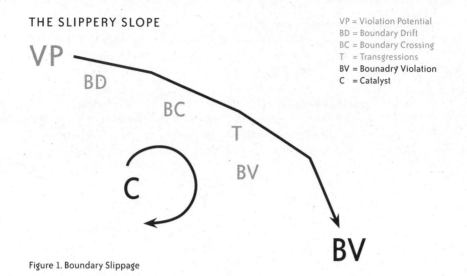

VP = Violation Potential
BD = Boundary Drift
BC = Boundary Crossing
T = Transgressions
BV = Bounadry Violation
C = Catalyst

Figure 1. Boundary Slippage

BOUNDARY SHIFTS

The nature of Child and Youth Care practitioners' clientele—that is, young people who have experienced dysfunctional relationships and who are uncertain about boundaries—demand that we work on a daily basis to address boundary violations and that we understand boundary management very well. Experience with intentional boundary management is essential for young people to develop close interpersonal relationships (Mann-Feder, 1999).

> We find our interpersonal boundaries pushed to the limit
> because this is precisely what our clients need to relearn.
> If we do not stay aware and active in setting boundaries,
> we miss an opportunity to help clients revise their sense
> of self. This does not contradict relatedness.... Managing
> boundaries need not contradict the need to connect but
> requires primarily that we remain aware of boundary
> issues. Knowledge of clients' early history is critical in
> understanding how they will position themselves in relation
> to others. Clarifying boundaries to enhance development
> also requires that we attend to three important aspects
> of our interventions: relevant limit setting; separations
> and reunions; and observing our own boundaries as they
> inevitably emerge in our interactions with clients. (Mann-
> Feder, 1999, n.p.)

Mann-Feder examines boundaries from the client side of boundary shifts. *Limit setting*, as a component of intervention, is critical to helping children develop a sense of self. It teaches children to establish a boundary around self; it is also essential to the worker's self-protection. For example, for a worker to say "no, I can't do that now," can protect the worker from over commitment. At times, the worker may consciously "shift" boundaries to set different limits. Such changes and shifts are part of day-to-day enactment of personal boundaries, and yet somehow we have developed the idea that professional boundaries are fixed.

Legalities of Fencing: How Society Governs our Boundary Setting

There are, of course, laws about fencing. How high can the fence be? Who pays for erecting the fence, and how far back from the property line must it sit? What types of activities and constructions, such as a swimming pool, require a fence? In addition, what type of fence should it be? There are laws about trespassing. The violation of a space owned by another, whether it is protected by a fence or not, is considered an intrusion of that person's space. Society prohibits such intrusions without permission and has encoded these prohibitions in the laws of the country.

The Changing Technology of Fence Building: Boundaries Redefined Through the Centuries

The great walls of the world—China, Berlin, and Rome—were built slowly over time with much human effort. The workers who constructed these walls were slave labourers, military workers, and people without choices. They built at the whim of the government of the day, which comprised the powerful elite of society. These walls created barriers by way of collaborative human effort for the benefit of the culture and society being protected. The walls formed barriers that were impenetrable to other humans, even when left unguarded. Until technology advanced and flight became possible, the size and extent of these great walls provided time to defend the fence when required, and time to observe others and plan for foreign visitors. Durable, heavy materials meant the barrier protected the people and the culture within, and outsiders either required force to break down the wall and claim the territory, or they were invited in. The material was protective because the people could not see beyond it, could not reach beyond it. It could not be moved except by super-human force.

The information age has significantly affected the nature of professional "fences," or boundaries. Just before the 21st century, the issues associated with technology and boundaries pertained to confidentiality, inter-professional communication, the impact of technology, electronic file systems, specialized IT members of the team, the security of networks, and voicemail systems (Gelman, Pollack, & Weiner, 1999; Rock & Congress, 1999).

The literature of that time focuses on networked computers and the threat of hackers. Rock and Congress (1999) described three levels of sensitivity that can be used to develop guidelines and practices for determining the appropriate procedures for security related to electronic storage and communication of client information. They recommend that the level of sensitivity be discussed with clients and based on the potential damage accorded to the client if confidentiality were breached. Threats to confidentiality were determined by the human factor—whether or not the computer user actually followed appropriate procedures. Proposed changes included five levels of security implemented according to the sensitivity of the material and the potential threat level:

1. Use of passwords to access computers
2. Use of passwords to access programs and operating system (including the implementation of an automatic "lock" function after a period of non-use)
3. Limited ability to change client data and information within a given program
4. The removal of hard drives at the end of the day and their storage in a secure location
5. Data encryption

At the turn of the 21st century, there was no discussion of the Internet and its role in open information retrieval and information sharing. The only concern expressed was how use of the Internet for information retrieval can place clients at risk for data-mining (Gelman et al., 1999) when their confidential information is held electronically. The concern was that individuals who did not have a relationship with clients might gain access to private data. Use of technology and electronic record keeping can enable such access by those who do not have a relationship with the client and who are not bound by a professional code of ethics. Confidentiality and security are provided for in the context of the relationship between the caregiver and the client, and outside the context of this relationship, the caregiver is expected to understand the implications of technology relative to confidentiality and security. The caregiver must often rely on someone with technical expertise to ensure that personal information is secure. In the literature of the day, there was no discussion of the implications of social networking on the Internet (e.g., Facebook, MySpace) because this is a more recent phenomenon.

Contemporary fence technology buries electricity and signals underground, rendering the "fence" invisible but shocks those who try to escape. One can see beyond the fence but cannot come close to or explore either side of the boundary unless it is "turned off." Invisible fences generally "target" particular people or animals because the signal only affects those wearing a receiver. The territory on both sides of the fence is open for exploration by those who have not been outfitted with specific hardware.

When clients are identified as having a given illness or disorder and are labelled, invisible boundaries are created. These boundaries can be shocking for clients initially, although habituation to the new boundary may occur eventually. A different issue, from the shock of being labelled and discriminated against, is how visible or invisible the boundary is, and how the client participates in negotiating what that boundary is. For example, children placed into protective custody are labelled by the community as troubled "problem kids," or "welfare kids," and local families try to limit the time their children spend with these outsiders. The placement of group homes and residences are subject to NIMBY[1] attitudes and, consequently, youth in these homes grow up on the edges of residential neighbourhoods. Children and youth rarely participate in negotiating where they stay or how boundaries might be developed around them and limit their potential.

The changing technology of fence building allows machinery to quickly and efficiently erect and take down fences to re-define territory and changing ownership. Only those more natural fences and boundaries that are developed as man manipulates nature are unaffected by the modern technology and consequent speed of change. Cedar hedges grow and evolve slowly into fences that are trimmed and shaped by their owners, inviting or blocking interaction with other people. There are always two sides to the fence, including fences in professional relationships. Both

---

1   Not in My Back Yard

client and therapist can participate in the trimming and shaping of the fence, even though only one likely participated in the initial planting.

A review of the literature of other helping professions reveal several critical analyses of ethical codes. There has been no review of the ethical codes employed in Child and Youth Care practice relative to boundary violations and the limits of professional behaviour. Why? First, the technology of fence building is different in Child and Youth Care practice. Boundaries are created within the child's milieu. The specific time, place, and cost of the therapeutic relationship is unclear. The practitioner comes to the child and therefore the child experiences little separation from his daily life. This demands a different approach to boundary setting on the part of the practitioner. Second, a review of three Canadian provincial codes of ethics and the *Code of Ethics: Standards for Practice of North American Child & Youth Care Professionals*[2] indicates that the profession has avoided explicit rules for behaviour and has chosen an approach to ethics that requires self-awareness and ethical decision-making. These codes recognize that personal and professional or therapeutic relationships are different and that there is an obligation to explicate and articulate this difference. If the relationship becomes non-therapeutic, the practitioner is obliged to refer elsewhere. The specifics of how to recognize a boundary crossing and what a non-therapeutic relationship looks like are left to the practitioner to determine. The only activity clearly prohibited to a Child and Youth Care worker is sexual intimacy.

The healthy therapeutic alliance is essential to successful outcomes for the client, and proper boundaries provide safety and ensure that the clinician will act in the client's best interests. The establishment of clear boundaries between the parties is a standard for clear communication and reduces the potential

> for misinterpretations of the therapist's messages, motives, and behaviours. Given this definition of treatment boundaries, it is clear the boundaries are regularly transgressed by even the most competent therapists, and such transgressions are not always to the detriment of the client. (Smith & Fitzpatrick, 1995, p. 500)

---

2 Please visit the websites for these professional organizations to review their codes of ethics. Child and Youth Care Association of Alberta, http://www.cycaa.com/ehtics. htm; Child and Youth Care Association of British Columbia, http://www.cycabc.org/ code-ethics.htm; Ontario Association of Child and Youth Counsellors, http://www. oacyc.org/page4.html; Association of Child and Youth Care Practice, http://www.pitt. edu/~mattgly/CYCethisc.html

Child and Youth Care practitioners meet the child in their milieu, where boundaries are not as clear as they might be in an office setting. The fence building technology, to return to the metaphor, is different from that of other professions. As I completed my initial review of the literature, I realized that the technology employed by other professions raises questions but provides few answers for establishing and shaping boundaries within the Child and Youth Care practice context.

UNANSWERED QUESTIONS: CREATING ENVIRONMENTALLY FRIENDLY BOUNDARIES

As a metaphor for the concept of boundaries, the fence raises some interesting questions about the definition and implementation of boundaries in Child and Youth Care practice. *How does one deal with virtual boundaries in the age of electronic communication?* The fencing metaphor is only marginally useful when it comes to the communication of boundaries in the context of the Internet and electronic communications. There are many additional issues to be considered.

Establishing a boundary between people tends to be an interactive activity that must address real and tangible issues for those participating in fence construction. Social networking sites like Facebook, while interactive, are not interactive in the same way that a face-to-face client–practitioner relationship is interactive; instead, a person sits alone with her computer and interacts with virtual images and information in an asynchronous timeframe. As practitioners begin to explore the use of e-counselling and youth find practitioners in social networking sites, the implications for boundary setting in the context of Internet technology will need further exploration.

Personal and professional boundaries are supposed to be different from one another. How are they different? *What is the flexible line between authenticity and professional boundaries? How is this line different for Child and Youth Care practitioners who work day to day in the milieu of the child and family?* The daily milieu does not impose, nor is it necessarily subject to, the characteristic limits or boundaries of time and space of the office setting. What does this mean for the permanency of boundaries and for the negotiation of boundaries?

An intuitive understanding of boundaries fits with the fencing metaphor, but intuitively I also know that fences are constructed, removed, adjusted, broken open, and made visible or invisible within the context of the daily milieu that we work in. Child and Youth Care practitioners need a counter-intuitive understanding and expression of boundaries to deal with their professional reality. Intuitive approaches are based on common sense, which varies for each person. However, common "professional" sense is typically defined by the professional culture of the practitioner. As a young profession Child and Youth Care has been guided by the common sense of other professional cultures (various of which have been discussed above), when in reality boundaries need to be considered in a manner counter intuitive to these other professional cultures. *How can educators and supervisors work to develop a counter-intuitive understanding of boundaries in new professionals—an understanding that appears instinctive and spontaneous but which both builds and protects relationships at the same time that it protects individuals?* The second half of this chapter explores these questions, relying on the first half as a foundation, and keeping these thoughts in mind:

> Chain link represents all that is wrong in this world.
> A fence discourages communication and collaboration.
> A fence marks private property and silently says
> "my mom never taught me how to share."
> A fence symbolises apathy towards community and
> public spaces, drawing a line of responsibility at the end
> of one's lawn.
> Each time we take down a fence, we open up a new space.
>
> http://www.publicspace.ca/defence_photos.htm

ASPECTS OF INTERPERSONAL BOUNDARIES IN CHILD AND YOUTH CARE: HOW DOES THE FENCE HOLD UP?

Relationship boundaries, and in particular relationship boundaries in the context of professional Child and Youth Care practice, are the focus of this discussion. I have defined boundaries as the interface of intimate communication between people, yet professional literature in other disciplines takes a different approach. Most professions define personal and professional boundaries as different structures; in reality, however, personal and professional boundaries are the rules that we each make up for how we participate in relationships. Thus, the potential for confusion is high. The expression of this confusion occurs in the processes of a boundary violation.

Child and Youth Care practitioners must be knowledgeable about and personally aware of all of the nuances of boundaries present in the fence metaphor. However, the answers to the dilemmas of boundary setting that are posed by other professions are ones that we have struggled with and rejected at some level. Why? What is the appropriate metaphor? What is it that we do with boundaries? Manage them? Cross them? Shift them?

I like the idea of using the metaphor of naturally evolving environmental boundaries and fences and engaging with children and youth to shape and develop those boundaries. Boundary shaping is therefore a time-consuming, life-long process and fits comfortably with Child and Youth Care theory. Practitioners make a time-limited contribution to a child's ongoing growth and development, but we leave an indelible impression. This section addresses some of the issues that are part of the milieu-based context that we work in as well as some of the new issues that have arisen because technology can now be used by everyone for social networking.

Imagine, as you read, that the child or youth "owns" a large property, perhaps a forest tract, and that the practitioner is the manager, caretaker, or cultivator of one of the adjoining properties. As such, the practitioner has permission from the child to enter and explore the forest and to work the other side of the boundary to help the child define and create a natural, environmental "fence," a cultivated cedar hedge, perhaps, that grows out of the forestland. As the practitioner, you don't come and work just an hour a week or even an hour a day: you are always there, ready to trim your side and help the child trim her side. This occurs in an ongoing developmental process.

In the context of professional practice as a Child and Youth Care worker, understanding interpersonal boundaries requires you to address issues such as emotional freedom, personal storytelling, secrets between people (e.g., youth and workers) and trust, physical closeness, and the (recent) incorporation of relationships that do not occur face to face (Facebook, MySpace) but that constitute relationships nonetheless. Practitioners who inhabit a common milieu with children and youth (such as a group home, school classroom, or community centre) find these issues pervasive. They must also consider the one-way and the two-way nature of communication about boundaries, as well as the vague and hard-to-define "space" between individuals and within the relationship.

Client satisfaction research shows that reciprocity in the helping relationship, along with love, friendship, and caring, is important to effective work. According to Maidment (2006) love develops through searching for the unlovable characteristics (as well as appreciating the loveable characteristics) of a client and knitting together the bonds of a relationship in spite of what is unlovable. Child and Youth Care practitioners are confronted daily with unlovable characteristics and young people who demand that they be real and genuine. Statements like "You get paid to care!" are a reality. Child and Youth Care practitioners have entered the field because they care. We are faced with negotiating this boundary between loving and caring for someone and minimizing any emotional reactions to the unlovable demands of children and youth who are uncertain about how to receive or give love and caring. Skott-Myhre and Skott-Myhre (2007) argue that capitalism has created a materialistic sense of community in which "love" is perceived as power-based and is therefore considered inappropriate and is frowned on in discussions about boundaries and of the nature of youth–adult relationships. They argue for a new type of love—political love—that encourages working together toward common ends and promotes a mutual relationship that is creative, infinite, and self-sustaining. This requires a new approach to developing and negotiating boundaries.

Freud and Krug (2002) argued that social work adopted "the psycho-analytic constraints of anonymity, neutrality, and abstinence" (p. 483), and that these restrictions run counter to social work's mandate. Clinical relationships and clinical counselling are very different from social justice work, child protection work, community development work, and other types of family work that require forming personal relationships, "working" side by side, and doing home visits. Freud and Krug argue that boundary violations in clinical work would actually be "day-to-day work" in the latter and therefore are not considered boundary violations. Like social work, boundaries in Child and Youth Care practice become flexible and co-constructed within the day-to-day milieu of the child. Out of daily events and based on the emotional reactions associated with those events, we co-create boundaries and mutually communicate. The creation of boundaries is intentional, purposeful, and is guided by the practitioner.

While practitioners in other professions discuss boundary violations, boundary crossings, and boundary shifts, these terms imply action and responsibility only on the part of the professional. In a context of emotional freedom, however, the co-creation of relationships and boundaries must involve mutuality. As the Child and Youth Care practitioner co-creates a sense of love and caring, the practitioner is responsible for identifying his and the youth's emotions and to adjust the boundaries as emotions emerge. Perhaps boundary shaping is the appropriate term.

Manning (1997) argues for the necessity of a moral citizenship framework to guide ethical decision-making. Moral citizenship requires using awareness, thinking, feeling, and action to guide ethical behaviour. For example, the practitioner is aware of the dilemma and then thinks rationally (with intention) and respectfully about the dilemma and any consequences, it may generate for the client. Feeling or caring for the person is part of this consideration. Emotion, then, motivates or drives action or ethical behaviour. Action when grounded in moral citizenship involves acting for a "cause" within society. This social justice approach to change is more commonly associated with social work; in Child and Youth Care practice, in comparison, we act for and with the child and mutually shape the boundaries of our relationship. Our moral citizenship means that the child or youth is our "cause."

Being Personal

Professional literature advises against interacting on a more personal level on the part of the counsellor. Self-disclosure and gift giving, examples of the more personal approach to caring and providing service, are discouraged in some professions. For Aboriginal people (and for some other populations), self-disclosure and storytelling establish authenticity in the helping relationship. Self-disclosure is a method of establishing mutuality in a relationship and serves to reduce the power imbalance inherent in a practitioner–client relationship, and thus facilitates client empowerment (Maidment, 2006). Children and youth are still in the concrete phase of understanding the world and therefore value and learn from concrete examples and stories about the lives of others. Being personal occurs in many forms in Child and Youth Care practice; practitioners can disclose basic feelings and reactions, personal histories and solutions to their own problems, their current issues and concerns, unresolved dilemmas and conflicts, stories about others and their reactions. Any of these forms of communication offer the youth something personal from the practitioner. Which approach the practitioner chooses depends on personal ethics and rules for behaviour, the practitioner's boundary around self-disclosure, and the nature of the youth's boundaries and needs at a given time. This is part of the co-creation of the boundary between practitioner and youth.

Being personal with youth requires an initial examination of your own "fence," or how you construct your boundaries around personal information. We all grow up learning boundaries and norms that pertain to personal disclosure. The stereotypical "stiff upper lip" associated with the British, the "Latin lover," the reserved and unfailingly polite Japanese—these are exaggerations of the boundaries we learn in our families, communities, and cultures. As practitioners entering into the community that works with children and youth, we must begin to assess, examine, and re-assess these fences and identify our own comfort levels and the comfort level of each child.

Children who have been physically and, or, emotionally abused are guarded when disclosing their feelings. In the past, disclosure of true feelings may have been associated with abuse or an increased risk of abuse. Children who have experienced sexual abuse do not have a clear sense of what appropriate emotional boundaries are, nor what boundaries of personal disclosure are appropriate. They are particularly confused by feelings of love and caring because the abuser may be someone that they love and care for. On the other hand, "system kids" can often tell stories about their personal histories that appear to be forms of deep self-disclosure; in fact, they may have told their stories so many times that there are no emotions connected to those tales. Any emotional response lies in the listener, who feels sympathy for and cares for the youth. In each of these circumstances of disclosure, the Child and Youth Care practitioner must consciously decide how best to work with the youth to shape the boundaries of disclosure and emotional involvement. If performed effectively, the shaping and trimming of these boundaries will stay with the child for life, particularly when the current practitioner-gardener, -cultivator, and -manager of the "hedge" moves on and a new professional engages in a relationship and begins shaping the hedge.

> *Bonsai: the Japanese art of cultivating miniature trees through careful trimming and shaping.*

Separateness

Working in the child's milieu regularly raises issues of power and control that compete with love and developmental needs. Practitioners who began in milieu-based care and who move to clinical care (a term that invokes antiseptic, clean contact in an office environment) bring with them the value of milieu-based work. Doucette (2004) describes an alternative to "office work" with adolescents that she calls "Walk and Talk": "Interpersonal relationships are a process of continuous reciprocal interplay of each person's internal working model with others. It is not possible to hold oneself apart from this interplay" (p. 375). A basic principle of this model is that one understands oneself in relation to others and to one's understanding of how others view us. These apparent violations of the traditional rules for professional boundaries in a helping relationship involve refusing to hold oneself separate.

There is reciprocal space present between people in a relationship. Reciprocity means both parties exchange, influence, and exist in that space. It is a joint space. When one considers parenting a child, the parent attends to the child's needs and must balance the adult authority, power, and control with love and caring to provide the necessary safety. As the child develops and becomes more capable of understanding the dangers of the world, parental power and control is reduced, but love and caring remain constant. In fact, love and caring strengthen as children begin to reciprocate. Child and Youth Care practitioners lack the shared history with children that parents experience as they develop relationships, and provide safety, in the context of a challenging relationship. When practitioners begin to maintain a shared boundary, and perhaps enter into the child's territory, they do so without knowing what the previous environment, fence maker, or growing conditions were like. This makes discussion and the co-creation of boundaries and personal history essential. If I, as the practitioner, accept that I am not separate from the child and that, indeed, my relationship and co-involvement with the child IS the therapeutic process (Fewster, 2005; Garfat & Charles, 2007), then I need to employ personal disclosure, and I need to actively build common ground and understanding that clears, cultivates, and shapes both sides of the boundary.

Research indicates that social caregivers derive satisfaction from interactions with clients to the extent that such interaction keeps them motivated and brings them personal rewards in their jobs (Faver, 2004). In my personal experience, sustenance from and connection with my work occurs as a result of interpersonal relationships, and these interpersonal relationships are essential to my fuller understanding of the world and the nature of the world. This is the notion of relational spirituality. Spirituality is the process by which we develop a fuller understanding of ourselves, our lives, and the world, and it is how we receive personal fulfillment.

Client views about how effective their counsellors are indicate that good listening, assurance of confidentiality, and trustworthiness are the top qualities required in a counsellor. Child and Youth Care strategies, such as group work; games, exercise, and sports; sharing fun activities; eating; going out of the office, and so on were valued by clients as the most beneficial forms of interaction (Smith, 2004). These are all strategies that serve to develop personal history and reduce the interpersonal separation between the people in a client–counsellor relationship.

Touch

Agencies are fearful of accusations made by children and youths of abuse, and regulators believe that legal controls are the best means to ensure children's safety. Therefore, agency policies tend to discourage touch, and legislation focuses on children's right to safety. These tools are critical for the protection of both workers and children, but they are not supportive of children's developmental needs for affection, nor do they acknowledge the importance of human touch in the healing process.

> Properly managed horseplay is how boys (and many girls) get to know where the boundaries lie, how they can learn to play by the rules and, perhaps most importantly, how they can experience essential physical contact with other human beings in culturally acceptable ways. If we don't offer adaptive means through which kids can get this physical contact, they may well seek it out in maladaptive ways, through initiating restraints. (Smith, 2006, n.p.)

We cannot talk about boundaries in Child and Youth Care practice without talking about touch. It is one of the greatest concerns of most practitioners. It is also one of the greatest developmental needs that children have. Thus the dilemma:

> it appears safer for the discipline to promote overt boundary setting than to even engage in a discussion about healthy

forms of touch in practice. Nevertheless, respectful and appropriate physical contact between the client and worker conveys a sense of connectedness unparalleled by verbal assurance and empathy. (Maidment, 2006, p. 118)

Child and Youth Care practitioners must determine their own level of comfort with touch, and they must be knowledgeable about the developmental needs that touch fulfills and the individual characteristics of every child. Only when this level of comfort and knowledge is achieved can the practitioner effectively shape the boundaries surrounding touch with children and youth.

Facing Facebook

Facebook is a social networking tool designed to connect people over time and distance through the Internet. MySpace serves a similar purpose; it is a simple way to create your own web presence without creating your own website. However, practitioners still need to know how and when to use these tools appropriately and be aware that it is a forum for clarifying and expressing boundaries. The rules, or fences, discussed above govern Facebook and similar sites. For most people there is no explicit discussion or consideration of boundaries, and this is evident in the ways in which sites are created. Boundary decisions are made in isolation of the relationship that one might have with someone else. One can view the profiles, personal information, and pictures of others on Facebook, and in turn others can see your information. The site owner is unaware of who is interacting with their site, and in many cases you only need to be a Facebook member, not a "friend," to see personal information. Depending upon how public a Facebook site is, knowing the other person and developing a sense of relationship could be very one-sided. One could also spend a lot of time responding to the technological games or "applications" that others send your way and constructing one's site in accordance with the appropriate level of openness and professionalism. Questions remain, however: What are the appropriate boundaries for the personal information that you share, and how flexible are the boundaries? Can they be adjusted according to the nature of the person you are interacting with?

Young people who have a strong online presence tend to be more open, independent, and aware of difference and social inequity. They also believe that the Internet imposes fewer boundaries on them because they cannot be judged while online because of their age or appearance (Maczewski, 2002), unless they construct a site that makes these characteristics apparent. Prior to the advent of social networking sites, youth presence on the Internet required a reasonable command of technology, and contact tended to be anonymous because it was text based. Youth of today have grasped the social networking sites as a means of staying in touch with others and expressing themselves to the world. With this practice comes the danger of open disclosure.

In professional face-to-face life with youth, I can choose what to disclose, what photos to share, what information, and so on. A social networking site requires the user to make the same choices, but I have seen too many workers fail to consider what information is posted on their sites or how to adjust security settings to set boundaries. The apparent anonymity of the Internet means that the importance of boundaries is forgotten when a site is being created. A limited profile should be available to the general membership, those that are not "friends" and careful consideration should be given to the choices of who to accept as a "friend." There are several challenges to boundary setting on social networking sites. The first is technical skill: the user must know how to use the program to establish restrictions regarding what can be viewed and by whom, and the user must make decisions about how much information to share. Understanding how to use the software can be challenging. The second challenge is the black and white nature of computers and software: everything in the software world operates on 1s or 2s—yes or no. There is no room for "maybe." There is not a range of responses to enable the progressive development of relationships, and no co-construction or joint decision making about the shape of the boundaries that are established between two people.

On the other hand, Internet-based counselling has developed significantly over the last 10 years. "Kids Help Phone" is not just a crisis line aimed at helping abused children get protection. The organization introduced an interactive Internet-based service in 2002. Since then the organization website, www.kidshelpphone.ca, provides access to phone counselling as well as Internet-based discussion forums where counsellors respond to questions. The site provides clear guidelines to maintain anonymity and confidentiality and acts as a first contact for referrals and information for youth who might otherwise not ask. Discussion is organized by topic and responses come only from the counsellors, though others can read each question and response. A Google search for the phrase "counselling online" brings up many different options, including a certificate in cyber-counselling at University of Toronto, through the Faculty of Social Work, studies for which began in fall 2007 in partnership with the Kids Help Line service (http://newsutoronto.ca/bin6/070704-3271.asp). There are also numerous private counsellors available who use secure email systems. Each site outlines boundaries that pertain to privacy and confidentiality. The information on these sites typically conforms to that required in ethical codes, describes payment procedures, and identifies the types of issues that are best discussed in person or can be addressed by phone.

King, Bumbling, Reid, and Thomas (2006) concluded that while both telephone counselling and online counselling provided by the Australian Kids Help Line produced positive outcomes, the former was more effective. Surprisingly, client–counsellor alliance did NOT contribute to the effectiveness of the outcome, though counsellor impact did contribute. The authors hypothesized that the greater amount of time for communication provided for in a verbal exchange (in contrast to a written, online exchange) contributed to increased effectiveness because the counsellor was able to use both verbal and non-verbal strategies to have an impact; in addition, discussion was faster and therefore went further.

The anonymity and asynchronous timing of online counselling appear to provide several benefits that face-to-face counselling does not. The client feels safer and may be willing to take increased risks with disclosure when not confronted with the relational aspects of face-to-face counselling. The counsellor's response can be considered and reconsidered as the client achieves deeper understanding and presents reduced defensiveness (Schultze, 2006). In other words, the nature of boundaries is different in cyberspace, and we are just beginning to explore what that means just as the more established and more traditionally minded professions begin to re-examine the restrictiveness of the ethical codes that define their boundaries.

DEVELOPING A COUNTER-INTUITIVE UNDERSTANDING OF BOUNDARIES

The examination of boundaries and ethical codes that address how to establish appropriate boundaries has led other professions to re-examine the restrictiveness of their ethical codes. While few ethical codes for Child and Youth Care hold these same restrictions, it is worth noting what has developed in other professions as mechanisms for guiding practitioners with making decisions that pertain to boundary setting. Earlier I discussed the idea of the "slippery slope" (Holder & Schenthal, 2007). Evolving from this idea is the "boundary formula" (see Figure 2), which provides us with a method of understanding the potential for a boundary violation. How does this "formula" help us with shaping boundaries in relationships with children and youth?

> The Boundary Formula...gauge[s] a nurse's relative violation potential (VP).... Every nurse and every healthcare provider carries a VP. VPs are dynamic and change over time in response to life events, professional risk factors (RF), and personal vulnerability (Vul). This variation explains why a nurse may have a low VP at one moment and a high VP at another. Risk factors encompass a number of external elements such as work setting, patient type, and experience. Vulnerabilities represent psychosocial elements that influence our boundary interactions. These elements could include unresolved childhood trauma or shame-based injuries, just to name a few. A nurse may be resistant (r) to look at risk factor or vulnerabilities. This mindset magnifies the potential for a violation because it represents a blind spot. As risk factors and/or vulnerabilities increase, the violation potential shifts from a low VP to a high VP. Concurrently, if an unexpected "catalyst" (divorce, death, career change, provocative patient, etc.) encounters a high VP, it may propel a nurse across the thin line that separates ethical from unethical. Accountability (A) is reciprocal. Increased accountability (nurse-nurse, nurse supervisor, EAP, boundary consultations, etc.) equals decreased VP. (Holder & Schenthal, 2007, p. 28.)

The theoretical orientation of the therapy associated with the practitioner's training determines one's definition of a boundary violation, as does the nature of practitioner preparation. The boundary violation potential is zeroed if resistance to examine the vulnerabilities and risk factors is zero, and it is reduced significantly if accountability is increased. For Child and Youth Care practitioners, training and pre-service education focuses on self-awareness, and therefore resistance to examining vulnerabilities and risk factors should approach zero as the practitioner enters the field. Accountability increases because of the team approach used in practice. On the other hand, the number of catalyst factors that

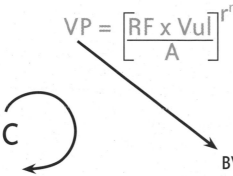

Figure 2. The Boundary Formula
° Professional Boundaries, Inc.

$$VP = \left[\frac{RF \times Vul}{A}\right]^{r^r}$$

VP = Violation Potential
RF = Risk Factors
Vul= Vulnerabilities
A = Accountability
r   = resistance
C   = catalyst

C

BV = Boundary Violation

are present in a milieu-based practice is greater. The catalysts present in on-line counselling, though, are less well defined.

A catalyst is usually an unexpected event that draws the practitioner's attention away from attending to boundaries. In milieu-based therapy, these are ongoing. It is a little like putting the gardener in a hexagon-shaped centre plot and requiring her to attend simultaneously to the boundary shaping of youth on all ten sides. It is essential to own good, sharp tools to minimize the resistance. One must also depend on the trimming expertise of the eight neighbouring property owners, knowing that things will go a little crooked sometimes but that corrections can be made, and that the resulting shape of the boundaries of the developing person, after the error, may be unique and beautiful.

Initially we understand boundaries intuitively because everyone has them. Professional boundaries are learned during professional education, and personal boundaries are learned in our interactions with family and community as we grow up. We need to move from an intuitive under-standing of boundaries engendered by our personal histories to an explicit understanding of boundaries established by our professional educations, and then move yet again to an understanding of boundaries that is counter-intuitive to other professional cultures and corresponds more appropriately with milieu-based therapy. We also need to consider the milieu of the Internet and its meaning in our practice. Through self-exploration and exploration of the other (in relationship), we come to understand and address the issues that bring to consciousness our relationship boundaries;

for those of us who work within the context of relationship, we define a new set of professional boundaries. We need to be able to resist, when appropriate, both our initial intuition (grounded in family based boundaries) and the explicit definition of professional boundaries, and then determine what is best for the specific relationship. Training in the specialty of drama, for example, includes explicit instruction and exercises to develop the actor's ability to be separate from the character, "move into" the character and portray him or her on stage, and then "move out" of character and become himself again without carrying the persona of the character into everyday life. It is this type of relationship that we need to achieve: oneness and distinctness.

Self-awareness and the exploration of values, behaviours, emotions, thoughts, and actions are critical for Child and Youth Care education. Only by defining the self are we free to come to know the other. Garfat and Charles (2007) observe, "self and the encounter of selves, is, in fact, the essence of the helping relationship. By being truly self with other, we are in the condition of helping" (p. 13).

> The new worker is attempting to become a competent care giver and trying to establish personal safety during the first year of practice. This stage of development is characterized by the worker's efforts to create personal safety and boundaries for him/herself before being able to create any therapeutic relationships with youth and families…. the new worker focuses on establishing external control and creating a safe environment for him/herself and the youths. The internal process for a new worker is characterized by frequent fight or flight reactions as he/she encounters intimidating situations…. Level 2 workers automatically think about individualized approaches and discard general descriptions and strategies as they plan interventions. At level 2, the process of living alongside the youth/family also becomes a living with them and the boundary dynamics become more intimate and more clear at the same time. (Phelan, 2003, n.p.)

As educators, if we stop at this revelation of the construction and building blocks of the self, we do the Child and Youth Care practitioner a disservice. Like the actor, the practitioner has to enter and exit a professional world of pain and ugliness and must make strategic decisions about where to place boundaries at a particular point in time, while maintaining a strong and open self. Tapping self brings the professional character forward in relation to the demands of the script and the reaction of the audience.

Donald Winnicott (1970), cited in Hardwick and Woodward (1999) in a public lecture, said:

> It may be a kind of loving but often it has to look like a kind of hating, and the key word is not treatment or cure but rather it is survival. If you [the CYC practitioner] survive then the child has a chance to grow and become something like the person he or she would have been if the untoward environmental breakdown had not brought disaster. (p. xv.)

Child and Youth Care practitioners must explore their definitions of love (Skott-Myhre & Skott-Myhre, 2007) and consider how these lead to ideas about boundaries and power within relationships. The idea of loving clients is often frowned upon. Love can occur without power, though in the minds of the children we work with it may often be associated with power. Thus, we need to "survive" their love and help them to redefine both love and boundaries. It is in this process that counter-intuitive understanding and the development of boundaries becomes essential. The intuitive response to hate and hurt is to build a wall for protection.

Boundary Shaping Techniques

Separations and reunions can be seminal times for learning about boundaries, for both worker and child (Mann-Feder, 1999). Identifying feelings during times of separation and reunion time, and building rituals that are representative of the unique relationship with each child, are activities that all workers can learn from. In my family, rituals like "drive safely," "love you," and a kiss on the cheek are the norm for potentially longer absences, and just a simple "have a good day" is common for short ones. A young friend likes to leap onto me or hug me from behind (as a surprise) each time she sees me. My French colleagues give me a hug and a kiss every time we greet. With others, a "high five," handshakes, and other gestures are all rituals of greeting that represent boundaries of touch and define our relationships. New parents teach their young children these rituals and the cultural boundaries that accompany them—consciously, by way of instructions, and unconsciously, through modelling. At three years of age, every time I meet Rachel, her father directs her to "Say hello to Carol. Shake hands." "Tell Carol good-bye and have a nice day," he'll say (in the grocery store), or "Give Carol a hug and say Happy New Year, because we're leaving now" (at a holiday party). The boundaries (and the appropriate circumstances) are being set at an early age. For children with social and emotional problems who are cared for by strangers, these rituals need to be created specifically for each child. The worker has to observe and negotiate the child's shifting boundaries and create opportunities to establish boundary rituals as they interact; the worker must also look ahead to predict and teach other rituals and routines that the child will experience in future social circumstance and networks.

With the increasing integration of technology into our social networks, we also need to address boundary issues in relation to technology. Child and Youth Care workers must address with youth the issues engendered by technology, and educators must address them with youth workers as they become professionals working in children's milieus. Social networking tools like Facebook provide concrete activities that we can do with youth and with youth workers. Exploring Facebook together creates many opportunities to discuss questions like these:

1. If a potential employer looked you up on Facebook, what would they see?
2. Who do you *not* want to find you? If they did find you, what would they learn about you?
3. If your future school roommate looked you up, what would they learn about you?

Internet- and email-based counselling services raise new issues about the role of relationship and boundaries when we work with children and youth in the new age of technology. Relevant questions to ask include these:

1. What advantage is there to anonymity?
2. How can safety requirements be met in an anonymous environment?
3. What are the characteristics of the Internet milieu, and how do we work with them?

Accountability is one mechanism used to reduce the potential for a boundary violation. Accountability operates in several contexts, only one of which is that of the supervisor and practitioner. Stacey et al. (2002) describe "Youth Partnership Accountability." *Empowerment* is defined as a process of addressing power within relationships between workers and youth. They advocate for identifying power imbalances and having explicit discussions between youth and workers about power imbalances, along with a discussion of how to implement appropriate decision-making processes when power issues arise. In their model, Stacey et al. co-create boundaries, trimming, and shaping the resultant fence that arises; this purposeful cultivation of the boundary provides for looseness and gaps that enable the youth to cross over and become a "worker" within an empowerment project and then move back again to be youth. This type of crossing back and forth is essential to an empowerment model. Accountability is mutual on both sides of the fence.

The shaping of boundaries in Child and Youth Care practice is a mutual activity. It is not random, without purpose, or unguided by the practitioner. The practitioner and youth co-create and shape an environmental fence that will offer the child protection, safety, and openness to future relationships throughout the child's life. The practitioner makes use of self-disclosure, rituals, and routines built into relationships, appropriate touch, overlapping social networks that are based on technology and community, and develops a counter-intuitive understanding of the nature of boundaries. Boundaries are not yours or mine: they are the set of points between you and me where we are both accountable and responsible for communicating and shaping the distinction between us so that we maintain our unique identities and shape a relationship that is specific to us.

REFERENCES

Doucette, P. A. (2004). Walk and talk: An intervention for behaviorally challenged youths. *Adolescence, 39*(154), 373–388.

Faver, C. (2004). Relational spirituality and social caregiving. *Social Work, 49*, 241–249.

Fewster, G. (2005). Making contact: Personal boundaries in professional practice. *Relational Child and Youth Care Practice, 18*(2), 7–13.

Freud, S., & Krug, S. (2002). Beyond the code of ethics, part II: Dual relationships revisited. *Families in Society, 83*(5/6), 483–492.

Garfat, T., & Charles, G. (2007). How am I who I am? Self in child and youth care practice. *Relational Child and Youth Care Practice, 20*(3), 6–16.

Gelman, S. R., Pollack, D., & Weiner, A. (1999). Confidentiality of social work records in the computer age. *Social Work, 44*(3), 243–252.

Hardwick, A., & Woodward, J. (Eds.). (1999). *Loving, hating, and survival: A handbook for all who work with troubled children and young people.* Hants, England: Ashgate Publishing Co.

Harper, K., & Steadman, J. (2003). Therapeutic boundary issues in working with childhood sexual-abuse survivors. *American Journal of Psychotherapy, 57*(1), 64–79.

Holder, K. V., & Schenthal, S. J. (2007). Watch your step: Nursing and professional boundaries. *Nursing Management, 38*(2), 24–29.

King, R., Bambling, M., Reid, W., & Thomas, I. (2006). Telephone and online counselling for young people: A naturalistic comparison of session outcome, session impact and therapeutic alliance. *Counselling & Psychotherapy Research, 6*(3), 109–115.

Kocet, M. M. (2006). Ethical challenges in a complex world: Highlights of the 2005 ACA Code of Ethics. *Journal of Counseling & Development, 84*, 228–234.

Maczewski, M. (2002). Exploring identities through the Internet: Youth experiences online. *Child and Youth Care Forum, 31*(2), 111–129.

Maidment, J. (2006). The quiet remedy: A dialogue on reshaping professional relationships. *Families in Society, 87*(1), 115–121.

Mann-Feder, V. (1999). You/me/us: Thoughts on boundary management in Child and Youth Care. *Journal of Child and Youth Care, 13*(2), 93–98.

Manning, S. S. (1997). The social worker as moral citizen: Ethics in action. *Social Work, 42*(3), 223–230.

Phelan, J. (2003). The relationship boundaries that control programming. *Relational Child and Youth Care Practice, 16*(1), 51–55.

Ricks, F., & Charlesworth, J. (2003). *Emergent Practice Planning.* New York: Kluwer Academic/Plenum Publishers.

Rock, B., & Congress, E. (1999). The new confidentiality for the 21st century in a managed care environment. *Social Work, 44*(3), 253–262.

Skott-Myhre, H. A., & Skott-Myhre, K. S. G. (2007). Radical youth work: Love and community. *Relational Child and Youth Care Practice, 20*(3), 48–57.

Smith, D., & Fitzpatrick, M. (1995). Patient-therapist boundary issues: An integrative review of theory and research. *Professional Psychology: Research and Practice, 26*(5), 499–506.

Smith, J. M. (2004). Adolescent males' view on the use of mental health counseling services. *Adolescence, 39*(153), 77–82.

Smith, M. (2006). Don't touch. *The International Child and Youth Care Network, 94.* [Retrieved January 28, 2008, from http://www.cyc-net.org/cyc-online/cycol-0611-smith.html]

Stacey, K., Webb, E., Barrett, K., Lagzdins, N., Moulds, D., & Stone, P. (2002). Relationships and power. *Youth Studies Australia, 21*(1), 44–52.

Schultze, N.-G. (2006). Rapid communication: Success factors in Internet-based psychological counseling. *CyberPsychology & Behavior, 9*(5), 623–626.

Wrenn, G. C. (1973, reprinted with permission 1985, 2001). The nature of caring: Part II: Caring for self. Original in "The World of the Contemporary Counsellor." Boston: Houghton Mifflin Company. Reprinted with permission in *The Child Care Worker, 3* [Retrieved January 8, 2008, from http://www.cyc-net.org/cyc-online/cycol-1001 wrenn2.html]

CHAPTER 6

The Virtuous Child and Youth Care Practitioner

Exploring Identity and Ethical Practice

Mark Greenwald, BA

ABSTRACT

In their desire to make ethics more real and practical, two workers employ "macro" and "micro" points of view to examine the relationship between identity and ethical Child and Youth Care (CYC) practice. Their exploration involves conceptualizing CYC identity according to three domains: relational, professional, and ethical identity. Finally, they apply a virtue ethics model to incorporate ethical practice into interactional CYC work.

INTRODUCTION

You are invited to join a conversation between two Child and Youth Care (CYC) workers who twice meet to explore ways to make ethics more practice-oriented. In their discussion they employ "macro" and "micro" points of view as they examine the dynamics between identity and ethical practice. Their exploration involves conceptualizing Child and Youth Care identity according to three domains: relational, professional, and ethical identity. In their second meeting they use a virtue ethics model to incorporate an ethical orientation into interactional CYC practice.

Please note that italicized words are expressed with emphasis by these two workers. A bibliography follows the end of their conversation.

> ### Setting the Context
> *We have two CYC workers. Susan, a senior worker and manager with many years of experience, serves as an ethics advisor to staff in this agency. Workers are encouraged to consult with her on ethical questions and concerns. Bob is new to the professional field. Since graduating from a pre-service CYC worker training program, he has been working in Susan's agency for roughly a year. Bob has arranged to meet with Susan to discuss some concerns with her.*

Bob: Thanks for seeing me. I'm about to celebrate my first anniversary here, and I've been reflecting on myself and my work.

Susan: It's not unusual for CYC workers to go through some introspection at this particular time. Please tell me more.

Bob: It's been a good year for me here. My training has prepared me well in developing relationships with the kids and in performing many of the tasks and responsibilities of a CYC worker. I know for sure that CYC work is what I want to do, and I'm ready for more learning and more challenge.

Susan: So, what are you thinking about?

Bob: Lately, I have been taking a closer look at how I interact with the kids and staff. I've grown a lot in my work with the kids, their families, and staff; and yet, when I reflect on everything I've learned and know about CYC work, I can't help but feel frustration and confusion. In considering the extent of my professional and practical training, one could say I have all the packaging for this line of work; but even though I've come a long way in developing as a professional worker, I'm not sure my CYC formation is sufficiently complete. I have acquired all this theory, information, and skills and techniques, and yet it all seems so splintered—with no coherent body or shape. What's my guiding force or purpose? Is it my own set of beliefs and values? Is it the professional standards and ethical codes teachers and supervisors drilled into me? What role, exactly, do ethics play in my CYC work?

Susan: Sounds like you're looking for some comprehensive framework that can help you incorporate more ethics into your work. Is this correct?

Bob: Yes! In my gut I believe ethics ought to play a more dynamic role in everything I do, but I just don't know how to include ethics in my continuous interactive work. In my training I learned about ethics within a hypothetical "What do I do when?" situational context. Now, when I focus on the basic interactive nature of my work as a CYC worker, I can't help but see this situational approach to ethics as somewhat random and remote, perhaps even irrelevant, to continuous practice. I ask myself: "Is there anything more to ethics that can make it more real in my CYC work?" I want to incorporate a "What do I do now?" orientation into my work. I know that it's important to be familiar with legalities, professional standards, ethical codes, and agency guidelines, as well as my own values and beliefs, but how can I translate all this into the moment-to-moment of CYC interactive practice?

Susan: Good. Now I have a clear idea where you're coming from. I also view your desire to discuss this concern with me as a type of inquiry driven by your frustrations, questions, and, perhaps, your transition from a beginning worker to a more aware and reflective worker.

So let's continue this inquiry by exploring how we can make ethics more real for you. The first step is to acknowledge the relationship between *identity and ethics*. This suggests that the way we view ourselves plays an influential role in determining what we value and what we do. It is my opinion that by examining ourselves as CYC workers, we can develop a comprehensive ethical orientation for CYC practice. Therefore, we will explore two ways of looking at CYC identity. One is a *macro* point of view, and the other, a *micro* point of view.

Bob: By bringing up identity, I'm now focusing on what goes into my sense of self and my CYC identity.

Susan: Whoa! Hold on! Your enthusiasm is great, but it's driving you to move too fast. You're already running when I'd like you to slow down and take a big step back. Let's take a macro point of view and stop thinking about what goes into your identity; instead, let's view your identity within a larger context of experience, time, and interaction. Later we will take a micro view and amplify specific aspects of identity, but first we need to explore how a macro viewpoint can help us incorporate an ethical orientation into interactive CYC work.

Macro means that we initially take an important step back and look at the *whole* of CYC work—with all its inherent *parts*. But how do we look at this rich constellation of the whole and its parts? Do we consider these parts individually, observe how each part functions, and consider how each part relates to the others? Or do we initially refrain from focusing on individual parts and, instead, start by figuring out what point of view, what particular theoretical lens—or as Goffman calls it, what "frame"—we will use to perceive this whole with all of its parts?

Bob: Would this be similar to *deciding* to put on sunglasses to see more clearly without the glare?

Susan: Yes. The important point is to acknowledge that whatever approach or lens we use will *shape* what we observe, think, and do. For example, a behavioural lens will influence our understanding of CYC reality quite differently from one that is psychodynamic or ecological.

In our desire to integrate ethics into interactive work, I suggest we take a macro view according to the holistic, systemic theory of Senge. His particular orientation views the whole as a constellation of parts in which *each* part, in some way, *reflects* characteristics of the whole. In other words, we will view the whole as existing in each one of its parts.

Bob: So according to this systemic, macro point of view, each thing I do in my work says something about the *whole* of me. Is this correct?

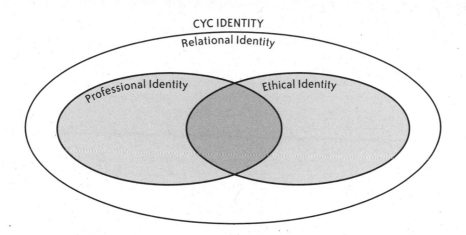

CYC IDENTITY

Relational Identity

Professional Identity

Ethical Identity

Susan: Yes, and to make ethics more real, we need to perceive it as not just one distinct, isolated aspect of your work, but rather as a standard that informs the *entirety* of your CYC identity. In my opinion, this particular perspective can help you incorporate ethics into your work more creatively and comprehensively. So let's continue with a macro approach to describe the first of three identities that bear upon ethical interactive CYC practice. This first one we'll call Relational Identity.

Bob: Three identities! Is this what I have to look forward to? How complex will this be?

Susan: I can't tell you. That will depend on the meaning you make of what I present to you. You say that you want to make ethics more real for yourself in your interactive work as a CYC worker. To do this we need to examine the dynamic connection between identity and ethical practice, and we will do this by breaking down your total CYC identity into three identity domains: *relational, professional,* and *ethical.* Please remember, we are starting with a wide-angle macro view of Relational Identity. We will then go micro to *amplify* Professional and Ethical Identities. It is my hope that this framework will help you incorporate ethics into your interactive work, but please be patient and consider this inquiry as an emerging process, and let's continue by exploring a Relational Identity. Perhaps this graphic representation can be helpful. Notice that the two overlapping domains of Professional Identity and Ethical

Identity lie within the contextual whole of a Relational Identity, which is the one we are about to examine. Take a look.

Bob: OK. Now I'm ready to take my step back and go macro. So what exactly do you mean by Relational Identity?

Susan: We're CYC workers. We embrace creativity in our work, so let's do some creative inquiry. I have two things for you to do. The first task involves using imagery. Give me an image that says something about *your* sense of CYC identity. What would it be?

Bob: Well, I could envision my identity as a sailboat, a cloud over my head, a pair of eye glasses, a favourite pet, or maybe even a fantasy friend.

Susan: Let's choose your fantasy friend. Describe your friend for me.

Bob: My friend is Joe. I'll let you figure out what Joe's gender is. I became aware of Joe's presence as I drove home after an unusually difficult shift. I found myself talking to Joe as an old friend who would openly listen to my thoughts and feelings. Our relationship is somewhat strange, because Joe doesn't say anything. Joe serves as a quiet presence, observing everything I do and what happens to me. I guess my relationship with Joe helps me gain a clearer sense of myself. I feel Joe's presence all the time.

Susan: Joe sounds interesting. Makes me think about the power inherent in one's silent presence. Let's now perform a second creative task. Please give me one important sentence that has always stayed with you. It could be a sentence that plays a guiding role in influencing how you work and live your life. What's your sentence?

Bob: Here it is. My sentence is a question: "How do I keep an open mind without having my brains fall out?"

Susan: So, what I have to play with is this: Joe, a quiet presence and observer; and a sentence that presents an image of a person who seeks to balance a desire to be open with all its inherent risks. Now, what I want to do is to use your imagery to articulate a sense of identity that can help guide your CYC interactional work. Let me elaborate. It's interesting that you mention Joe's presence as influencing your self-awareness. Perhaps your envisioning of Joe as a representation of your

CYC identity may have something to do with you viewing identity as a way of *being, thinking,* and *acting.* This means that right now we will view your identity not as a concrete, descriptive, content-laden "Who am I?" but, instead, as a dynamic manifestation of your unique *presence* of self. Another way to conceptualize this is to think of your Relational Identity as a flow of particular states of mind and body *when you interact with another person.* As you interact with another in your CYC work, you become conscious of several states: you experience and become aware, you make meaning, and you act. These states can be referred to as *being, meaning,* and *acting.* This is what is meant by a Relational Identity. It addresses the question, "How do I see myself *when* in interaction with another?"

Bob: Oh, I understand. I think. My Relational Identity involves my awareness of various states of mind when interacting with kids, their families, and staff. Fair enough. But I believe I'm a bit lost. I don't know where to go with this way of looking at identity.

Susan: OK. This may help. Let's scan these three states of mind—of being, meaning, and acting. As we discuss them, we can see how they influence your ethical practice.

There's so much to say about being in CYC work. Gerry Fewster has even written a book with that title. Let's relate your sentence to a state of being. The first part of your sentence is about your desire to keep your mind open, but open to what? Keeping an open mind can mean opening oneself to time, experience, and thought. Heidegger refers to this as "being-in-the-world." Senge calls it "presence," and Guttman calls it "immediacy." In general, being means experiencing oneself *in time*, in that moment, and then in the next. In our interactional work we attend to a specific moment of experience through our own mental suspension of time within a continuous flow of time.

Bob: I wonder. Would one become more aware of this sense of being, this experience of oneself in time, when, for example, one gets drunk or high?

Susan: Oh, I knew you would bring that up, and I won't completely disagree with you. What's important, though, is to take this experience of time, dare I say it, to a higher, more practical level by focusing on the *meaning* we generate from our experience of being in that specific moment. How we *interpret* that temporal experience of being brings meaning and utility to what we eventually do in our interactive work. To use your sentence as an example, perhaps you can more productively address your concern about not "having your brains fall out" by internalizing a sensibility of *knowing* that you will *always* make some meaning from your openness to experience.

In addition, we generate meaning when applying the cognitive frameworks we acquire from our purposeful and incidental learning in the world. Thus, we use acquired philosophical, theoretical, and personal lenses to organize and interpret our experiences; and we know how easily we can distort objective reality and delude ourselves as a result. That's what makes your sentence so good and wise. You emphasize both the concerns of being open and the inherent danger of being open without having some cognitive mechanism that brings you to meaningful understanding. This all falls into the realm of Relational Identity.

Bob: Now I'm getting energized. You've interpreted my sentence in a more substantial way. What I'd like to explore is what results from my making of meaning from experience. To suggest that the end product of this process is to act seems too simplistic, especially when we're exploring a different way of looking at identity and ethical practice.

Susan: You're absolutely right. We need to put an identity- and ethics-based spin on our understanding of action. I suggest that when we act we do more than problem solve and make decisions in the moment. We also bring a sense of engagement, ownership, standards, and integrity to what we do in interactive practice.

Let me summarize these three states of mind of a Relational Identity in a way that invites an ethical sensibility into CYC practice. Take a look at this breakdown of what I think goes into an interactive moment.

MY RELATIONAL IDENTITY MEANS THAT
IN THE INTERACTIVE MOMENT

Being   I am open to myself and to the other person.
I experience myself with the other person.
I observe myself with the other person.
I become aware of myself with the other person.

Meaning   I make meaning using these components:
my observations of myself and the other person
my reflections on these observations
my recognition of what's important in that
        interactive moment
my cognitive frameworks of acquired knowledge
my consideration of actions, or non-actions, to take
my consideration of skills to use

Acting   I act with the clarity and purpose.
I act with a desire for excellence in whatever I do.
I act according to standards and values of the
professional CYC field.
I act with the commitment that my decisions
and actions will consistently reflect qualities of
responsibility and accountability.

Bob: Yes. I can see this breakdown helping me to be more ethically alert when I am performing interactive practice. Let me ask you something. Are you saying that my CYC Relational Identity reflects my practice of *all* these principles within these three states of mind?

Susan: Why not? Ultimately, it's up to you to figure out how to incorporate these items into your work. In addition, with sufficient attention and practice, I can see these three states of mind flowing so naturally that they may appear to blend into one fluid state. However, at this time it's not important, nor realistic, to consider one complete state of mind as an immediate goal. Probably the best way to look at this would be as a new sensibility or attitude—a way of *being, thinking,* and *acting* in practice.

Now I think it's time for a break. But first, I want to return to your friend Joe. Will Joe still be with you as you perform your CYC work?

Bob: Yes, I presume so.

Susan: Well then, let's use self-observation and reflection as additional forms of inquiry, and let's see how this new way of looking at identity may become more evident to you. During this next week I would like Joe to observe you through the lens of your sentence: "How do I keep an open mind without having my brains fall out?" Joe will observe to see how you manifest this sentence in your interactions as a CYC worker. Are you willing?

Bob: Yes. This particular task makes me think of Dumbo with that feather that enabled him to fly. I wonder whether my awareness of Joe's observational task will influence my state of mind and consequent thinking and actions.

Susan: Maybe, but Joe's task is also to communicate with you. After all, if you can converse with me, why not with Joe as well? So, I expect Joe will share observations with you.

Bob: Why not? I guess you want me to record what Joe shares with me?

Susan: In any way you want. I could present you with some outline to use, but I don't think it will be necessary. I have full faith that you will employ your sensitivity and creativity to learn more about what you experience, think, and do. Let's see what happens. Remember, next time we meet we'll take a micro point of view to examine those other two CYC identities, which will focus on what I know and who I am as a CYC worker.

Setting the Context
A week later. Same meeting room. A time and place to relax and talk.

Bob: We meet again. Before we go micro, I have something to share with you.

Susan: I'm all ears.

Bob: Well, after our talk I initially planned to use a journal to record observations of myself. Then I remembered my task was for my friend Joe to observe me in my openness as I performed CYC work. I really did feel like Dumbo with his feather, because my awareness of Joe projected me outside of myself as I interacted with the kids and staff. Consequently,

I found myself becoming more aware of my being with the kids and enjoying myself more with them, too. Whenever I had the opportunity, Joe and I had our discussions. We had an excellent talk after one interesting experience. Let me describe it to you.

Towards the end of an evening shift, a senior staff member suggested that I go upstairs into Steve's room to, as I was told, "settle him down." A short while before, Steve had had a fierce argument with this staff member, who wanted to know why Steve had returned to the house much later than an agreed-upon time. There were a lot of loud words, which led to Steve storming up to his room, slamming his door, and ranting out loud. I could hear the sounds of things being thrown around in his room. At the time I wasn't sure why this worker wanted me to speak with Steve. After all, it was this worker who, in my opinion, should be continuing with his, let's say, "intervention." As a new staff person, I automatically agreed to go upstairs to settle Steve down, but then I felt regret over my willingness to follow this suggestion. In any case, as I went up those stairs, I shifted my focus onto Steve. I mentally reviewed what had occurred downstairs and what I knew about Steve: his background, his temperament, his needs, his issues with staff, his family issues, and his intervention plan. I was thinking of all those things that a CYC worker would be considering in addition to entertaining questions about "why me?"

I was feeling uptight as I approached his room and anxious about what would await me after that first eventful knock on the door. Holding my breath, I knocked. Steve yelled out a sarcastic "Yeah?" I identified myself and asked to come in, knowing full well that he could have easily refused my request with a loud "No!" I immediately realized that I might have goofed by posing a question that gave Steve the option to refuse me when I really didn't want him to entertain such a choice. I felt stupid. I really didn't have much of a relationship with him. Why would he agree to my entering his room? To my surprise, he said "OK." I lucked out! Was it my subdued tone of voice, my purposeful under-talking rather than over-talking, or something else? In any case, I had an opening. I entered his room, which was a mess. I was about to offer help to restore his room, when he resumed his ranting—straight at me. I waited a short while, which seemed like hours, allowing the hot air to blow by me. Then

I prompted him to cool down. I told myself: "Make your words sound calm, short, and clear." No luck. He continued his verbal tirade. My mind raced. If I talked too much, asked questions, or threatened to call other staff upstairs, he would probably escalate even more, or just completely shut down to me. Here we were, both standing in the center of his small room, not too close but still face to face.

As Steve's rant goes on, and I'm figuring out what to say, I sense time becoming slower and longer. This situation of complete disconnect seems to go on forever. Out of the blue, my perspective changes. Joe enters my consciousness, and I remember my sentence. I felt that I was actually experiencing the chaos of my brains falling out of my head, and then, to my absolute surprise, without any strategic thinking, but with a deep feeling of exhaustion, I sit myself on Steve's bed. Looking down and taking a deep breath, I say quietly: "I'm tired." Nothing else. Silence. After a short while, Steve sits down next to me and says softly that he's tired too. After a few silent moments, both of us looking straight ahead, I say: "Well then, let's be tired together." We sit silently for a little longer. Then I say something to invite him to talk, and we talk. Upon my leaving, Steve begins to clean up his room.

Later, feeling somewhat bewildered, I manage some quiet time to have my dialogue with Joe. "Joe," I say, "what just happened? It all occurred so naturally. Some people would say I took a big risk inserting myself into Steve's space, especially when he was in such an emotional state. Others might say that my actions as a CYC worker should not be influenced by my feelings." Joe tells me that in that moment with Steve, for whatever reason, I liberated myself from thinking about what I should do as a CYC worker. Steve and I connected after I allowed myself to be open to that very moment. Joe then asks me what made this moment work for both Steve and me. Upon reflection, I wondered whether my genuineness of voice and body in that moment expressed to Steve a true picture of me without the judgmental noise of a standard behavioural intervention. How easy it could have been for him to escalate if I were to say those very same two words, "I'm tired," with a judgmental tone of voice. I realized that my action in this situation reflected an experiential openness to be myself in that moment. It created an opportunity for connection with Steve and then for some compassion and care.

Standing on the Precipice

Upon further reflection, I realize that I should be careful with what I take from this experience. Yes, I am now more attuned to the beneficial potential of being open in an interactive moment, especially in regard to its value for creating interpersonal connection; however, I'm also aware that expressing this openness can possibly lead to precarious states of self-absorption, insensitivity, and misunderstanding. This is where my sense of responsibility and an ethical sensibility comes into the picture. What do you think?

Susan: You've made productive use of your relationship with Joe. Your interactions with Steve, as well as your comments, suggest that an active openness and attentiveness to self has become a more valued and dynamic aspect of your work. As for whether you broke policy by inserting yourself into Steve's personal space—that's a typical CYC judgment call. Workers make these decisions all the time. This is where your self-awareness, comfort, knowledge, and sound judgment enter into the picture.

I also share your concern that an overactive attention to self can lead to undue self-absorption and insensitivity. Keep in mind that we've only macro-focused on Relational Identity. We have yet to explore the more regulatory functions of Professional and Ethical Identities, which we will soon examine with a micro perspective.

In addition, your interaction with Steve not only stresses the importance of openness to experiencing oneself in a CYC encounter, it also underscores the value of making meaning and then acting upon it. I recognized this in your invitation to Steve—"Let's be tired together." You reinforced what I discussed with you last week when I described how every moment is not just a state of being, it's also a state of reflection and action. In that moment you could have said a variety of things. You stayed focused in that moment and attended to yourself and Steve, and you *decided* to create a climate that would encourage connectedness, sharing, and care. You practiced Child and Youth Care!

Now, before we reverse our lens and go micro to amplify CYC identity, let me briefly review our previous discussion. You expressed a desire to acquire a framework that would enable you—one that would help you integrate ethics more fully into CYC practice. My response was to take a macro view, and we stepped back to look at interactive CYC work as grounded in time, experience, and openness to self. This I called a Relational Identity. We then used your sentence about staying open minded, with its inherent risks, to articulate those experiential and reflective states of mind that influence interactive practice. Finally, I presented you with a holistic, systemic approach for considering the totality of one's CYC identity as composed of individual parts, and these parts, in various ways, reflect the primary qualities of the whole of one's identity. Please hold on to this last concept. We will make more practical sense of it when I return to it later. Does this review cover what we discussed?

Bob: Yes. It does.

Susan: Good. Let's now go micro. As I mentioned before, this point of view conceptualizes identity as having two overlapping domains within the contextual whole of a Relational Identity. These two domains respond to the question "Who am I as a CYC worker?" and provides two answers:

1. I have a professional identity.
2. I have an ethical identity.

The first answer refers to the professional formation of acquired CYC-related information, knowledge, and skills. The second answer reflects a CYC ethical formation that comprises professional standards and codes, personal values, a sense of one's own moral agency, and an understanding of oneself as a "Virtuous CYC Worker." Here, this may help. Take a look at this more descriptive overlay of that first graphic I showed you.

Bob: Professional Identity is something I'm familiar with from my training, but the idea of an Ethical Identity is new and intrigues me. You have been emphasizing this connection between identity and ethical practice, and now it's making more sense to me that you are identifying ethical practice as one complete component of one's total CYC Identity.

Susan: That's right. If we're talking about ethics and making it more real in interactive practice, then why not emphasize an Ethical Identity that informs all our CYC actions? But before we explore an Ethical Identity, let's first amplify CYC Professional Identity.

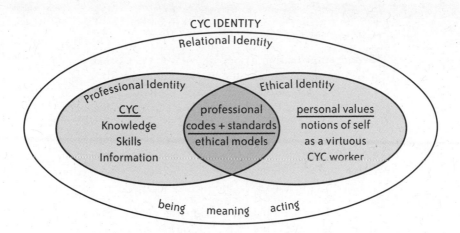

CYC IDENTITY

Relational Identity

Professional Identity

Ethical Identity

CYC
Knowledge
Skills
Information

professional
codes + standards
ethical models

personal values
notions of self
as a virtuous
CYC worker

being   meaning   acting

When considering a CYC Professional Identity, we need to keep in mind that all that we do in CYC practice is a function of what we've learned from our experiences in the practice field and from all those cognitive and theoretical frameworks presented to us in pre-service and in-service training. Whatever approach we use, whether it is behavioural, psychodynamic, ecological, systemic, or phenomenological/constructionist, we are all in some way products of our acquired professional knowledge. To give you one clear example, I'll use myself as a case in point with one particular conceptual framework that has influenced me in my CYC work.

Many years ago in my training as a CYC worker, I was exposed to the work of Polsky and Claster and their application of a sociological, role-function model to CYC work. I found myself attracted to their ideas because, in my opinion, they envisioned CYC work as a form of reflection and action-in-process. In their research in examining role performance of workers, Polsky and Claster used a social interactive model to observe the what, how, and when of CYC work. Their observations and analyses influenced me to view the CYC worker as a kind of juggler who, in continuous time, handles four balls or, let's say, four role functions: *monitor, nurturer, teacher/counsellor,* and *integrator.* The magic came in viewing the CYC worker as this dynamic, creative juggler who could exercise a high degree of fluid, focused, creative responsiveness in deciding, from one moment to the next, which specific role to perform. As the moment changes—so do observations, so do decisions, so do actions.

This conceptualization helped me view CYC work as a dynamic process in which the worker continuously and creatively responds to any interactive moment. Although I have expanded my repertoire to include other orientations, I've stayed loyal to this particular vision of CYC work. Whereas you see yourself as wanting to be open and in control of your mind, I view myself as wanting to be open, creative, and responsive as I juggle those four role functions. Maybe my CYC fantasy friend would be a juggler.

Bob: Why not? I can see a juggler serving as a most relevant metaphor for a CYC worker. But doesn't your image of yourself as a juggler influence your experiential and relational state of mind, and thus your CYC Relational Identity?

Susan: Yes, you're quite right. This way of looking at CYC practice derives from my professional learning. It is a research-based conceptualization that I have adopted as my frame—my orientation, my lens—when I perform interactive practice. As a *learned* theoretical framework, I regard it as part of my Professional Identity. *And*, as a *sensibility* that influences how I perform interactive work, I also incorporate it into my sense of Relational Identity. Please notice that these identities are not mutually exclusive. They work together dynamically as parts reflecting the whole.

So let me complete this CYC Professional Identity. In addition to learning theoretical models, clinical and professional skills, and a wide range of related information, we are also exposed to the values and standards of the professional field. Now, you might assume these values and standards would be viewed as part of one's CYC Ethical Identity—and, for obvious reasons, they are. However, they should also be seen as part of one's CYC Professional Identity. It is my hope that your pre-service training has exposed you to this profession's historical narratives, its inherent values, its professional standards and codes, and relevant ethical models. I include history here because evolving social values have influenced historical changes in the CYC professional field. Consequently, much of what we do today as CYC workers reflects current social values that emphasize respect, inclusion, equality, participation, and self-determination. We may have personally internalized these values in our own Ethical Identities, but we need to acknowledge that these values also reflect explicit principles of the CYC profession, and thus they also belong to one's CYC Professional Identity.

Bob: Yes. I recall being exposed to these principles and professional codes, and also being encouraged to explore my own values to see how they influence my CYC work. I also remember applying several ethical models to particular dilemmas. While I found this material helpful for situational ethical analysis, I frequently wondered how I could apply these models to any CYC interaction. Professional codes of ethics have also helped me recognize the importance of accountability and standards in professional work. I hope I have incorporated this knowledge into my practice—but to what degree? I really don't know. Now I'm wondering whether this idea of a CYC Ethical Identity will address my concerns.

Susan: Let's find out.

The first thing we need to do when examining a CYC Ethical Identity is to confirm our sense of moral agency. You tell me that you want to make ethics more real for your CYC practice. Well, the first step is to recognize that your moral agency underlies all that you think and do as a CYC worker. This is especially important when you consider all the responsibility you assume, all the decisions you make, and all the things you do to provide safety, nurture well-being, and encourage growth. Whether you want to or not, you act as a moral agent in all that you do as a CYC worker.

Bob: So, would it be fair to say that my sense of moral agency serves as a sort of contextual glue that binds all that I think and do in my work?

Susan: This is interesting…contextual glue. My answer is yes. What a powerful way to envision the role of moral agency! Context heightens awareness and understanding, and glue strengthens the relationships of parts. You're quite productive in using imagery to create your own clarity and meaning.

Let's, then, explore the notion of a Virtuous CYC Worker. This model may help you to more comprehensively incorporate ethics into your interactive practice.

If we are to consider ethical practice as a reflection of identity, we must ask ourselves, "What kind of person am I when performing ethical CYC work?" To answer this question we would need to identify those valued traits within ourselves that enable us to perform ethical CYC practice. We have to go back in time to explore the Greek philosopher Aristotle and his notion of a virtuous person. His major premise argues that in striving for excellence, people guide their actions according to internally embraced virtues. In general, these virtues include wisdom, integrity, justice, courage, respect, and benevolence. It should also be noted that virtue-based models of ethics have been applied in the CYC field. Schools are introducing more character education curriculum into their programming. In fact, you can go online and explore over one million hits on "character education" alone; and we can't discuss this model without acknowledging Vorrath and Brendtro, and their extensive work in developing a variety of "positive peer" cultures over these recent decades.

Bob: OK. I see relevance here, but how do we use this model in practice?

Susan: When handling specific situations of ethical complexity or conflict, you would probably continue to make full use of professional standards, and ethical standards and codes; but when performing interactive work, your actions would reflect more of your own sense of Ethical Identity as framed by how you see yourself as a Virtuous CYC Worker. In addition, according to Aristotle's model, virtues mean little if they are not *habitually practiced*. It isn't enough to just acknowledge that you have particular virtues. To possess a certain virtue means you display it as a functional, observable aspect of *who* you are and *what* you do. Finally, if this model is to be useful in practice, it requires an examination of its basic features and how they relate to CYC work.

Bob: Please continue. I'm anxious to see how this model connects to my CYC work.

Susan: Our consideration of this model leads us to the work of Peterson and Seligman and their ambitious effort to identify, measure, and classify virtues and their related character strengths. I found their descriptions of these virtues and related qualities to be quite exciting, because I readily saw how these character traits reflect so much of what we strive to do as CYC workers. We can see CYC practice in their breakdown of six basic virtues:

1. Wisdom
2. Temperance
3. Humanity
4. Justice
5. Transcendence
6. Courage

Bob: So, are you saying that all CYC workers ought to strive to practice all these virtues, with their related qualities of character?

Susan: Good question. I'm not one to expect workers to walk on water. These virtues, described as various strengths of character by Aristotle, Greenwald, and by Peterson and Seligman, are traits we see—or do not see—within ourselves. The interesting thing is that when I consider these virtues and related qualities of character, I can't help but see their role in CYC practice. Actually, I see a quality of practice that both training programs and agencies actively encourage. We can make numerous CYC connections as we examine Peterson and Seligman's classification of virtues. So let's begin with the first virtue of wisdom.

According to Peterson and Seligman, wisdom is the appreciation and exercise of intellectual responsibility through open mindedness—there's your sentence again—creativity, flexibility, critical thinking, love of learning, and perspective. So let's have an interesting discussion here. Explain to me your CYC meaning of wisdom.

Bob: I'll start off with creativity, and say that I believe creativity is more than just doing something different or unique. Some people could say that what I did in Steve's room—plopping myself down on his bed and telling him I was tired—was creative. Perhaps. It was definitely unexpected. I allowed myself to experience and share a moment and, fortunately, I made a connection. For me, creativity involves curiosity, flexibility, experimentation, and play, as well as courage. When talking with a young person, I'm creative in acting on my curiosity and excitement about seeing where this interaction may go and what my next response may be. I can also see myself exaggerate or dramatize an expression in order to emphasize a particular message or learn more about a person's state of mind by provoking a response.

I'm now realizing how much creativity, curiosity, and flexibility also play a role in learning and inquiry. Your creative use of inquiry with me reinforces my own love of learning, and maybe also a love of teaching, which, as you mentioned previously, is one of those four role functions a CYC worker juggles in interactive practice. You're making me realize and appreciate how my creative use of inquiry can contribute to my practice of this virtue of wisdom.

Susan: Sounds good, but there's more to say about wisdom, intellectual responsibility, and critical thinking. According to Watts, and to Ricks and Bellefeuille: if we want to reason in a critical, responsible, and productive manner, we must first embrace the cognitive state of "not knowing" and then process information in an open, focused, and responsible way. In our desire to avoid making erroneous inferences, assumptions, or interpretations, we need to take certain steps: suspend judgment, attend to the moment, reflect on what we know or don't know, and then make an informed response.

Bob: I like this. As you did last week, you're placing experience, thought, and action within a context of responsibility, but this time you're connecting it to a valued quality of character. And now I see the application of this virtue to my sentence.

Susan: Good. The final thing to say about wisdom is the most obvious: wisdom means the exercise of sound, insightful judgment rooted in sensitivity, knowledge, and understanding. Whatever you do to aspire to this virtue, your intentions should reflect an ethical concern for thinking and acting with compassion, concern, respect, safety, kindness, and responsibility.

Bob: Yes. I agree; but as I listen to you, I can't help but think about all that I do as a CYC worker. I experience. I attend. I reflect, and I respond. Now, in addition to all that, you introduce one initial virtue involving the importance of exercising intellectual responsibility in all that I think and do.

Susan: So what's the problem?

Bob: I don't know. It just seems like so much, and we haven't even begun to cover the other virtues.

Susan: Don't sweat it. You seem to be articulate, aware of yourself, and knowledgeable. Perhaps when we get to that last virtue of courage you'll achieve some peace of mind. Have faith in this inquiry, and let's continue with the virtue of temperance.

According to Peterson and Seligman, temperance serves as a protective function. Qualities of forgiveness and mercy protect us from hatred and resentment. Humility and modesty protect us from arrogance. Prudence, as a proactive and pragmatic sensibility, protects us from the mistakes we make when employing expedient, short-term thinking. Exercising prudence means suspending our attention to short-term concerns and focusing on long-term success through pragmatism, farsightedness, and consequential thinking. The final strength of character is self-regulation, which involves moderation and self-control. It also protects us from acting on impulse and extreme emotions. Peterson and Seligman also indicate that self-awareness and self-monitoring are instrumental in the exercise of self-regulation.

Bob: Qualities of self-regulation and prudence sound like some of the skills I encourage when I do the life-space interviewing of Redl and Wineman, or when I teach social skills and problem-solving skills. I also see how I display these qualities in my interactive work. I practice prudence when I hold myself back from responding and look at the bigger picture surrounding the young person. I then decide to continue my actions, change gears, or just wait and see. Of course, there are those moments when I self-regulate. When dealing with a young person's provocative behaviours, I step back, monitor my own mind–body experience, and get in touch with my emotional reactions. I can then focus more clearly on the young person's needs and hopefully make a meaningful response.

I'm just beginning to become aware of how forgiveness and mercy, and humility and modesty, play out in my work. I see the relevance of these qualities when working to maintain respectful and productive relationships with co-workers, teams, and families.

Susan: Yes. I'm pretty sure that as you gain more experience working with staff and with families that these two qualities will become even more evident. It will be interesting to see how they play out in your work.

It's now time to tackle the virtue of humanity. I don't think I have to spend much of our time describing it, because this virtue encompasses so much of CYC practice. Greenwald initially referred to this virtue as "compassion and care" and "the air that CYC workers breathe." Peterson and Seligman describe humanity as the interpersonal qualities of "love, kindness, and social intelligence." They describe love as not only unconditional acceptance and comfort, but also commitment and sacrifice. Kindness refers to care and all the things that CYC workers do in furthering safety, support, growth, and general well-being.

Social intelligence involves sensitivity and understanding when dealing with the emotions of others. This quality includes empathy as well as emotional and social awareness. In addition, a person who displays social intelligence would emphasize mutuality, emphasizing the *we* rather than the *me* when interacting with others.

Bob: I understand most of this, but what I'm really interested in is exploring care within that context of moral agency and ethical practice. I've had so many sources drill into me the general principle that care work needs to be consistently grounded in "respect for the dignity of the individual." There's got to be more to it than that.

Susan: You've read my mind. When considering care work, we can't ignore ethics. That's why we have this phrase, "an ethics of care." In CYC work ethical practice means becoming familiar with an ethics of care as articulated by Gilligan, by Noddings and by Austin and Halpin. For them, an ethics of care is grounded in relationship and human encounter.

Let's begin examining an ethics of care by focusing on the work of Gilligan and Noddings and their proposition that people have natural inclinations to form relationships, to become interdependent, and to care for one another. As with Peterson and Seligman, qualities of generosity, compassion, and empathy are quite evident in their view of an ethics of care. In addition, Gilligan suggests our sense of moral agency reflects a "moral predisposition" towards justice and care, which then influences how we interact with others. For Noddings, the primary theme is an ethics of care grounded in "receptivity, relatedness, and responsiveness." She views ethics as a "moral impulse," or "moral attitude," that guides our actions as care practitioners.

Bob: OK. That's a beginning for me. What about something more specific and practice-oriented?

Susan: This is where Austin and Halpin come into the picture. They include a strong ethical sensibility in their envisioning of care as making a "caring response." Rather than my going through their breakdown, let me give it to you here. Take a look at this.

> ### THE CARING RESPONSE
>
> *The caring response...recognizes the other as valued and important.*
>
> *The caring response...recognizes the other as a being and not an object.*
>
> *The caring response...respects the authenticity of the other.*
>
> *The caring response...must be sufficient in itself and not dependent on any expectation of tangible or intangible reward.*
>
> *The caring response...involves self-knowledge and knowledge of the other.*
>
> *The caring response...is non-judgmental.*
>
> *The caring response...focuses on the possibility of help with an assumption that the other can be helped, but will not necessarily be helped.*
>
> *The caring response...reflects commitment, availability, and courage.*
>
> *The caring response...adapts to the particular needs and styles of the other.*
>
> *The caring response...reflects the self of the care worker and his or her way of being in the world.*

Bob: That's quite a thorough and concise analysis. This breakdown can help me incorporate an ethical sensibility into care work. Now, I'd like to make my own sense of all this.

- The virtue of humanity, with all its qualities, speaks directly to the many tasks of CYC care work and an ethics of care.

- An ethics of care suggests that our sense of moral agency—described as a "moral pre-disposition" or "moral attitude"—involves our attention to interaction, connection, and relationship in CYC practice.

- One way of practicing an ethics of care is to practice the guiding principles of a "caring response."

Susan: Not bad. You bring together the virtue of humanity, care work, an ethics of care, moral agency, and interactive practice. Let's move on to justice.

It's good that we're following humanity with the virtue of justice, because I can once again see many instances where our sense of justice, as defined by notions of fairness, fidelity, and social responsibility, influences interactive work. Peterson and Seligman take a broad approach and apply justice-based qualities of citizenship, leadership, and fairness to activities in the greater community. I'd like to make our own meaning of this virtue by applying it to the smaller social arena of interpersonal relationship.

To begin, I want to attend to a particular point made by Peterson and Seligman in their description of citizenship and leadership. They suggest that a person who displays these qualities acts with a strong sense of "duty" in working toward a "common good." So tell me, what does this mean to you?

Bob: On a larger scale, I see how this sense of duty toward a common good may have influenced my decision to take up this line of work. I also see a connection with my recent involvement in agency committees, my union, and professional organizations. On a smaller scale, I see how this sense of commitment may influence my style of work with individuals, groups, and families. However, in striving for that common good, I wonder how creative, persistent, or even neurotic I may become when sensing possible failure. When dealing with such a possibility, I would hope that my actions reflect additional qualities of the self-regulation of temperance, the flexibility and creativity of wisdom, and the social intelligence of humanity. Finally, in considering justice as a virtue that I practice in my CYC work, I can't disregard the importance of being honest and trustworthy.

Susan: Yes. I like the expansive way you're considering these virtues and related qualities, but let's pay more attention to fairness as a quality of justice. Let me share a short anecdote.

Once, when coordinating a unit of early adolescent youth who exhibited a generous amount of overly active, defiant, and provocative behaviours, I supervised "Rose," a short, rather petite female worker. In her work she seemed to have the least difficulty with the kids over issues of control. Out of curiosity, I asked the kids for their perception of Rose, particularly with respect to the qualities that they saw in her. They told me that they saw Rose as not only a good, attentive listener, who would under-react to their behaviours, but as someone who was consistently fair with them. They strongly emphasized this fairness, because it was something that was important to them. Rose would work with co-workers who had more experience using management skills, yet she seemed to be more effective in connecting with the kids because they saw her as being consistently fair.

I retain that memory of Rose's fairness. Her virtues of wisdom, as shown in her flexibility, open mindedness, and sound judgment; humanity, as displayed in her kindness, compassion, and understanding; and temperance, as revealed in her prudence and self-regulation—these were quite evident when she turned potentially loud moments into quiet, effective moments. What struck me most, from what the kids told me and what she shared with me in supervision, was her strong commitment to a moral standard of fairness. Her consistency, or as Aristotle would say, her "habitual practice" of fairness, made this quality quite evident in her work.

Bob: Yes, and where does advocacy fit into this picture of justice?

Susan: Oh, we could be here forever! If we were to explore CYC-related philosophical orientations of inclusion, normalization, and empowerment, then it would be impossible to avoid a lengthy discussion of the essential and pervasive role of advocacy in CYC work. For now, let's say that your work as an advocate includes not only the virtue of justice, but also your commitment to virtues of humanity and courage. Now before we complete this inquiry with an exploration of courage, let's focus on the virtue of transcendence.

Peterson and Seligman describe transcendence as reflecting our efforts to make meaning out of our lives. It displays itself in qualities of appreciation of beauty and excellence, gratitude, hope, humour, and spirituality. The way I would prefer to examine transcendence is to view this virtue, with its related qualities, as a powerful influence on our *style* of practice.

Bob: This sounds interesting, but I'm not sure how the appreciation of beauty relates to CYC work.

Susan: Actually, it is appreciation of beauty and excellence. The key word here is appreciation and not our own notions of beauty and excellence. Appreciation suggests an openness to experience, a sensitivity of recognition, and some manner of celebration. Some people exhibit this quality with loud exclamation. Others show it more quietly with subdued expressions of acknowledgment and praise. So, let me ask you. If you were to observe a worker exhibiting this quality, what would you notice?

Bob: I would see something special in the interaction. It wouldn't just be plain talk. I would notice a sense of openness and engagement and some degree of animation, and maybe even excitement. Wait a minute! Would I be witnessing something of passion?

Susan: Perhaps. Passion can be viewed as a particular manifestation of one's personality or personal style. We have known people who appear to act passionately in many things they do. On the other hand, passion could characterize a type of animated response. It could be a response to a specific situation that celebrates a job well done, a good deed, a created object, or a shared insight.

Let's continue with other qualities of transcendence. As with appreciation of beauty and excellence, gratitude assumes openness to experience; but in this case, gratitude is a response of being grateful that reflects both appreciation and goodwill.

Bob: ...and once again, we have an active recognition of something of value, whatever that may be, which strengthens connections between people.

Susan: Yes. You may be onto something here. With hope as our next quality, we can think of optimism and one's view of a positive future. Now I am not suggesting a type of mindless optimism with which we delude ourselves and others about happy days always existing around the corner. The hope I am presenting here is strength of character that keeps us focused, coping, and energized. However, we have an ethical responsibility to exercise our sense of hope realistically, combined with sensitivity to the needs, abilities, and situations of others. We need to stay alert to how our own conception of the future can potentially lead to unrealistic expectations that cause unnecessary disappointments and failures.

Bob: That's where sensitivity and balance are important in interactive work. I know that my understanding of a given child or youth will determine the expectations I communicate. Now I'm *thinking* about how my own sense of hope and optimism may influence how I interact with another, but I don't want it to overly intrude into our relationship. My hope is that my expression of optimism will encourage a genuine and receptive response without inadvertently setting anyone up for confusion or failure. Does this sound reasonable to you?

Susan: Yes it does. The ethical implications for our use of expectations in CYC work deserve another encounter for us, but not now. Let's get into humour. The amazing thing about humour is how it involves a mental stance of stepping back, looking at a person or situation differently, and finding the contradictions and absurdities that can help someone gain a new awareness of themselves or their situation. Another type of humour, referred to as "good cheer," can help in coping, reducing tension, inviting participation, and in getting along with people. We also know its flip-side, when humour becomes a weapon to ridicule, embarrass, or overpower. This is where the virtue of humanity steps in to ensure that displays of humour reflect strength of character and does not serve as a weapon or personal outlet.

Bob: Yes, and I've learned that humour works if it's genuine, and if you feel comfortable with yourself and with the other person. If it's forced—not really you—and you're not comfortable, forget it. It's so easy for humour to serve as an outlet for our frustrations and resentments, and frequently at someone's expense. I realize that a bit of gentle, humorous sarcasm can help when relating to adolescents, but again, it's a balancing act involving sensitivity and moderation.

Susan: That's right. Now, before we finish off this virtue with an exploration of spirituality, let me ask you something. What familiar theme that we've discussed before ties these four qualities together?

Bob: My hunch is that transcendence-related qualities of appreciation of beauty and excellence, gratitude, hope, and humour all have something to do with open and receptive *states of mind*, which lead to actions of sharing and celebration.

Susan: Good! You got it! Now let's finish up with spirituality, which is, in my opinion, a popular topic in society and in the CYC field.

For me, spirituality is difficult to pin down because it can mean so many different things to different people. It can also provoke an automatic connection with religion and divine faith. For example, I am aware of agencies that describe their spiritual programming as exclusively focused on taking their kids to religious services. They don't indicate much more besides that. I'd prefer to leave religion and divinity out of our discussion. We are focusing on spirituality as a particular strength of character. However, the specific religious faith a person embraces does not reflect such a strength; how one performs in life and with others as a *function* of their faith—whatever it may be—does. And that's what I want to explore with you. Let me begin.

Peterson and Seligman describe spirituality as a belief system that helps to explore and articulate a sense of purpose in life. To put it in everyday language, spirituality addresses this question: "Where is my place in the universe, and what meaning do I make of this in determining how I live my life?" Whether one's sense of purpose is grounded in a belief in the divine, or nature, or a particular political consciousness, or something else, is of little importance to our discussion. What is important is that *guiding* sense of purpose, because we are exploring how one's quality of spirituality influences our actions as Virtuous CYC Workers.

On another level, one's spirituality can also be viewed as a continuous, life-long, emerging process of self-exploration and discovery. This begs the question of whether one's spirituality demands a well-articulated belief, or maybe just a general sensibility—or maybe we're talking about a sense of personal spirit, or even, dare I say it, *soul*. I'll leave it up to you to make your own sense of your spirituality and how it guides you in what you do as a CYC worker.

Bob: Again you're making me return to my sentence, which does reflect a specific belief of mine, but I don't think it speaks to my sense of spirituality. Should I consider another sentence that articulates more of a spiritual belief?

Susan: Noooo! Please don't! If you did, then we would have to go down another long path. Let's not do that. You could create your sentence at another time, perhaps as you go home today, or later when you're getting comfortable listening to some good music. Actually, to create a single sentence that defines your guiding sense of purpose would be a fascinating exercise of inquiry. It would be interesting to see how your particular belief guides you in your personal and professional life. What would emerge from such an inquiry could become part of your Ethical Identity. Think about it.

Bob: I'll think about it, but to get a better handle on spirituality, how would someone with this quality of character perform CYC work? For example, would a worker who displays serenity or enthusiasm in their work be considered to have that quality of spirituality?

Susan: Why not? It would be interesting to know what influences such a worker to be serene or enthusiastic. Perhaps it may have something to do with a sense of spirituality. Who knows?

Another way to explore your question about describing someone with a sense of spirituality is to imagine a worker who embodies very little of this quality. Although some may say that everyone has some sense of spirituality, let's imagine a person who lacks this quality of character. How would you describe this person?

Bob: This individual's CYC work would seem to lack a sense of purpose. Although this may sound simplistic, I would imagine that such a worker would display generous degrees of cynicism, negativity, low expectations, and, in particular, low productivity. On the other hand, such a person may just be downright flat in their interpersonal work, and I'm sorry to say that I have, on a few occasions, worked with co-workers who resemble both of these profiles.

Oh, wait a minute! Could it be that someone who exhibits these spiritually-challenged behaviours would be short in displaying many of the virtues we've discussed, and their related qualities of character? Does this mean that any person who exhibits the qualities of a Virtuous CYC Worker has some sense of spirituality, regardless of the content of their spiritual or religious beliefs, and that this spirituality shows in his or her CYC work?

Susan: Why not? They may have their own spiritual sentence or belief system, which in some way enters into their work. However, we ought to be careful when considering spirituality in CYC work, particularly if one's spiritual beliefs are sufficiently ego driven to intrude too much into CYC interactions and relationships. This is where other virtues—I'll let you identify them—play a regulatory role in ensuring responsibility, sensitivity, balance, and a clear focus on promoting well-being and self-determination. Now, let's move on to our final virtue: courage.

We need to be especially focused here in examining courage. We could relate this virtue to situational ethics and the handling of difficult, complex dilemmas, as Kidder and Ricks do. Their view of courage within this context of overcoming inhibiting personal and social factors is quite relevant to the CYC professional field, but what is necessary is to examine courage with respect to continuous interactive practice. We need to create our own meaning for applying courage-related qualities of bravery, persistence, vitality, and integrity.

Now I don't think it's necessary to go into much detail in describing these four qualities of courage. They are self-evident in that we can easily picture a person acting with courage as embodying these particular qualities. And according to Peterson and Seligman, we can also view qualities of bravery, persistence, and vitality as specific manifestations of integrity. So tell me, what is your understanding of integrity?

Bob: Honesty. Taking ownership. Having a strong sense of commitment to performing good work. Acting according to a clear set of values and beliefs. I guess there's a lot of self-awareness too.

Susan: Yes. Ricks makes a case for self-awareness by viewing courage as grounded in "consciousness," which she equates with self-awareness in the interactive moment, and "conscience," which serves as a guiding ethical, moral lens.

Bob: ...and would my "conscience" influence how I see myself as a moral agent in all I do as a CYC worker?

Susan: Yes. That pervasive sense of your moral agency would definitely be related to your conscience. Remember last week when I introduced this systemic way of looking at the relationship between the *whole* and its *parts*. The whole is reflected in all its parts. Thus, the whole of our CYC Ethical Identity—which comprises our sense of conscience and moral agency, values, knowledge of professional standards and codes, and our view of ourselves as Virtuous CYC Workers—will in many ways trickle down and become evident in whatever we do in our interactive work.

Bob: That trickling down of my Ethical Identity into the specifics of my work is where I want to go. Can we?

Susan: Very soon. It's my belief that one last look at courage may give us an opportunity to develop a more elegant and coherent understanding of all that we've explored this last week. Let's give it a try.

Let's view courage as a type of personal potency, and let's begin with you describing to me how *your* potency would reveal itself when you perform CYC work. Specifically, what indicators would be evident when you are acting with a sense of potency?

Bob: When interacting in that moment, I would feel a certain strength in my own presence. I would be aware of my attending to myself as well as to the other person. In addition, I would see myself interacting with a clear sense of *purpose*. My actions and thoughts would suggest a clear direction in what I was doing or planning to do. If I were to act with purpose, I would also see my actions reflect the sound and comprehensive application of both my personal and professional knowledge.

Susan: Good. Tell me more.

Bob: My potency, reflecting a clarity of presence, would involve a clear focus on the individual with whom I'm interacting and any particulars in the immediate environment; and, of course, an attention to myself as I experience, reflect, and act...wait a minute! Last week when we went macro, didn't you present me with a framework for conceptualizing Relational Identity as a dynamic of these very same three processes? Oh, I am in a mental loop here, but I sense more clarity, too. I've just made a connection between clarity of *presence* and Relational Identity. As for clarity of *purpose*—guess what? Clarity of *purpose* connects to both my Professional and Ethical Identities.

This is strange! Right now, as I think about my working with courage and potency, I'm turning myself inside-out, and my brains are on the edge of falling out of my head! You've given me all these frameworks for Relational Identity, Professional Identity, and Ethical Identity, with the Virtuous CYC Worker at the centre of each one. Now I'm realizing that my consideration of courage as a virtue is helping me bring all this together. I see more clearly how my internalization of these three identities can enable me to perform interactive work with more clarity of *presence* and *purpose*, which can also help me work with more courage, satisfaction, and effectiveness. But what about this notion of a Virtuous CYC Worker? As a major component of an Ethical Identity, I can entertain how virtuous qualities of character influence CYC work, particularly with respect to ethical practice. But again I ask: How do I make practical use of this way of viewing *myself* as a Virtuous CYC Worker?

Susan: With one last task of inquiry. Now that you have a comprehensive understanding of the connection between identity and ethical practice, I want to give you an observational tool that also summarizes our examination of a Virtuous CYC Worker. By using this framework—here it is—you can generate your own examples to identify how your CYC practice may reflect these virtues. It would be interesting to see what particular virtues, and their related qualities, you display in your work. I also wonder whether your use of this tool may help you become aware of these virtues and qualities *as you perform your interactive work*.

Bob: Thanks. Now I have a comprehensive package for integrating ethics into my CYC work. By using your summary, I hope to find out whether or not this notion of a Virtuous CYC Worker has any real practice value for me. If it does, then this model may help me become a more effective CYC practitioner. Who knows…right?

Susan: It's good that we end with a question.

SUMMARY AND OBSERVATIONAL TOOL

THE 6 VIRTUES OF A VIRTUOUS CHILD AND YOUTH CARE WORKER*

Identify your examples of working as a Virtuous Child and Youth Care Worker

1. WISDOM: The Virtuous CYC Worker makes decisions that reflect sensitivity, curiosity, creativity, knowledge, understanding, and sound judgment. In avoiding erroneous inferences, and in making sound judgments, the CYC Worker is a critical thinker who exercises open-mindedness, self-awareness, and intellectual responsibility.
Examples:_____

_____

2. TEMPERANCE: The Virtuous CYC Worker practices prudence in making decisions that reflect pragmatism and far-sightedness. In practicing self-regulation, the CYC Worker monitors one's self and stays focused on the presenting issues inherent in CYC interactive practice. Qualities of forgiveness and humility may also enter into the picture, especially when working with co-workers and families.
Examples:_____

_____

3. HUMANITY: The Virtuous CYC Worker practices an ethics of care that is displayed in respect, acceptance, availability, sensitivity, compassion, understanding, and authenticity, and in a commitment to conscientiously promote safety, well-being, and growth.
Examples:_____

_____

* Adapted from Peterson and Seligman (2004) and Greenwald (2007).

4. JUSTICE: The Virtuous CYC Worker values the importance of honesty, trust, and fairness in all aspects of CYC work. CYC practice in clinical, administrative, professional, and co-worker domains would also reflect one's commitment to working toward a common good.
Examples:_____

_____

5. TRANSCENDENCE: The Virtuous CYC Worker displays transcendence as a style of practice that reflects the worker's interest in extending one's sense of self to a larger reality. He or she interacts with an active openness to experience that leads to sincere recognitions of beauty, excellence, and gratitude, and to authentic, sensitive expressions of hope, humour, and passion. One's spirituality, as in a distinct personal belief or general sensibility, may also be evident in responsible, sensitive, balanced, supportive CYC practice.
Examples:_____

_____

6. COURAGE: The Virtuous CYC Worker acts and makes decisions according to what he or she thinks is "right" because he or she judges it to be the "right" thing to do and not because he or she feels obligated to do so. In addition to working from a base of personal and professional values, decisions and actions stem from clarity of presence, purpose, and from one's sense of integrity and moral agency.
Examples:_____

_____

REFERENCE

Austin, D., & Halpin, W. (2007). The caring response. *Relational Child and Youth Care Practice, 20*(2), 62–64.

Aristotle. (1976). *The nicomachean ethics.* (J. A. K. Thomson, Trans.). London: Penguin Books.

Fewster, G. (1990). *Being in child care: A journey into self.* New York: Haworth Press.

Garfat, T. (2001). Developmental stages of child and youth care workers: An interaction perspective. *CYC-Online: Reading for Child and Youth Care Workers, 24*, retrieved June 2, 2008, from http://www.cyc-net.org/cycol-0101-garfat.html

Gilligan, C. (1988). Remapping the moral domain: New images of self in relationship. In C. Gilligan, J. V. Ward, J. M. Taylor, & B. Bardige (Eds.), *Mapping the moral domain.* Cambridge, MA: Harvard University Press.

Goffman, E. (1974). *Frame analysis: An Essay on the organization of experience.* Boston: Northeastern University Press.

Greenwald, M. (2007). Ethics is Hot...So What! *Relational Child and Youth Care Practice, 20*(1), 27–33.

Guttman, E. (1991). Immediacy in residential child and youth care: The fusion of experience, self-consciousness, and action. In J. Beker & Z. Eisikovits (Eds.), *Knowledge utilization in residential child and youth care practice* (pp. 65–84). Washington, DC: Child Welfare League of America.

Heidegger, M. (2004). *Being and time* (J. Macquarrie & E. S. Robinson, Trans.). New York: Harper and Row. (Original work published 1962)

Kidder, R. M. (2005). *Moral courage.* New York: Harper.

Noddings, N. (1984). *A feminine approach to ethics.* Berkeley: University of California Press.

Peterson, C., & Seligman, M. P. (2004). *Character strengths and virtues: A handbook and classification.* Washington, DC: American Psychological Association & New York: Oxford University Press.

Polsky, H. W., & Claster, D. S. (1968). *The dynamics of residential treatment: A social systems analysis.* Chapel Hill, NC: University of North Carolina Press.

Redl, F., & Wineman, D. (1965). *Controls from within: Techniques for the treatment of the aggressive child.* New York: Free Press.

Ricks, F. (1989). Self-awareness model for training and application in child and youth care. *Journal of Child and Youth Care, 4*(1), 33–42.

Ricks, F. (2003). Relatedness in relationships: It's about being. *Relational Child and Youth Care Practice, 16*(3), 70–77.

Ricks, F. (2007). Thus conscience does make cowards of us all: The need for moral courage in these times. *CYC-Online,* 100. Retrieved June 2, 2008, from http://www.cyc-net.org/cyc-online/cycol-0507-ricks.html

Ricks, F., & Garfat, T. (1998). Ethics education in child and youth care: A Canadian study. *Journal of Child and Youth Care, 11*(4), 69–76.

Ricks, F., & Bellefeuille, G. (2003). Knowing: The critical error of ethics in family work. In T. Garfat (Ed.), *A child and youth care approach to working with families* (pp. 117–130). New York: Haworth Press.

Senge, P., Scharmer, C. O., Jaworski, J., & Flowers, B. S. (2004). *Presence: An exploration of profound change in people, organizations, and society.* New York: Doubleday.

Vorrath, H., & Brendtro, L. (1974). *Positive peer culture.* Chicago: Aldine.

Watts, A. (1951). *The wisdom of insecurity: A message for an age of anxiety.* New York: Vintage Books.

Becoming Aware and Challenged by the Complexities of Relational Practice

After crafting a mindful approach to relational practice and understanding its critical aspects, practitioners usually become aware of and are challenged by the complexities of practice. Practice is complex because of the multiple elements that are involved and their interaction within the relational practice context: the practitioner, family members, the agency, the ever-changing influences that affect government funding and policies, and the access and availability of services. Practitioners must be mindful of their reactions to all that emerges and changes within the practice context. The chapters in Part Three explore the complexities of relational practice and promote inquiry into whether or not—and how—to participate, express one's voice, and deal with differences.

CHAPTER 7

Presence and Participation

Being at the Heart of Change

Tam Lundy, PhD

ABSTRACT

What does it mean to "be the change" I want to see in the world? How do my inner experiences come to life in my actions and my behaviours? In other words, how does my *being* shape my *doing*? How does paying attention to my inner development make my actions more effective? And how does this enhance my professional capacity as a Child and Youth Care practitioner?

This chapter explores ground-breaking thinking and practice approaches for catalyzing effective and sustainable change—in people, in organizations, in communities. Readers are introduced to new ways to understand participation in change-making, and to *presencing*, a promising new approach for dialogue, deliberation, and making decisions. With new thinking to accompany new tools, Child and Youth Care practitioners expand their capacity to promote positive change.

INTRODUCTION

Gandhi said it best: "Be the change you want to see in the world." But what does this mean in a world so focused on *doing*? In our professional lives—in our work with children and youth, with families, and with communities—it's our doing that is expected, and it's our doing that is rewarded. Typically, a Child and Youth Care practitioner gets paid to take action: to engage with clients and colleagues, to develop programs, to teach, to collaborate and build partnerships, to advocate for more effective policy and practice. In most aspects of our work, it seems, we are valued for what we do.

Recently, though, I've begun noticing that my doing alone—no matter how passionate, no matter how professionally rewarding—just isn't making the changes I'd like to see in the world. It's not even making the changes I'd like to see in my own life, or the lives of the people I work with. And so I'm wondering just what it means to be the change I want to see in the world.

BEING AT THE HEART OF CHANGE

My inquiry begins with a question: *What if I am the catalyst for the change I want to see in the world?* Yes, that makes sense to me. I know that even the smallest action can make a difference. So, every day, I can do my part to make the world a better place. And my doing is most effective when it is inspired by my highest intelligence and deepest wisdom. I agree.

But another question follows close behind: *What if I am the being at the heart of change?* This sounds a little different. I think it means that by my very being I make change in the world. That my moment-to-moment existence makes a difference. I make a difference even when, to all appearances, I do nothing. And it's not, I suspect, simply my being, but my becoming as well; as I grow and change, the world grows and changes. My inner experience is not contained by my skin; it seeps out and solidifies in the world, as change in the world.

Now this is a different way of thinking about change. A little more mystical, perhaps. But also a little more practical. By peeking into the mystery of life, I become better able to be the change I want to see in the world—not merely in my activist moments, but in every moment. I've heard this called "walking the spiritual path with practical feet." It's a path

I'd like to explore a little further. But first I need to know a little more about these three key elements—being, heart, and change—because each seems to play an important role in world-making. I'll start by taking a closer look at being.

Being

Over the years I've facilitated a lot of meetings in a lot of community settings. Knowing that it is sometimes difficult for ordinary citizens to participate on an equal footing with highly educated professionals, I developed a simple practice to address this issue. At the beginning of each event I would ask participants to reach up and, metaphorically, take off their professional hats and place them under their seats. I requested that they remain "hatless" during the meeting, knowing that they'd happily pick up their hats and plunk them back on their heads once the discussion was over.

On most occasions, this worked well. People willingly took their hats off, fully recognizing that professional status frequently confers a little more voice, and a little more authority, than a non-professional person might experience. Once the hats were off, and safely stowed under the seats, the meeting proceeded. Even though the hats were imaginary, people were willing to play along; this simple exercise did seem to level the playing field a little.

One day, however, when asking folks to take off their professional hats, I met with some resistance. A public health nurse in her late 30s made one of the most honest statements I'd heard in that sort of setting. She said, "I don't want to take off my professional hat, because then I'd feel naked. I wouldn't know who I am. I wouldn't know who I'm supposed to be." You could have heard a pin drop. Her brave statement resonated with many in the crowd and opened a wonderful discussion about the being that does the doing.

So, what is being? To me, *being* describes conscious existence. The book you are holding exists: you can see it, touch it, feel it, and perhaps even smell it. But while it exists, it doesn't possess consciousness. A book, therefore, is not a being. I, on the other hand, exist, *and* I have consciousness. With conscious existence, I am more than a body. I am a being. A human being. I have subjective awareness and an inner capacity to experience and make meaning of my experiences.

In other words, I am a *self*. And this self shows up in all settings, in all situations. This self walks, talks, and sips cappuccino. But there are many parts to this self that can't be seen in my body, my actions, or my behaviours. And yet they show up in every room I'm in.

So, who is the self that is behind all this being? How do I get to know her? One way is to engage in self-inquiry. A few questions I might ask of my self are these: What's in my awareness, right now? What am I feeling, right now? What's important to me? What do I need? What are my values, my assumptions, my sense of what is right? These questions are at the subjective heart of me, the heart of my self. They're at the heart of each of us.

Heart

When your self and my self come together in any form of relationship, a we is created. This we-space is intersubjective space in which communication between conscious beings generates shared experience, shared meaning, shared values, and shared beliefs. This is cultural space, a shared heart-space in which we generate the worldviews, norms, and ethics that shape our relationship and to which we hold each other accountable. This, of course, is the interrelational space in which Child and Youth Care is practiced.

There's another side to this heart—an interobjective side—that shows up in the systems and institutions that we create to structure our collective lives. Sometimes these structures show up as buildings, roads, schools, parks, and playgrounds. They also show up as economic systems, as educational systems, as governance systems, as justice systems. And within these systems, they show up as laws and policies, services, programs, and "best practices." These are the systems and structures within which Child and Youth Care is practiced.[1]

What's important to note is that at the heart of these structures are the collective values, beliefs, norms, and ethics that have been created in we-space. And what's at the heart of our collective values, beliefs, norms, and ethics are the interiors of our selves—each and every one of us. We are not only shaped by society, we shape it with every breath we take.

---

[1] See An Integral Map of Community (Appendix I) for a more detailed look at the subjective, objective, intersubjective, and interobjective territory in which Child and Youth Care—like all professions—is practiced.

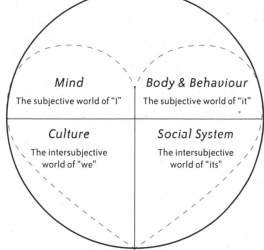

Figure 1. An integral look at self, culture, and society

Mind
The subjective world of "I"

Body & Behaviour
The subjective world of "it"

Culture
The intersubjective
world of "we"

Social System
The intersubjective
world of "its"

Because all individual experience takes place in relational space. And all interpersonal relationships take place in the context of social structures and systems. It's all interconnected. And it's ever-changing.

Change

Change happens. It's always been so. Half a century before Christ was born, Heraclitus observed that change is a universal constant. "Everything flows, nothing stands still," he noted, "nothing endures but change." We often take this ancestral wisdom to mean that if change is the only constant, we'd better get used to it, learn to flow with it. But what if we came to understand our selves—our very beings—as generators of change and not merely pawns in its game?

I live in a society obsessed with change. Most often this obsession runs to the mundane: fashions change, automobiles change, computers change. Recently, however, our obsession with change has become more meaningful as we come to terms with the changes required to ensure human sustainability on our planet. We know we're not pawns in this game; we are the authors of our own encroaching calamity.

But in either context, mundane or meaningful, when our conversation addresses change, there's an underlying assumption: change occurs when we do differently, when our actions are amended, our behaviours modified. But, as I've already discovered, my acting self, my doing self, is just one part of the equation. Every action, every behaviour, has an interior generator. And sometimes things change when I take no action at all. So, to understand the dynamics of change I need to have a better understanding of the generativity of interiority—my own and others'.

Here's an example. In my work-a-day world, change is all around. Policies change. Programs change. Organizations change. Governments change. Funding sources change. Sometimes it's hard to keep up. When I look in the mirror, I see that I am changing too. A few more grey hairs. A few more laugh lines. Bones that don't bounce as they once did. These are all exterior changes. But change is also an interior event that takes place in both me-space and we-space.

In so many ways I'm just not the same person, or the same practitioner, that I was twenty years ago. It's very evident that my exterior doing self has changed: I have a larger inventory of skills, tools, and techniques at my disposal, which enables me to navigate complex situations with greater confidence and competency. But those changes mirror changes within, changes that one can't see just by watching me in action. My self has continued to develop—I am more aware, can take more perspectives into account, and can be more compassionate. My values have shifted, and "doing the right thing" looks a little different than it did at age twenty. I am more self-authoring, less dependent on the agenda-setting and approval of others. I have more emotional intelligence, more relationship intelligence. And of course it is these changes, not just the tools in my professional tool belt, that make me a more effective practitioner. So, my practice isn't just what I do, my practice is also what I be.

I'm also noticing how changes in me-space are influenced by changes in we-space. Since I entered my teen years in the early '60s, cultural norms that once seemed impenetrable have cracked open, bursting with possibilities that my grandmother could never have envisioned. Notions that my culture once pronounced impossible are now not only possible, they are the new norm; in my own lifetime I have seen the emergence and cultural embedding of children's rights, environmental consciousness, gay marriage, the Internet, global governance…and the list goes on. This emergent flow of ideas and forms has shaped me just as surely as my family has shaped me. That I am a product of culture and society is not a surprise; as a student of the social sciences, I learned a lot about this in university. What I didn't learn at school, but what is currently exciting researchers and practitioners alike, is how my developing self—my being and my becoming self—participates in shaping this ever-creative and emergent universe.

And here's the newsflash! There is growing evidence that the underlying catalyst of change is actually *a dynamic inherent in our own development.* Yours and mine. Generativity, it seems, is not merely a by-product of our actions, but of our being and our becoming. And this is where it gets really interesting: I'm coming to understand that I'm not only influenced by the world around me, I participate in making that world. With my own developing consciousness I participate in reality making. My evolving self, my inner being, is a change agent, a world-maker.

Of course, I have to be careful here and not imagine that my very own ego is in charge of making the world. Thankfully, it's not. But there's a deeper part of me, a spiritual essence at the core of me, that has an enduring connection to the creative force by which the universe unfolds. By tapping into that creative force I participate in change-making, in reality-shifting. And here's where it starts to sound a little mystical, but I'm ready to walk the spiritual path with practical feet, and willing to take this inquiry a few steps further.

PARTICIPATION: A DEEPER DIVE INTO THE DYNAMICS OF CHANGE

One of the ways that change shows up in the world is through evolution. Explaining evolutionary processes, biologist Rupert Sheldrake describes nature as "essentially habit forming" (Mishlove, 1998, p. 4). But habit is one of two organizing principles within nature. The other principle is creativity: "creativity essentially involves the appearance of new patterns or new forms or new structures" (Mishlove, p. 4). And this, of course, describes evolution in action.

Habits are patterns of the past, those forms and structures that keep showing up much as they always have. The human body is a good example: seemingly the same as it has been for millennia. But, as scientist/ philosopher Peter Russell (2000) proposes, humanity is "still evolving as a species; …what is evolving, and evolving very rapidly, is the human mind and the ways in which we apply it" (p. 50).

From this perspective, the evolving mind is a product of creativity, with consciousness unfolding in new patterns, new forms, new structures. But, one wonders, whose creativity is at play here? As humans, does evolution just happen to us? Or do we, as conscious beings, play a part in directing our evolutionary unfolding?

A few years ago I set out on another learning journey. The questions that guided that inquiry were, again, both mystical and practical: What does it mean to be a human participant in an inherently participatory universe? And how might a deeper understanding of the essence of participation make a positive contribution to the unfolding of human potential?

Participation and Potential

First, a few words about human potential and development will help to set the context for this inquiry. Evidence that human evolution continues to unfold can be found in the research of the myriad scientists and scholars who study human development—in children, in adults, and in societies. But one doesn't need a string of academic degrees to observe human development at work. Each of us knows something about this—from our own experience and from our observations of others. We notice, for example, the changes in the children in our lives as their development unfolds in leaps and bounds. Over time, we see significant shifts not only in their physical and kinesthetic achievements, but in their cognitive, emotional, psychological, and spiritual development as well.

To illustrate, I need look no further than my three-year-old buddy Liam, a bright and loving child who is curious and caring about the world around him. Liam is also egocentric; while he cares about others in his world, it is rarely at the expense of caring for himself. And, for someone who is three, that is developmentally appropriate. Liam is acting on his newly acquired sense of "self." This nascent self-concept has slowly emerged from a growing awareness that he is an individual, separate from an important circle of "others" in his life, including his mum, his dad, and his orange cat, Clem. This differentiation of self and other is a huge developmental achievement. And he's only just begun!

By acquiring a strong sense of self, Liam is building the foundation upon which his future development will continue—not just in childhood, but throughout his life. At six or seven, with a healthy and well-formed sense of self, he will begin to transcend the egocentric, or selfcentric, stage, and make the transition to the next significant level of development. But even when he makes this transition, he will retain the selfhood that he has worked so hard to claim. The next step on his lifelong journey will take him to the sociocentric stage, sometimes called ethnocentric. Here,

Liam's capacity for care and concern will be extended to a larger circle of others. At this stage of development, he'll discover, it is not only our own personal needs and wants that determine our sense of self, but those of a larger society. Here he will become socialized into the norms and expectations of the community around him. And when he has fulfilled the developmental curriculum that the sociocentric stage has to offer him, he has the potential to reach toward the worldcentric stage.

At the worldcentric level of consciousness, Liam's capacity for care and concern will expand once again. While still caring for himself, and for people like himself (his family, and those of his religion, community, and country, for example), when Liam achieves worldcentric consciousness his circle of care and concern will become universal, expressed as a call for fairness and justice for all people, regardless of nationality, status, wealth, culture, ethnicity, or religion. And any other differences that keep us separate from one another.

Keeping Liam's developmental journey in mind, let's explore a very simple three-stage model of human development:

Figure 2.

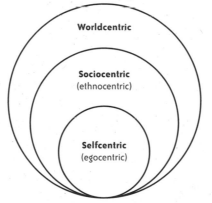

As this diagram summarizes, the span of human consciousness can be condensed into three general stages: selfcentric, sociocentric, and worldcentric. Each marks a developmental stage in which care and concern becomes increasingly inclusive: it begins with "me" at the selfcentric stage, expands to include "us" (i.e., people like me) at the sociocentric stage, and, finally, "all of us" at the worldcentric stage. With each evolving stage, narcissism decreases and consciousness increases, which expands our "capacity to take deeper and wider perspectives into account" (Wilber, 2000, p. 20). Everyday we see evidence of this range of human experience in ourselves and in the people around us.

While a three-stage model is inadequate to map the expansive territory of human development and human potential—in children and in adults—it does accurately describe the direction in which development proceeds. And it provides a helpful entry point for a more in-depth discussion of the evolving complexities of human experience throughout the lifecourse and throughout evolution.

To explore this further, we could choose among many models of human development that emerge from a growing body of empirical studies. Abraham Maslow, we know, identified a hierarchy of human developmental needs that range from deficiency needs to self-actualization and self-transcendence needs. Jean Piaget is familiar to parents and educators alike for his pioneering work in the area of child development. His work has been expanded and extended by Robert Kegan, who continues to research cognitive development in children and adults. Jane Loevinger and Susanne Cook-Greuter have made influential contributions to our understanding of the development of self-identity. Research into multiple stages of spiritual development was pioneered by James Fowler, and his work has become foundational in diverse faith traditions. Lawrence Kohlberg's work revealed important stages in moral development, and Carol Gilligan extended his work to address moral development in women. Clare Graves articulated a developmental sequence based on value systems; his work has been popularized by Don Beck and Chris Cowan in a model widely known as Spiral Dynamics.

Each of these researchers are storytellers, weaving a rich and revealing narrative of the experience of being human. This narrative illuminates a more complete picture of the complexities of human experience and of human potential. Because each storyteller is navigating somewhat different territory, or lines of development—morals, faith, values, and ego, for example—each describes the landscape a little differently. Even when the terrain is different, however, each author maps a developmental pathway that is defined by multiple steps and stages. And, regardless of the terrain they traverse, these stages are remarkably alike in their structure and their progression. Clearly, a pattern is emerging—an unfolding pattern of human development.

Development, of course, is complexification, an ever deepening change process that can be observed over a lifecourse and throughout evolution. My earlier inquiry into the mysteries and practicalities of participation revealed that as the human mind complexifies, we become more aware of our capacities as participatory beings in a participatory universe. At the higher stages of human development, we become aware that we participate in the unfolding of life and evolution.

But just what do I mean by *participation*?[2] Typical, taken-for-granted definitions, such as this—"to take part, or have a share in common with others"—are deceptively simple. From this perspective, participation is understood simply as a physical interaction among individuals that involves "doing" (e.g., taking part in a program, a service, or an event), with an underlying assumption that participation is something that I engage in some of the time. But participation, I've learned, involves much more than my doing. And it's happening all of the time.

Science is revealing that participation is an ever-present pattern in the universe, a pattern of relationship found everywhere in nature. Like change, participation is a universal constant. Participation is the dynamic process pattern that underpins the phenomenon of relatedness in all contexts throughout the universe. To illustrate, I point to three habits of nature that can be found in all corners of the cosmos. These universal habits, present everywhere, are interconnectedness, agency, and influence.

Interconnectedness describes a basic holistic pattern within nature: there is not one entity in the universe that is not both a whole and a part of a whole. Everything alive in the universe is simultaneously a whole in itself and a part of something larger and more complex—a whole/part. Evidence of this interconnecting pattern can be found everywhere in the material world, from planets to photons, from brontosauri to bacteria. This pattern shows up in human domains as well—in actions and behaviours, as well as in social systems and structures, in the subjective world of mind, and in the intersubjective realm of culture. In other words, interconnectedness is a pattern that pervades self, culture, and society at all levels of complexity.

Agency refers to the resource, or the means, by which change occurs. It stems from the Latin *agere*: "to do.". For integral philosopher Ken Wilber (2000), agency is the "pattern or regime governing or regulating the action" (p. 2) of any whole/part. As I see it, agency is a *force of emergence*, an emanation of *will*, that manifests physically and mentally as new forms, new structures, in mind, body, culture, and society. Agency is the "juice" that fuels action and drives change in all domains.

---

2   See Appendix II for a short summary of the essence of participation.

Influence, in this context, is a noun that describes that which is emerging; it is the *emergent form* that flows in and gives shape whenever agency is enacted. Influence can emerge as habit or as creativity, the primary organizing principles within nature. As habit, influence manifests as well-embedded patterns—the form and shape that the past gives the present, as in the example of the morphogenesis from acorn to oak tree. As creativity, influence arises as potential, revealing ever-new possibilities—as, for example, the potential for the human mind to develop to deeper levels of complexity. These possibilities, emerging first as creative newness, may, over time, become habit.

Taken together, these universal habits form an equation that defines the dynamics of participation: *interconnectedness + agency + influence = participation*. This cosmic equation shows up in all relationships between wholes and parts everywhere. It describes their relationships and evolutionary trajectory in all realms of reality—in the inner and outer experience of individuals and collectives.

Willing Participants in our Own Evolution

Common assumptions to the contrary, then, participation is not simply something we do—in a game, at a meeting, or in the classroom. Participation is more: it is also what we *be* and what we are *becoming*. As a fundamental universal pattern, participation is a primary human process, present everywhere. We are, in every minute of every day, participating. No matter where we are, or what we're doing, it's impossible not to participate. The only real question is, how conscious is our participation? We are also, each of us, in the midst of our becoming. Consciously or not, we are, at this moment, participating in our own evolution and in the evolution of the human species.

To understand this process more clearly, and to engage it more purposefully, a deeper understanding of human agency is needed. My online dictionary describes agency as "the capacity, condition, or state of acting or of exerting power" (http://www.m-w.com/dictionary/agency). This fits with common assumptions about agency that focus on external action. But my research, as well as my own lived experience, shows that human agency comes in two types: outer agency and inner agency. In humans, outer agency is a force that emanates through exterior means: my actions, for example, and my behaviours. When I engage this agency, I make things happen. But I possess a greater power than can be accounted for by my actions and behaviours. My interior is also agentic; I make things happen without ever lifting a finger.

I suspect that this concept is familiar, although not, perhaps, part of everyday conversation. Most of us, however, at one time or another, have uttered a cautionary "be careful what you wish for," or "be careful what you pray for." What is the agency at work here? It's an interior part of my self, an inner agency, emanating from deep within me as volition, as will. It shows up in various forms, including emotion, thought, wish, feeling, hope, imagination, choice, inner knowing, intention, and conscious creativity. Each of these forms of inner agency is generative. And each one is a little juicier, a little more generative, than the ones preceding it.

The juicier, more generative forms of inner agency become more available to me as my own development progresses. For my egocentric self, inner agency most frequently arises as emotions or magical wishful thinking. As I develop a stronger sense of self, I have more reliable access to my feelings, my hopes, my imagination, and a growing awareness of their generative capacities. With a highly developed self-sense, I know I can imagine new realities, make choices among competing potentials, rely on my inner knowing to guide my choices, and by activating my intention I can influence the future, moment to moment.

And there's more. As my self development soars into the higher reaches of cognitive, psychological, and spiritual development, something amazing happens. Here, I recognize myself as connected with all of life, as an integral part of the single dynamic living organism that is the universe. And I recognize that where there is consciousness there is divinity. Here, I begin to recognize my inseparability from divinity, my oneness with All That Is. With this awareness, I become conscious of a creative capacity that I once assigned elsewhere. As a conscious being, I am imbued with a spark of that divine creativity. As a participatory being, a co-creator with divinity, I am an evolutionary participant. And co-creativity is juicy agency indeed.

Thought creates. Wish creates. Intention creates. By engaging volition, by activating will, I make change in the world without moving a muscle. Further, the higher my development soars, the greater the probability that this inner agency is engaged as "willingness,"not merely "willfulness." The willful self is the egocentric self, the one that is focused on getting my own needs met while not surrendering an ounce of my personal power. My egocentric self is my three-year-old self, showing up as my need to get my own way. On my good days, at least, I can claim that my personal development has transcended this stage.

It's at the higher stages of development that my willing self is more apt to show up. This is the self whose awareness, values, morals, and interpersonal accountabilities are in service of a greater good. This is the self who knows that, despite my own natural genius, insight and innovation are more likely to emerge when I practice mindfulness, when I tap into a source of knowledge and creativity that is greater than me. Sometimes known as "letting go and letting come," I give up my attachment to a specific outcome, no matter how rational, no matter how well planned, and trust the creative process that occurs when I tap into and participate in the greater flow of divine creativity.

I experienced the power of this phenomenon when I began meditating. On most days I now take the time to sit and go inward, shining a light on my inner experience and drawing it into my waking awareness. I began this practice nearly twenty years ago and have noticed the change it has brought into my life. I am calmer, more grounded, and more self-referencing. I trust inner wisdom more than external opinion, no matter how well-intentioned. At the same time, I am less reactive to outside opinion, knowing that the validation I need emanates from an inner voice. Most surprisingly, I tap into a creativity that I had never previously suspected. It wells within, then bursts out in a juicy flood of information and energy. With creative agency I reach deep within, floating future potentials in the stream of present experience. With a nod toward mystery, I notice my participation in the unfolding of my being and becoming.

In recent years, I've begun wondering how to extend this experience into other parts of my life. If mindfulness makes me more insightful and more creative as an individual, what would happen if we could be more mindful in group settings? Would it help organizations and collaboratives to work together more effectively? Would it help humanity to be more responsive to pressing problems? Would it help us to live more fully into our potential? Would it help us to make the world a better place?

Figure 3. Mindfulness: Being at the heart of change

Awareness

Possibility

The change we
want to see in
the world

Action

Mindfulness
Attention to Being

PRESENCING: A PROMISING TECHNOLOGY FOR MINDFUL PARTICIPATION

Of course, I wasn't the only person pondering these possibilities. As it turns out, a team of researchers and practitioners at the Massachusetts Institute of Technology have been exploring these questions for years, pioneered by Otto Scharmer and Joseph Jaworski, in collaboration with such leadership luminaries as Peter Senge, Adam Kahane, and William Isaacs. The result is an innovative group facilitation approach called U-Process, popularly known as *presencing*; it has been described as a social technology for addressing highly complex challenges. In *Presence: An Exploration of Profound Change in People, Organizations and Society,* the authors describe presencing as "seeing from the deepest source, and becoming a vehicle for that source."

This methodology is emerging as one of the more promising practices for engaging groups in learning, dialogue, deliberation, planning, decision-making, action, and evaluation. Perhaps its most significant contribution is the manner in which it supports participants to approach each of these very practical activities with open heart, open mind, and open will, tapping into a source of creativity that far surpasses the rational work-a-day mind.

To begin, here's a simple overview. Think of the U as a map that guides a group on a journey of learning, discernment, and action. As our group moves along the U, we expand our collective awareness, imagine a broader range of future possibilities, and engage mindfulness before taking action to create the change we want to see in the world. Mindfully engaging a deeper and richer source of creativity and wisdom before we leap into action, we find ourselves tapping into the being at the heart of change.

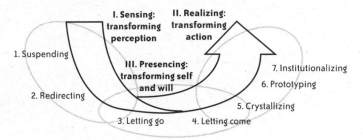

Now, a little more detail. U-Process guides participants through three major movements. The *sensing* space involves learning, taking the pulse of the current situation, uncovering assumptions, and transforming perceptions. In the presencing space we tap into the deepest source of creativity, transforming self and will. *Realizing* is the space in which we take action to generate new realities.

As Figure 4 illustrates, the journey through the U engages seven essential capacities:

1. The *suspending* capacity calls us to "observe, observe, observe," and to make new meaning of what we observe. Suspending asks us to be comfortable with not knowing, to acquire "beginner's mind." From that place of inquiry, we uncover current realities by gathering background information, developing a shared understanding of the problem or the potential to be explored, identifying participant learning needs, and creating a trusting environment for learning. With the capacity to "suspend," we learn about ourselves as well; we examine our assumptions, our judgments, and our typical responses, those taken-for-granted ways of thinking and doing that have historically informed our efforts to make change. In other words, we learn how to "see our seeing." We explore the ways in which this particular problem or potential is part of a larger system, and we learn to view the system with "fresh eyes."

2. *Redirecting* our focus, we bring our fresh eyes to the problem or potential at hand, seeing the situation from different points of view, transforming old perceptions, inviting the new. By re-directing, we re-imagine and re-frame our typical taken-for-granted responses and explore a range of new potentials from multiple perspectives. We envision several versions of the future and examine each from diverse perspectives and landscapes, including how a particular scenario might play out over time, how

it might be experienced differently by different populations and in different contexts. As Zaid Hassan (2005) says, "the ability to re-direct means being able to put ourselves in another's shoes and in other places. It means expanding our sense of place and time" (p. 7). Approaches such as dialogue, storytelling, and scenario-building offer just a few ways to explore future potentials.

3. By *letting go* we give up our attachment to perceptions, ideas, and outcomes. Opening to the unknown, we surrender, inviting newness to emerge from a creative source that runs deeper than our everyday rational and performing selves. At the bottom of the U, walking the spiritual path with practical feet, we invite the inner knowing that emerges when we tap into the flow of universal creativity. Those who prefer a more secular description can be inspired by a leadership training initiative in Halifax; they call this process "sitting in the soup." In his research conducted with high-level achievers in a variety of disciplines, Otto Sharmer (2007) discovered that this is the space from which inspiration, innovation, and peak performance always emerges—in art, in sports, in business, in science, in all human endeavour.

4. *Letting come* is the receptive capacity with which we welcome the wisdom that is emerging from deep within. Zaid Hassan (2005) describes the locus of this experience as "the space between waking and dreaming, where your mind is floating free" (p. 9). It usually happens when we step outside our typical routine… for a walk in nature, a contemplative moment, deep breathing, meditation, a prayer…whatever frees us from the usual stream of thoughts and actions. Sometimes it comes when we least expect it—when we're out for a run, when we sing in the shower, when we write in our journals. At times we experience this receptive moment as a peak experience, a huge "aha!" But often, information comes in quiet ways, too—as intuition, as insight, as inner knowing. For me, it is a small still voice within, a voice I've learned to trust. When we hear the voice, we know what we must do. A clear direction has mysteriously emerged.

5. *Crystallizing*—While presencing involves connecting with a deeper source of creativity, crystallizing, says Scharmer (2007), "means sustaining that connection and beginning to operate from it" (p. 195). Here, with insights emerging as we let go and let come, we clarify the vision and intention that will guide us, and set out together on the path to the future. With this capacity, says Hassan, "we almost let our insight propel us towards and into action" (p. 10). An emergent plan; not a strategic plan: in many ways this means simply getting out of our own way, out of the way of the future that is wanting to be born.

6. *Prototyping* describes the co-creative capacity to take quick and provisional actions in rapid succession, paying close attention to the feedback, identifying patterns, making adjustments, and trying again. This capacity is often called *rapid prototyping*. "Instead of planning and designing," says Hassan (2005), "you just start. You take the first step as quickly as possible. You try something out, and then evaluate it. You walk around it, test it and then change it" (p. 10). Hassan's advice? "Fail often, fail early...we learn best from making mistakes" (p. 11).

7. *Institutionalizing* is collaborative future-shaping: taking the best of our insights and inspirations and embedding them in every-day practice. By institutionalizing, we integrate new approaches into our systems and structures, giving solid form to the innovations that have proved most successful during prototyping. In professional and community settings, these innovations come to life as new organizational systems and structures, policies, protocols, programs, and services. And, from there, into our own day-to-day practices.

Professionals and practitioners in the public and private sector are recognizing U-Process, or presencing, as a practical process for addressing complex challenges, a promising methodology for accessing untapped potentials in people, organizations, and communities. When we take into account the four dimensions of change (inner self, actions and behaviours, culture, and systems), and when we take into account the stages through which human development unfolds (selfcentric to sociocentric to worldcentric), presencing supports our intention to be the change we want to see in the world, and it enhances our capacity to be at the heart of that change.

PRESENCE AND PARTICIPATION: BE THE CHANGE YOU WANT TO SEE IN THE WORLD

In Child and Youth Care, as in most other professions, the objective is change. When our work is working, we achieve positive changes that serve children, youth, and families. Sometimes we look to changes in the system. Sometimes the change is in the client. But what shifts when the change we're seeking is in ourselves? And how do self-changes help generate the changes we want to see in the client and in the system?

Recently, colleagues and I have been having a discussion about just this. We're noticing that as professionals in the human services sector we're always on the lookout for new techniques and new tools to support our work with groups. For example, in recent years a bundle of innovative facilitation approaches have captured our attention: Appreciative Inquiry, Open Space, Future Search, Dynamic Facilitation, Generative Dialogue, World Café…thirty leading methods are profiled on the website of the National Center for Dialogue and Deliberation (http://www.thataway.org). And there are many, many more, each bearing gifts for our professional practice and our community lives.

We love new tools. We collect checklists, guidebooks, resource kits, and facilitation techniques that promise to make our work easier and more effective. For years, in the organizations I consult with and in the communities I visit, I have heard a common plea: just tell us what to do, and show us the tools to do it! But after many years of discovering new tools, and sometimes designing them myself, I'm no longer convinced that they hold the secret to our success. There's more.

For one thing, no matter how brilliantly conceived and designed, a tool is merely a tool. Like a craftsman's hammer, like a weaver's loom, the tool has no life, no purpose, no practical value until it is activated in the hands of a conscious and creative being. And that conscious being will make use of that tool from the perspective from which he or she makes sense of the world. Using the simple three-stage model introduced earlier, that person may be operating from a selfcentric/egocentric perspective, a sociocentric/ethnocentric perspective, or a worldcentric perspective (Torbert, 2004; Wilber, 2000)[3] . So, the developmental perspective of the practitioner is as important as the tool in her hand.

Perspective evolves as humans evolve. As human perspective unfolds toward worldcentric consciousness,we open our arms a little further and are better able to take more and more into account—more complexity, more compassion, more awareness of our own divine nature.[3] We have more information available to us and receive that information in more mindful ways. With worldcentric vision, we recognize the power of our own agency, inner and outer, and the ways in which we influence outcomes—sometimes with our actions, sometimes with our thoughts and intentions.

---

3   These stages are alternatively described as preconventional, conventional, and postconventional.

.Which has led my colleagues and I to pose a provocative question: What if the new tool is the new you? Hmmm. If the new me is more mindful, then I bring that mindfulness to all of my work, day to day, moment to moment, no matter which tool or technique I'm using. If the new me is a more conscious participant in life and evolution, then I am more consistently aware of my interconnectedness, my agency, and my influence. And, as a worldcentric self, I'm more aware that it's not just my doing that generates effective agency: it is my very being and my becoming. If the new me is a more compassionate person, then my care and concern will be more inclusive, more able to embrace people and situations that may have previously triggered selfcentric or sociocentric reactions. At the worldcentric stage of consciousness development, I am better able to walk in another's shoes. And that is an important aspect of presencing.

Being and Change

Presencing is more than a methodology to apply in group settings. It's a potent personal practice, an unfolding journey of self-discovery. Each turn of the U is a self-inquiry as well as a group inquiry; it asks each of us to be on intimate terms with the "you" in the "U." By presencing, we invite self-awareness and other-awareness, self-responsibility and systems responsibility. We become increasingly self-authoring; we own our own practice. We become more intentional, more consciously creative. We become more responsible and more response-able.[4]

My friend and colleague Gail Hochachka (2006) describes this well:

> Becoming more present in the moment, I also become more "available" to other people around me. This helps me to engage more completely with my work, see interpersonal dynamics more clearly, and to hold with more respect the varied ways that other people go about their lives ... my practice includes simply being present as the moment unfolds. (p. 113)

---

4   "Response-ability" is the term with which Fred Kofman (2006) acknowledges our ever-present ability to respond to whatever life offers. This doesn't mean taking responsibility for the causes of any given situation; it means acting on the awareness that we always have the ability to choose how to respond. Response-ability, says Kofman, "is a direct expression of our rationality, our will, and our freedom. Being human is being response-able" (p. 32). According to Kofman, an important human developmental goal is "unconditional response-ability"—a shift from viewing oneself as a victim to acting like a self-empowered "player" (p. 33).

Gail's description reminds me of a similar statement by Harvard psychologist Robert Kegan, who proposes that by developing greater self-awareness and presence, we inevitably become more recruitable to other perspectives. As Kegan (1982) explains,

> what the eye sees better the heart feels more deeply. We not only increase the likelihood of our being moved; we also run the risks that being moved entails. For we are moved somewhere, and that somewhere is further into life, closer into those we live with. (p. 16)

As I am recruited more fully into life, moving more fully into conscious participation, I become more open, more vulnerable, and less attached to outcome. This is my experience in my personal life, in my intimate relationships. It is equally my experience as I move more fully into my professional life. As Robert Kegan (1982) observes, "it is our recruitability, as much as our knowledge of what to do once drawn, that makes us of value in our caring for another's development" (p. 17). When I am more recruitable to other perspectives, I am more helpful because I am practicing more from a place of love, and less from a place of fear. With the healthier and more inclusive perspective that love brings, I am potentially recruitable to the entire human race.

With an expanding openness, I see myself and others as we are and as we have the possibility to be. As a more vulnerable being, I hold myself open to the reflexive principle by which the universe unfolds, a radiant and receptive turning that takes my intention and directs it back toward me as my experience. As I recognize this process at work in my own life, I am better able to see it at work in the lives of others. As I invite expanded capacity in others—in individuals, in organizations, and in communities—I recognize that spiritual principles are at work.

Conscious participation is one form of presencing; as a participatory being in a participatory universe, my agency and my influence help to shape the unfolding of life and evolution. U-Process is another form of presencing; it supports the practice of conscious participation in each member of a group. Participating in presencing, my agency and my influence shape my society and my culture, even as it reshapes my mind and my behaviour. I change myself, even as I change the world. With conscious participation, I become the change I want to see in the world. In my own development as an evolving human being, I find myself at the heart of change.

REFERENCES

Hassan, Z. (2005). Connecting to source. [Online.] Available: http://www. generonconsulting.com/publications/papers/pdfs/Connecting.pdf

Hochachka, G. (2006). *Developing sustainability, developing the self: An integral approach to international and community development.* Victoria, BC: University of Victoria POLIS Project on Ecological Governance and Drishti Centre for Integral Action.

Kegan, R. (1982). *The evolving self.* Cambridge, MA: Harvard University Press.

Kofman, F. (2006.) *Conscious business: How to build value through values.* Boulder, CO: Sounds True.

Mishlove, J. (1994). The universal organism. *Thinking allowed: Conversations on the leading edge of knowledge and discovery.* [Online.] Available: http://www.intuition. org/txt/sheldrak.html.

Russell, P. (2000). *The global brain awakens: Our next evolutionary leap.* Boston: Element Books, Ltd.

Senge, P., Scharmer, C. O., Jaworski, J., & Flowers, B. S. (2004). *Presence: Human purpose and the field of the future.* Cambridge, MA: The Society for Organizational Learning, Inc.

Scharmer, C. O. (2007). *Theory U: Leading from the future as it emerges.* Cambridge, MA: The Society for Organizational Learning, Inc.

Torbert, W. (2004). *Action inquiry: The secret of timely and transforming leadership.* San Francisco: Berrett-Koehler Publishers, Inc.

Wilber, K. (2000). *A theory of everything.* Boston: Shambhala Publications, Inc.

Wilber, K. (2002). *Kosmic karma and creativity* (draft excerpts.) [Online.] Available: http://www.wilber.shambhala.com/

Wilber, K. (2007). *The integral vision.* Boston: Shambhala Publications, Inc.

Appendix I. AN INTEGRAL* MAP OF COMMUNITY

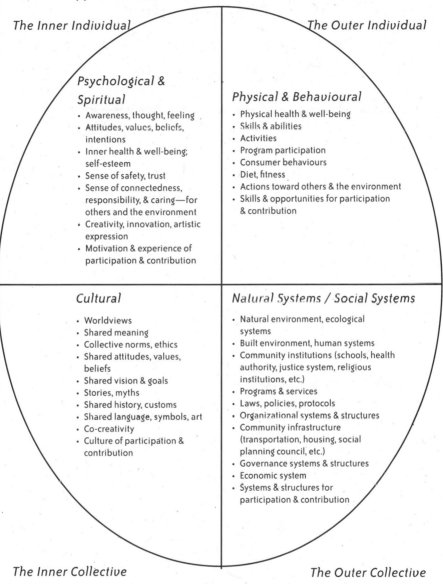

The Inner Individual

Psychological & Spiritual
- Awareness, thought, feeling
- Attitudes, values, beliefs, intentions
- Inner health & well-being; self-esteem
- Sense of safety, trust
- Sense of connectedness, responsibility, & caring—for others and the environment
- Creativity, innovation, artistic expression
- Motivation & experience of participation & contribution

The Outer Individual

Physical & Behavioural
- Physical health & well-being
- Skills & abilities
- Activities
- Program participation
- Consumer behaviours
- Diet, fitness
- Actions toward others & the environment
- Skills & opportunities for participation & contribution

The Inner Collective

Cultural
- Worldviews
- Shared meaning
- Collective norms, ethics
- Shared attitudes, values, beliefs
- Shared vision & goals
- Stories, myths
- Shared history, customs
- Shared language, symbols, art
- Co-creativity
- Culture of participation & contribution

The Outer Collective

Natural Systems / Social Systems
- Natural environment, ecological systems
- Built environment, human systems
- Community institutions (schools, health authority, justice system, religious institutions, etc.)
- Programs & services
- Laws, policies, protocols
- Organizational systems & structures
- Community infrastructure (transportation, housing, social planning council, etc.)
- Governance systems & structures
- Economic system
- Systems & structures for participation & contribution

* *Integral* means "comprehensive, inclusive, balanced...not leaving anything out."

Appendix II. THE ESSENCE OF PARTICIPATION:
A SHORT SUMMARY

1. Participation is a fundamental aspect of human consciousness and human experience. No matter what we are doing—waking, sleeping, dreaming—we are always participating.

2. Participation is more than we typically think it is. Participatory patterns are present everywhere in the universe; where there's life, there's participation.

3. Participation is a dynamic that engages three universal habits: interconnectedness, agency, and influence.

4. A new way of thinking about participation: interconnectedness + agency + influences = participation.

5. There are two types of agency: inner agency (volition, will) and outer agency (action, behaviour, physical force).

6. Inner agency is a force of emergence. The form, or influence, that emerges is the new reality.

7. Expressions of inner agency include emotion, thought, feeling, wish, hope, imagination, choice, inner knowing, intention, and conscious creativity. Some forms of inner agency are more effective for influencing outcomes than others.

8. At higher stages of consciousness, such as interconnectedness, agency and influence become intentional and creative; conscious participation in human evolution becomes possible.

9. Through conscious participation in life and evolution, we become the change we want to see in the world.

CHAPTER 8

Inquiry into Issues of Voice in Relational Practice

Jennifer Charlesworth, PhD

ABSTRACT

This chapter discusses issues of using voice in Child and Youth Care practice. It identifies what is meant by voice, specifies how the absence of voice shows up in practice, and offers the opportunity to examine one's presence/absence of voice. It also explores strategies that can be used by practitioners to overcome barriers to voicing.

Practice Story

Ten of us file into the meeting room. I bring up the rear
with Ellen. I am Ellen's key worker in the care home and
this meeting is all about her, or at least this is what we say it
is about. Around the table is the guardianship worker from
government's child protection service, the psychologist who
has met with Ellen a few times, someone from the school,
my team leader, Ellen's aunt (who is the one family member
that has stayed connected with her), the outreach worker
that has known Ellen the longest, and a few others that I
don't even know. The coordinator calls the case conference
to order and we proceed to discuss parts of Ellen's life—how
she is doing in school, what the psychologist thinks, what
has taken place in the care home and so on. Ellen sits beside
me. She seems to be monitoring what is being said about her
but she is quiet. Several times the coordinator asks Ellen a
question or inquires about her views on what's been said,
but each time Ellen looks down at her hands and in a barely
audible voice replies with single words, short phrases, or a
simple "I don't know." Her aunt, too, seems overwhelmed
by the number of people in the room and the pace of the
conversation. I notice who speaks and who doesn't. I notice
my own anxiety about speaking and offering my views
as a new practitioner. I had come well-prepared for the
discussion, but I hold back and contribute only a fraction of
what I had intended to share.

INTRODUCTION

This very typical Child and Youth Care story addresses "voice" in Child
and Youth Care practice. Who has voice in this context and who doesn't?
Are we doing our best work for the people that we serve when we only
have parts of their life pictures and particularly when we don't have their
voices clearly at the table? What is our responsibility as practitioners to
support or foster voice with the people that we serve? How might we do
this? What is our responsibility to use our voices in our practice? What
does it take to become more attuned to our own voices and silences?

In this chapter, we will explore the topics of silence, voice, relational
practice, and personal and social change. Drawing on my research into
girls' and women's experiences with silence, voice, self, and change, as

well as the literature on these topics, we will consider the implications of this knowledge for Relational Child and Youth Care practice.

By engaging in this exploration you will

- have a language and framework to work with and apply within your practice
- explore your own experiences with silence and voice and be more curious about your own voice, sense of self, authenticity in practice, and discomforts with having and using voice
- understand that silence, voice, and voicing is complex, multi-faceted, and influenced by contexts and relationships
- appreciate the significance and relevance of these topics in Child and Youth Care practice
- be better prepared to practice in relational ways that support voice, a positive sense of self, and personal and social change

DEFINING VOICE

In my studies I discovered that there is no "shared voice" about what is meant when we use the term *voice* as a construct in human service practice. At one level we might understand it to mean "speaking." If I speak, then I have voice; if I speak out loudly, then I have strong voice. I do not believe that it is so simple. Does the mother who screams at her child and berates her for her inability to tie her shoes have voice? Does the youth who loudly protests a change in curfew have voice? It is possible that each of these people has voice, but I believe that it is not indicated or evidenced by whether or not they speak or the volume with which they speak.

As an illustration of the ambiguity with which the term *voice* is described in the literature, I refer to the description offered by Carol Gilligan in the new preface to her 1993 edition of *In a Different Voice*:

> By voice I mean voice. Listen, I will say, thinking that in one sense the answer is simple. And then I will remember how it felt to speak when there was no resonance, how it was when I began writing, how it still is for many people, how it still is for me sometimes. To have a voice is to be human. To have something to say is to be a person. But speaking depends on listening and being heard; it is an intensely relational act.

> When people ask me what I mean by voice and I think
> of the question more reflectively, I say that by voice I
> mean something like what people mean when they speak
> of the core of the self. Voice is natural and also cultural.
> It is composed of breath and sound, words, rhythm, and
> language. And voice is a powerful psychological instrument
> and channel, connecting inner and outer worlds. (p. xvi)

As Carol Gilligan's (1993) comments suggest, voice is not a simple or straightforward concept to define. It is a noun and a verb, a name for something and an act. It is not a simple matter of it existing or not, of one having it or not, of one using it or not. The topic of voice cannot be separated from the cultural and social context, from experiences of voice and voicing, silence and silencing, or from the relational act of speaking and listening. Voice is a complex and fundamental concept within human, social, and cultural development.

For the purposes of this chapter, voice represents a connection with the core of the self, and it arises in and through relationships with self and with others. The following excerpts of interviews with women[1] who moved through silence and into voice illustrate what "having voice" means to them and how it shows up in their experience:

> It was years of a reclamation project but I feel like my self is
> what I got back. Before I was almost unrecognizable, there
> was no "me." So getting that back, and self-knowledge and
> self-awareness, and confidence that I won't have to go back
> there. That I'm safe now. I'm well-shored up. I won't ever
> get into that same situation.

> Now I'm comfortable in my own skin and able to hold my
> own and not apologize for my existence. A real being able to
> move into my body and mind and fully engage in activities,
> and things that I want to, ways of thinking, doing what I
> like to do, or thinking the way I like to think, speaking how
> I like to speak.

---

[1] To illustrate key concepts I will draw on the words of the women who participated in my doctoral research from 2004 to 2005. Throughout this chapter, quotes from the interviews and group discussions have been used. The speaker's names have been changed to protect confidentiality.

WHY VOICE MATTERS

As the excerpts above illustrate, voice is a construct,[2] a strategy, and an outcome that is relevant to Child and Youth Care practice.

As a construct, it gives us one way of understanding the experience of the people that we serve. For example, if I am working in a neighbourhood that is gripped by fear due to widespread violence, crime, abuse, and addiction, and I set up a community meeting to discuss what might be done to reclaim the community and no one shows up, does this indicate that no one cares? Or might it indicate that citizens feel voiceless and unable to effect change? If I am working with a youth who has been involved in a series of abusive relationships and is struggling to break free of the latest unhealthy relationship, I might wonder whether she has a sense of self and voice. I might be curious about the messages she has received in her family and community about her right to safety, and about her entitlement to her own voice and mind. These questions might guide my assessment of her situation and context and inform the choices I make about the way in which I try to engage with her.

Voice is also a strategy. Through the intentional nurturing and encouragement of voice, we may be able to facilitate or effect change in individuals, families, and communities. For example, in the neighbourhood described above, I might try to build individual connections and relationships and listen to the perspectives of people who live in the community about what is going on, how it affects them, what they wish for, and so forth. I might engage a few people in informal kitchen table conversations that enable them to hear their own voices, to connect with and express their frustrations and hopes, and to hear the voices of others who share a desire for a safer neighbourhood. Over time, we might be able to draw out and nurture individual and shared voice, help develop a sense that issues can be talked and thought through, and encourage action within the neighbourhood. In my work with the youth who is struggling to break free of an abusive relationship, I might encourage her to tell me stories or write in a journal to help her build or regain some capacity to listen to her own voice and give value to her self.

Voice is also an outcome. In my work with communities, teams, and groups that are struggling, a successful outcome is often indicated by the

---

2   A *construct* is something that has been systematically put together to help organize or explain an experience or phenomenon.

participants' ability and willingness to engage in difficult conversations and their ability to participate in dialogues with each other while respecting differences. They are able to see the context that they are in, gain voice in relation to this context, and creatively engage in ways to give expression to their hopes and dreams. For example, in the neighbourhood described above, voice could be an outcome of our work together. That is, citizens will have connected with their right to have and express voice, and they will have discovered ways to use their individual and collective voices to effect change in their situations. In my work with the youth, a voice-related outcome might be that she begins to pay closer attention to the small voice inside that still believes she has a right to be safe and valued.

Practice story

I knock on the door, and as I wait for an answer I look around the exterior of the house. The curtains are drawn on this bright sunny day, heaps of debris litter the front yard and driveway, the grass is a foot long, and the flower beds have long since been taken over by weeds. I am overwhelmed, and this is not even my home. Eventually the door opens and Ella welcomes me. She takes my hand, pulls me into the front room, and tells me where to sit down. She heads off to get her mother and then thoughtfully looks back at me and asks if I would like a glass of water. She is just 9 years old, but she has a mature way about her. When she returns she tells me that her mom has been sleeping, so she'll be up to see me in a few minutes. In the meantime, Ella launches into an animated conversation about what's happening at school, what she thinks of her teachers and the other children, the trouble that her brother has got into in the neighbourhood, and a dozen other snippets of conversation. I don't know whether this means that she feels safe with me, if she's nervous and trying to fill in time, or what, but I find her refreshingly open and candid.

Eventually Ella's mother, Cassie, arrives and tells her to "shut up" and to stop telling stories. She tells her that I am not interested in what she has to say. Ella falls silent. She looks at me as if to say, "Do you really not care?" I open my mouth and begin to say that I am interested in what Ella has to say and then I stop myself. I am not sure why, except I feel torn now—do I oppose Ella's mom and run the risk of undermining her in front of her daughter, or do I remain silent and run the risk of Ella being less trusting of her own voice and our new relationship? What message has Cassie just

given to her daughter about her right to voice? What messages
has Cassie received about her own voice? What message have
I just given to them both with my awkward silence?

As the above story illustrates, the concept of voice frequently shows
up in our work with vulnerable and marginalized children, youth, and
families. It may also show up in our work with other service providers, in

Table 1. Conceptual Framework for Understanding Silence and Voice

Section	Metathemes (Level One)	Themes (Level Two)
Experiences with Silence	Silencing in Significant Relationships	Silencing in Families
		Silencing in Intimate Relationships
	Silencing and Personal Context	Isolation and Disconnection
		Trapped and Responsible
		Not Entitled to Have Voice
		Can't Trust Experience
		High Stakes
	Consequences of Silencing for the Self	Unconscious/Don't Know—Disconnected from Self
		Experiencing Disability, Loss, and Death
Coming into Voice	Receiving New Information and Interrupting Patterns	Receiving New Information
		Connecting With Allies
	Seeing Life Situations Differently	Becoming Aware of the Struggle
		Assessing Risks to Self and Others
		Beginning to Question—Can I Have My Own Truth?
	Defining the Self	Discovering Entitlement to Have Voice
		Defining Personal Boundaries and Responsibilities
		Finding a Place to Speak From
	Working Around the Edges of Voice	Practicing and Experimenting with Voice
		Working Through a Long Process
No Turning Back—The Voicing Moment	Crossing the Line into Voice	
	Taking Action	
	Achieving Alignment—Voice and Self	Coming to Life
		Emergence and Congruence
Evolving Voice	Integrating Self and Other—Self in Relation	Authenticity and Identity
		Confidence and Shifting the Terms of Relationships
	Works In Progress	Voice and Context
		Voice and Growth

our teams, agencies, or service systems. It may show up in our work with communities, and in our own families and relationships. It is interesting to consider how attuned we are to our own voice and sense of self, how we use our voice in practice (and in our lives)—as either a construct, a strategy, or a desired outcome—and in what contexts.

THE JOURNEY FROM SILENCE TO VOICE: A CONCEPTUAL FRAMEWORK

In this section a conceptual framework for understanding silence and voice is described. This framework has evolved from my research into girls' and women's voices and from a review of the literature on voice, self, relationships, and change. The work is gender-based and its relevance to the experiences of boys and men has not been explored. Nonetheless, practitioners who work primarily with boys and men may still find value in the framework, either because it suggests some areas for inquiry or because boys and men are often in relationships with, or influenced by, the girls and women in their lives. Through better understanding of girls' and women's voices we might better understand the nature of relationships between girls, boys, women, and men. Furthermore, the majority of Child and Youth Care practitioners are women, and it is only through exploration of and reflection on our own voices and sense of self that we can be fully prepared to engage in the complex world of Child and Youth Care practice.

As each area of the framework is discussed, I have woven in descriptions provided by the women who have informed my research in the hopes that these concepts will come alive for the reader.[3] I encourage you to engage with this material by asking the following questions:

- What personal and professional experiences have I had that reflect this characteristic or aspect of silence and voice?
- How might this knowledge inform how I do my work as a Child and Youth Care practitioner?

---

3   Quotes and stories from my research with women are used to illustrate the meaning behind each of the themes identified in the framework.

EXPERIENCES WITH SILENCE

In the sub-sections below, we will examine the experiences that girls and women have with silence—what contributes to silence, what it feels like to be silenced, and what the consequences of being silenced are. As you move through this material, consider how knowing this information might help you to understand the behaviour and intentions of others (e.g., the children, youth, and families that you serve, colleagues, family members, and so on) and perhaps even your own behaviour and intentions.

Silencing in Significant Relationships

SILENCING IN FAMILIES

Girls and women who are disconnected from their own voices and selves may have had experiences as children within their families that silenced them and defined the relationship (or, rather, the lack of relationship) that they had with their voices. These early experiences may continue to define women's connection or lack of connection to voice and sense of self throughout adulthood. In *Women's Ways of Knowing: The Development of Self, Voice and Mind* (Belenky, Clinchy, Goldberger, & Tarule, 1997), the authors noted the strong link between women's silence in adulthood and childhood and family experiences of neglect and abuse. Their childhoods were lived in isolation from their family members and others outside the family. As they grew up, these women were passive, subdued, and subordinate. Belenky and Clinchy et al. (1986/1997) note, "The ever-present fear of volcanic eruptions and catastrophic events leaves children speechless and numbed, unwilling to develop their capacities for hearing and knowing" (p. 159). These women experienced themselves as mindless and voiceless.

My research affirmed these findings. The message that such women received from authoritarian, abusive, preoccupied, or unavailable parents and family members was that they did not have much value as girls or young women. They were expected to be quiet or obedient, "seen and not heard," and were discouraged from asking questions and "taking up energy" of other people by speaking. If bad things happened to them, they were either told that they were responsible or they silently assumed responsibility. Their sense that they had little value as girls or women was further reinforced when they observed their mothers silenced in their relationships. They grew up feeling no sense of entitlement or right to have voice or to have some influence over the way their lives unfolded. Meg, for example, described her childhood this way:

> I was raised in a very patriarchal household where I really didn't have value. My mom and I, we didn't get the same food as my brother and my father and things like that. There wasn't a lot of value to who I was as a human being. And I'd been abused as a child as well so that had left me not really having much belief that I had a right to voice.

Another participant talked about how her sense of not having value or a right to have voice showed up in her behaviour: "When I was younger [my speech] was so fast that people had a hard time even understanding it because I wanted to take up as little space as possible."

Even when support for voice is expressed within a family context, the young person's sense of self and voice may be compromised when these messages are confused or contradicted by other familial experiences. For example, Jess received lots of encouragement from her mother to have and use her voice for social justice, but she witnessed her mother's lack of voice within intimate relationships and the lack of regard for Aboriginal voice within her community, and so Meg began to doubt the positive messages that she received.

SILENCING IN INTIMATE RELATIONSHIPS

Early experiences such as these often define women's sense of themselves and influence how they enter into adult relationships. One woman talked about how she had "gone from being controlled by an abusive, controlling father to being controlled by an abusive husband." Another talked about entering into a very traditional marriage at a young age; although her husband was controlling and abusive, she had no concept of her right to have a voice, and she had such a diminished view of herself that she felt "lucky to have him." She continues:

> I was this bad rotten person. He was this beautiful guy that was with me so how could anything about me be of any importance or worth? And so when he hit me, it was my fault and when he belittled me he was right and all those kind of things.

Women who have grown up in families or contexts that have silenced them often describe how in their adult interpersonal relationships they have the experience of being disconnected from their selves. Linda remarked:

> There's something that happens where suddenly something overpowers you or the situation takes over or something shifts, where it's not like you're making a choice to not speak up anymore, it just becomes habit to be silenced. It just made me feel like part of me had gone away.

The common thread that connects silenced women's experiences of their childhood and adult years is that they have not felt entitled to claim voice or identity, or they have been confused about how to be "authentic" and "whole" within relationships. For women who have journeyed beyond silence and toward voice, this awareness has come about only with the passage of time and reflection: when they were in the midst of their adult relationships, they were not conscious of what they were giving up · in terms of self and rights to voice.

Silencing and Personal Context

ISOLATED AND DISCONNECTED

Girls and women who are or have been silenced often describe experiences of being isolated, disconnected, alone, and of not experiencing a sense of belonging. Sometimes this takes the form of not feeling connected to a part of themselves and their heritage. Laura described her experience of

> feeling like, "Oh, I'm the only brown-skinned person on the planet who doesn't fit in, who's a fraud, who's not Indian enough to be an Indian." So that's where my little voice of, "Who are you to be saying, thinking, doing?" That comes from that voice, "You're not authentic."

Some women describe how they are disconnected from others and even from information and knowledge. They are not encouraged or allowed to have relationships or connections outside of their immediate families, or they feel such shame and embarrassment about their situation and themselves. As a result, they either do not reach out and connect with others, or their circle of connections is very limited. Gabby talked about being unable to be with other people unless her husband was present or gave his permission:

> He could see that I had things to offer the world and he didn't want the world having them. He wanted only him having them so that was the only way he thought he could keep me was by keeping me enclosed in this world.

Another woman described how she was only allowed to read material for her children's schooling or home care. The impact of this isolation was that she had no way of accessing alternative perspectives and new information. She remarked, "There was no place of making that common connection, and even if it was there, I didn't see it as common." This kept her disconnected from and unaware of her voice and her self.

Sometimes women's unique circumstances—such as being an immigrant or being in a non-traditional relationship that others disregarded or judged negatively—resulted in their feeling even more disconnected and isolated.

TRAPPED AND RESPONSIBLE

Women who have been silenced often talk about carrying a sense of responsibility for the well-being of others and for the difficulties of their own situations. They feel highly responsible for others and often give themselves over to accommodate the interests of others and keep silent for fear of "hurting others with my words." Their descriptions convey a strong orientation to the interests of others and yet remain unconscious about "self." For example, Karen's sense of self only went so far as sensing a need to "survive." She had no awareness about self and entitlement, but she carried a burden of responsibility for others: "I had a friend who said, 'I hate it when you say you're sorry cause you really mean it. You really actually feel responsible for everything that's going on in the world.'" Karen did not tell anyone about the abuse that she experienced within her marriage. She described how a close friend of hers shared information about how her husband hit her, but Karen did not disclose that she, too, was hit by her husband. She didn't make the connection between their experiences or see them as similar. She understood that her friend's husband was at fault, but she didn't believe that her own husband was responsible for his treatment of her. She protected him (the "other") and never said anything about her experience: "I was afraid that if I said he hit me then she would think badly of him and that wouldn't be fair to him because it was my fault." Karen had no concept of self or of her rights.

Many women who live in silence describe how they give little or no consideration and care to their selves. Self-care is simply not within their conscious awareness. They have "no sense of self," and therefore have no capacity to care about something that they do not have. Joanne's comments about her lack of care for the self resonated with a chorus of other women whose voices and selves had also been subjugated:

> I think for me it's partly back to that hierarchy, you know Maslow's hierarchy. When you're sort of fighting for your life in your relationship everything else becomes submerged under many layers so that you can't access those needs that you might have because they're superfluous, really, because you're in survival mode. I remember just doing the bare minimum to get by, and if I did do anything outside of that it was just treated as such an indulgence, that it wasn't really necessary for the well-being of the family and I really wasn't entitled to it.

Sometimes women describe how they feel trapped. They feel responsible for how things are in their lives, that somehow they had created their life situation and have to live with it, or that they deserved it and this was the best they would get. They felt no capacity to effect change in their circumstances. Amy speaks to this:

> There was a period of time when I was in a state of recognizing that I couldn't continue but I didn't really know that I could survive, and I was afraid of being on my own. So I felt that I had to stay in the relationship because I wasn't going to be able to manage, you know, to look after children, and I felt that whole sense of giving up one problem but getting another one, and of being trapped, completely trapped. So that went on for quite a number of years.

NOT ENTITLED TO HAVE VOICE

Women speak of years of "feeling very much voiceless and silenced" and of not even being aware that they could have a voice. For Meg, it took years before she became aware that she was entitled to have a voice, and then some years again before she began to exercise that right:

> There was a time when I didn't think I had any right to have any voice or any sense that there was a notion of voice for me. It was very much a sense of I needed to do what I was

told and I didn't have that right to have voice, so there was a point where I moved to "I do have a right to have voice," and since then I've done a great deal of struggling. I continue to struggle about how to have voice, and when to have it and when not to, and be curious about when I'm okay with it and when I'm not. But there was a time where I really didn't think I had a right to it, whereas I know I have a right to it now, even though I might not exercise it all the time.

CAN'T TRUST EXPERIENCE

Flowing from this belief of no entitlement to voice, some women talk about having some sense of entitlement but of not trusting their own perspectives and experience, and of being confused about how to express their voices. They also speak of their frustration with others who did not talk truthfully about what they saw and who failed to assist them to find their ground and affirm their right to have a voice.

Jess had a sense of being entitled to use her voice, but within the context of a chaotic and abusive family she lost her perspective on what mattered to her and who she was. She remains puzzled about why others did not assist her at the time to regain her sense of entitlement to have a voice. The lack of participation by others contributed to her continued silencing:

> Sometimes I wish someone would have sort of shook me and said, "What are you doing? Why are you putting up with this?" That someone would have just maybe helped me a little more in that way?

> [Because of everyone's silence about what they observed,] I came to think that what was going on was acceptable to them. And then it was sort of like, well, if all these people that I love and respect know that's how I'm being treated in my relationship and they think it's okay, then I guess I'm not worthy of something else. I couldn't trust my own experience anymore.

Jess wondered, "Doesn't anyone else see this?" and she had a hard time hanging onto her sense of self and voice in the face of others' silences about things that mattered to her.

The doubts that women have about their own experiences, their perspectives, their right to have a voice, whether they have something meaningful to say, and where they stand contribute to a fear or reluctance to use their voices.

Women and girls often describe the risks they face in using their voice—the risk of physical consequences, such as being hit; emotional consequences, such as being blamed or judged; financial consequences; or relational consequences, such as losing their place in a group, their children, or other key people. Given their experiences of other people's words being harmful to them, some girls and women believe that their voice will hurt others, so they keep silent to avoid this potential hurt to others. Others speak with the intention to cause harm to others, but there is no authenticity to the voice. As one woman remarked,

> I didn't really care what I said or how I said it. I was pretty convinced no one would ever listen to me anyway, but that violence wasn't really me. I desperately wanted to not feel like I had to do that to keep myself safe.

For this young woman, she "screamed" in order to keep others away and to prevent further assaults on her sense of self, but she was clear that she did not have voice.

Consequences of Silencing for the Self

UNCONSCIOUS/DON'T KNOW—DISCONNECTED FROM SELF

Many girls and women are clear that having voice is not the same as "speaking." Some experience struggles with speaking as well as voicing, but others do not. One of the participants in my research described herself as always having been "the outspoken one," although she knew that this was not the same as being "the one with voice."

Many women who have journeyed into voice speak to the ways in which their voice and self are intertwined. Without a sense of self there is no place to voice from or no sense of what to voice about, and without voice there is no access to the self. Voice is connected to a deeper awareness or sense of knowing the self.

Girls and women who have had some experience of being disconnected from their voices and sense of self often talk of "not knowing," or being "unconscious," "unaware," or "submerged." Because they aren't conscious that there is a self to be discovered, known, or created, they internalize the ways in which others define them rather than creating their own definition and sense of self. Kate described it this way:

I think that I had lived with a lot of criticism, and huge amounts of self-denigration as a result of the abuse, the emotional abuse that I took within my family, and I had internalized a lot of that, so I had very little confidence and I really was, I thought of myself as fairly…did I think of myself as useless? I had internalized this view to some extent and I'd lost that sense of self.

Suze described her situation in this way:

> For the longest time getting up, and breathing and eating, and moving through life and not getting hit or hurt, was all I thought about, was how I could get through each day, breathe, eat and survive. I was in survival mode—there was no room for anything else.

Sometimes girls and women take on other personas as a way to avoid facing aspects of who they are, that they don't fully understand, and are not able to safely inquire about.

EXPERIENCING DISABILITY, LOSS, AND DEATH

There are significant consequences for many girls and women who are silenced, trapped, and disconnected from self and others. Some women describe significant health issues—their bodies "fall apart" as they become more and more "worn down" and disenfranchised from their voices and as the risks to their emotional well-being and safety increase. It is as if their bodies are signalling the seriousness of their situations through weight loss, illness, physical disability, chronic pain, anemia, and exhaustion.

Some women describe experiences of feeling like "something inside of me has died." Gabby reflected that, for her, what had died was "partially my voice and my ability to know where I was coming from." During the time when she lost her voice in her intimate relationship and with members of her family, she dropped out of university, stopped performing and writing, and had no contact with friends. She still has moments in which she grieves for the "loss of my self when I was silent."

Tory recounted how she was "unable to breathe," and was always "vigilant" and watching to see what she needed to do to make sure "bad things" didn't happen. This involved her children, too, as they were raised in a household that required vigilance and "watching over" each other. She and others talked about the extraordinary energy that it took for them to just survive, about the building awareness that they were "dying," that their sense of self had died, or that if things continued the way that they were they would surely die or make the choice to die as a viable and more appealing alternative. Karen described her situation this way:

> I was also kind of suicidal at this point in the sense that I'd be driving down the road and think, "Well gee, I could just go straight here and I'd go off the edge instead of turning the corner." And these kind of things, thoughts, would pop into my mind. It was interesting 'cause I didn't feel desperate or anything—these suicidal thoughts would come to my mind off and on.

COMING INTO VOICE

In this section we will explore the processes of coming into voice. One woman described this process as being like "building a scaffold." Different experiences, opportunities, and information slowly enabled her to construct a scaffold that allowed her to climb out of the silence and begin to see things differently and eventually act differently and make different choices. She said that sometimes she'd just be moving along the scaffold and gaining different vantage points, and at other times she'd be able to add new levels and draw closer to what she described as a more whole sense of her self, mind, and voice, and her right to be in this world. What is clear from both my own research and from the literature is that there are many different aspects to the scaffold and many different ways in which the scaffold can be influenced and constructed.

As you read through this material, I hope you will be inspired by the resiliency and desire for health and well-being that is reflected in the stories and illustrations presented. I hope, too, that you will begin to appreciate the opportunities and responsibilities that we have, as Child and Youth Care workers, to nurture, facilitate, and support the process of coming into voice with the children, youth, and families we serve. The practice implications will be discussed in a later section.

Receiving New Information and Interrupting Patterns

People who have moved from silence towards voice describe instances of receiving new information that interrupted or prompted them to question their established patterns and the formulations they had about their worlds. Sometimes this was information provided by or through external sources, such as teachers, friends, counsellors, and authority figures, and at other times this was information that individuals generated by noticing something about themselves for the first time.

Callie talked about noticing things about herself and was able to receive this as new knowledge and information that made her wonder about what was going on and where she stood. She noticed that she had stopped talking to others, even close women friends, about her life situation and relationships. She noticed that her respect for herself was slipping away. Callie also shared an experience with a counsellor in which she received new information about how relationships could work:

> One of the things I remember the counsellor saying was, "You know you can ask for things in your marriage." Like she was talking to me. I had always thought that you accept the person the way they are, that's who they need to be. It just really struck me. It didn't occur to me that I can set some ground rules here or I can say what's important to me or what I need. I kind of just left, realizing, I can say, "This isn't OK in my marriage, I don't want this, I won't accept this."

Joanne talked about instances when she received information about her talents and strengths in university, and she began to wonder about the validity of her husband's characterization of her as not capable:

> I had been feeling very much voiceless and silenced for a very long time. And a couple of points that I can remember when I was doing my degree where there was that sense of, give yourself permission to do this, to speak up, to say what you need to say, to lead this particular activity or group and realizing, "Oh I can!?"

Sara talked about experiences of connecting with others who shared a similar life path—that of adoption as an Aboriginal child into a non-Aboriginal family:

> I was adopted at birth into a non-Aboriginal family and I am Aboriginal. And I'd grown up believing I was the only Aboriginal adoptee in the world. Because I felt like I was the only one, I felt very silenced in general, from all different parts of society and just in general, the world, the universe.
>
> In the 1990s I met another Aboriginal adoptee and she opened the world to me of the Aboriginal adoptee world,

the Aboriginal adoptee universe. There's hundreds, there's thousands, there's a hundred thousand of us in Canada and I didn't know that.

Connecting with Allies

One of the most critical components for the construction of the scaffold is the presence of supportive relationships and allies that people experience in their voice journey. These allies often create a bridge to new experiences and new perspectives that enable women who have been silenced to begin to wonder and question. What they achieve through these relationships and experiences is a sense that "I am not alone" and "I am okay."

The following quotes illustrate how important allies are to the process of coming out of silence and into voice. This is particularly important to Child and Youth Care practice:

> That's how I got my voice because people gave it to me, and I feel lucky to have people in my life that have done that, and have been able to support me through the transition to give me voice when I didn't have it. And still having people now that help me keep it, you know? And so for me that's really important. I have to rely on external voices still, in order to trust my inner voice. (Linda)

> There are certain parts that I can think that I was still trying to go solo, and it generally doesn't work for me. But once I'm willing to, okay, get over it and just be willing to share what the struggle is, it's way easier for me. It works better when I'm able to do that. (Sara)

> When I looked at my own words written down and my own memories of experiences that had happened, and significant things that people had said, or just had heard me through a particularly difficult time, and I realized, my goodness… that's so powerful! (Kate)

Of interest is the diversity of types of allies and circumstances and places in which these alliances and supportive connections might arise. Supportive connections and allies included both male and female friends, colleagues, teachers and professors, physicians, counsellors, special interest group members, supervisors and mentors. One of the women spoke of a man she met in a college course many years ago that validated her strengths. She can't recall his name but recalls the experience and described how this had been tucked away in her memory and gave her a "glimmer" of hope. Another woman spoke of the supportive relationships that she had with her animals.

Laura talked about the connections that she has with her colleagues and how these have enabled her to go through both her adoption reunion and the pubic exposure of the very disturbing circumstances of her placement for adoption:

> This is the most incredible place to work, the most
> incredible team of people who love and support and lift
> me up as we love and support and lift each other up all
> day every day. Where I worked previous to here, if I had
> said, "I have to go and meet my biological family, I need
> three days off," they would have said, "Well, that's two
> days off without pay, you need to give us two months
> notice, blah, blah, blah." Just total bureaucratic crap. And
> here, it's "Laura's embarking on this amazing journey of
> self discovery," and they see it as part of the holistic being
> that makes up me in my spiritual, mental and spiritual and
> emotional way. And they're supportive, and I know that
> there're prayers for me. There's *no way* I could have done
> this working for McDonald's. I needed to have lots of love
> and support and care all around me. No, I couldn't have
> done it alone. They have all encouraged me to raise my
> voice, and helped me find new ways to do that, and better
> ways to do that, and stronger ways to do that. We all help
> each other have our voice in a big way.

Meg received the support of a variety of allies, and one of the first was an animal. She was extremely isolated, and her connections with other people were monitored and managed by her husband. As an illustration of the tremendous need for connection, the ally she found was a dog that had been rejected in its early life. What is notable, too, is that the loss of her ally resulted in her questioning many aspects of her life:

> And so her and I had a fine relationship. I could relate to
> her and to what had happened to her when she was young. I
> never had any problems with her and so she kind of felt like
> my ally a bit, you know what I mean? I could relate to what
> that dog was doing.

Meg's relationship with her dog was so strong and necessary that after the dog died, Meg felt that she'd lost an ally:

> It probably sounds really silly but you know, I *thought* [when I tended to the dog] every day for a number of years. I lived [in] an isolated world. But my relationship with her was totally unmonitored so I think because of that in some ways I was able to develop a different kind of relationship with her. So when she died it really kind of broke my heart. I really questioned what I was doing with my life, and questioned my relationship and where my loyalties lie and what I was doing.

There are common threads in what girls and women find to be significant about the way in which their allies treat or engage them. They value being listened to, accepted, validated, reinforced for having good ideas, acknowledged for their strengths and capacity, being given opportunities and encouraged to reach out and take some risks. Kate describes it this way:

> I think the biggest thing for me has been having people in my life who not only will tell me that they believe in me, or whatever, but will give me opportunities. In a way they put something on the line too. It's like a generosity of trust. There's no weird power-thing. It's like people wanting to share that with you and wanting you to be. So it's just people being really generous with wanting you to just feel like you're somehow important, or what you have to say is really valid, or what you're doing is. And, having people say, "You have something to say." And people being on board and just using the power that they have strategically to help you. Something about the way that I've been treated has made me think, "I can learn from this and I can grow."

For many people it is also important to connect with others who share similar interests, people who are either experiencing or have experienced similar things and have successfully worked through their challenges, or who are "living a principled life" that helps them reconnect with their sense of what is right. One woman spoke about connecting with others that were willing to engage in a dialogue about their experiences:

> There used to be a group of mixed race people and we'd meet and talk and write, talk about our families and write

and stuff. I'm trying to support myself through having people with common interests. Because it's easy, I think, to feel isolated especially if you are trying to speak out or make a difference. But there are people who want to have space for that kind of dialogue all around, so you just need to bring those people together. That feeds me a lot, just having more people in my life like that. I don't feel alone.

It is also interesting to note that the connections need not be long term, intense, or sustained in order to have a significant impact. Joanne talked about brief connections that she'd had that had been powerful. Reflecting on these recollections and their significance for her own practice and way of being in the world, she said,

I think that we tend to not to think of ourselves as having a great impact on others, but chances are we do. It's nice to think about that—that we have that opportunity to have that kind of significance in whatever journey others happen to be on.

Seeing Life Situations Differently

BECOMING AWARE OF THE STRUGGLE

Through receiving new information, being exposed to different perspectives, and having allies, girls and women become more aware of their situations and what is at stake for them. With evolving awareness they begin to see themselves and their situations differently and to question the way things are. Many experience a period of discomfort, conflict, or struggle. They distinguish this struggle from previous experiences when they felt they had no choice but to be uncomfortable. As they become more acquainted with themselves and their voices, they come to a realization: "I can't stay in this place of discomfort anymore." Sara described it this way:

Before I just accepted the pain. Before I wasn't aware that there could be something more comfortable. I think when you don't know something doesn't fit but it's all you know, it fits just fine. But as soon as you put something on that does fit properly, you realize, "Oh, that was really uncomfortable!"

Tory described how she became aware of her emotional struggles:

> I cannot put myself through that emotionally anymore.
> All of this energy that I've put into this and it's still come
> to nothing. I can't continue to fill that void all the time,
> whatever it is that I keep doing, I'm getting nowhere.

Joanne described a range of experiences that brought to mind a ticking clock or of walking slowly up a spiral staircase; each new experience shifted her vantage point and perspective. Over a number of years the array of new experiences and information enabled her to locate herself very differently in relation to her life situation. She had experiences of finding and losing allies that brought her new information and awareness, of reaching out and receiving help for her child, of going to classes with other women, of going back to school and learning that she had skills and abilities, of being with other women and learning that they didn't live in the way that she had had to live, of going into the workforce and being valued. She watched her teen children become aware "that this whole new exciting world was out there and it was open and there were all these things that you could do." Joanne recognized that she had never experienced that excitement and realized that she was in the midst of a struggle for her survival. She began to contemplate suicide and realized, "I will die if I stay here" and continue to try to live in the same way.

Tied to the growing awareness of the struggle, some women experience ill health or exhaustion, and they talk about "dis-integrating." The world as they know it is "falling to pieces" or they are "falling apart." Upon reflection, many women look back and see the significance of the disintegration process and the opportunity that the process created for them to re-create their identities. The following exchange between Meg and Laura illustrates such an experience:

Meg: It's almost like there's a "dis-integration" that happens at
different times, and to some extent the pre-voice place is a
disintegration. Things are falling apart as you have known
them to be. And then you find some place in yourself and
you see the world differently, you put things together
differently and therefore you walk in the world differently.

Laura: There's a Chinese character that is the same symbol for
crisis and opportunity. Sort of out of the ashes of one thing

grows something new. And it's because of that crisis that you have the opportunity to do that. So in some way I've sort of thought about that one, you know. Wouldn't I have liked the sort of regular, boring, ordinary type of normal life, and what would have happened? Would it have brought out certain things in me? Maybe it's better that it happened this way.

Meg: Yeah, when we're dis-integrating or in a space of disintegration, we're creating space for new things to grow and bloom which wouldn't be there otherwise. We have to be uncomfortable to want to move.

Being "uncomfortable" and more attuned to the struggles in their lives opens people up to seeing themselves and their situations in a different light. This signals a shift to being more attentive to and aware of the self and how the self was located in relation to others and what was at stake for the future of the self.

ASSESSING RISKS TO SELF AND OTHER

Becoming aware of the high stakes of staying silent is a significant shift for people who are silenced and voiceless. At some point they recognize that there are greater risks associated with keeping their silence than with using their voice. The risks include not being able to help others or make a positive difference in others' lives, children being damaged in some way, repeating unhealthy family patterns in a new generation, the continued absence of happiness in their lives, substance misuse, the loss of their principles and values, the loss of self-respect, the annihilation of their self, or death.

Jess assessed several risks of being silenced in relationships in her reflections about her mom's experience. Her mom had always been a vital encourager of Jess's voice and entitlement to speak and be heard and valued. However, Jess also sees clearly what has happened to her mom as a consequence of being silenced over many years and in multiple relationships and contexts, when being in a relationship was more important than being valued and supported. Jess recognizes the risks of her repeating these patterns because she has been in "tortured" interpersonal relationships herself. She sees that she's at risk of losing her sense of self, her passion for living, and the opportunity to make a contribution to the world. In talking about what happened to her mom and what she has learned from this, Jess says,

> I can see that she had a lot of passion that somehow got taken away through just being diminished in her relationships and then she couldn't get that back. Somehow the personal relationships took that out of her 'cause she got the wind taken out of her sails or something. So I think I've somewhat learned that I don't want to be silenced in my relationships. And I learned through my experience that it does take away your ability to then do what you are passionate about in the world.

Claire described what she came to understand was at risk for her if she stayed disconnected and voiceless about her experience as an Aboriginal person growing up in a white family:

> I met lots of Aboriginal adoptees and people who had been apprehended—like hundreds—and I met so many who I really related to and I saw them going down real self-destructive paths. And there was one woman in particular. I met her and I just thought she was fabulous, really enjoyed her company. And then we were at a party one night and I saw how she was when she drinks. And then I started seeing her more and more like that and thinking, "She's just like me. I'm looking at a mirror, and I don't want to go there because she's one step ahead of me on that ladder of self-destruction." And I don't want to go there. I really don't. I don't ever want to have those things [i.e., addictions] as part of my life. So it was more about avoiding something bad than it was about going towards something. It was seeing that that's the logical end of this pathway, and I don't like it, so I gotta do something different.

At this point in the journey to voice, women begin to be aware that the risks of not acting and of remaining silent outweigh the risks of acting and using their voices. Although they are not necessarily ready to use their voices and take action, some do begin to experiment with their voices and test the possibilities. They begin to shift from being aware of, concerned about, and feeling responsible for only the interests and well-being of others to having a glimmer of the self and what the self needs. They begin to be aware of both self and other and accord some importance to both.

Beginning to Question—Can I have my Own Truth?

The way in which I have presented the themes and threads that describe the process of experiencing, connecting, wondering, becoming aware, assessing risks, and preparing to act may suggest that it is a linear process. It is not. The image that I carry of the process is that of a river with slow-moving and fast-moving sections and many back eddies and whirlpools. For the most part, there is forward motion, and it would be difficult to turn back and swim upstream once one has jumped into the river of awareness. However, the back eddies and whirlpools characterize the swirling and blending experiences of women on the voice journey—having a new experience, wondering, questioning, assessing risks, and so on might all blend together and be difficult to differentiate.

This is particularly the case with the experience of "Beginning to Question." Here, women go beyond wondering and puzzling and begin to question themselves, their situations, and what they had thought to be the "truth." This questioning is illustrated by the following passages:

> I really questioned what I was doing with my life, and questioned my relationship and where my loyalties lie and what I was doing. (Gabby)

> I started to see that maybe I didn't need to do that...other people didn't live like that, maybe I didn't need to live like that. (Claire)

> When you're in a relationship that's with someone who's kind of manipulative or abusive or whatever, you start to justify things that don't really make sense to you. I just found that I didn't know. Well if I don't believe in that, if I don't believe in these principles and how women should be treated or whatever, what am I doing here? Like I'm somehow justifying all these bad things, then who am I? Where am I coming from? I just started to question all those things and I didn't know. (Sara)

Another characteristic of this process is that women become more likely to ask questions of others and stop simply accepting other people's versions of events, as Laura describes:

> Things that he said to me were making me really angry. I'd gotten to the angry stage about things and I started asking him questions like, "I noticed so and so is really loving with

his wife. Why don't you treat me like that?" He said, "Well you're not that kind of woman. You don't deserve that kind of treatment." I started to see that that was his problem, not mine. Again, there was a shift in my thinking.

Laura also described several instances when something happened to her and she expected her husband to respond with some concern and caring. But this wasn't his response:

> He started complaining that it was my fault he didn't come to help me and this was fairly typical. And in the past, I just would have felt bad, I would have felt, "Yeah, it was my fault," but I didn't. I thought, "Ugh, you jerk, you could have come to see if I was dead or not." It was funny, there were little things I started to notice. There was a shift in how I saw what he was saying and how I saw our relationship.

Claire described how she began to question herself, other people, and then systems when she discovered a new truth about her adoption:

> I definitely got just unbelievable rage and anger, and then I thought, "Well, what am I going to do about it? Am I just going to react, and be all raging angry? How am I going to address this, really? What is the truth that needs to be said here, and understood? Who is accountable? Who's going to be held accountable? Am I going to use my voice or not?"

Karen described the shift in her understanding about "truth," "the way things needed to be," and the significance that it had for her:

> I came from a very black and white childhood in that there was only one truth, and so finding out there's more than one truth was really helpful for me as well. Knowing that I could have my truth and it might be totally different than somebody else's. They look at the situation from a totally different perspective. It took me a lot of years to find that out, but that was a really important piece of information for me.

For many women the process of questioning and examining whether or not their situations have to stay the same, what other options exist, and how they could define their own truths is intertwined with their processes of discovering and defining self.

Defining the Self

DISCOVERING ENTITLEMENT TO HAVE VOICE

As the process of coming into voice unfolds, women begin to see and become acquainted with the self and realize that they have inherent value and rights, including the rights to have voice or choose to be silent. As Cassie observed of her transition, "I started to see that I had a right to breathe because people were telling me I did, and people were telling me I was an okay person."

When women are asked what is happening at this point in their journey, they often describe a growing awareness of self and the situation that they are living in, as Gabby describes:

> I had a feeling that I was holding back, that I was not
> fully able to participate, to relax, to enjoy, to embrace
> opportunities, sort of almost seeing myself out there. It was
> like I was looking out at the world but I wasn't in it yet, and
> I wanted to be more in it.

Some women describe an interesting twist to the concept of voice and voicing:

> For me, having the choice not to speak was huge. It was
> just as big as having the choice to speak, because I didn't
> think I had the right not to give out information about
> myself. And there were certain things that I did not want to
> share with people [such as abuse]. So I spent a lot of my life
> avoiding certain conversations and certain places, because
> I didn't want somebody to ask me a question that I'd have
> to give the answer to. So I can't even begin to tell you
> how much energy it took to constantly be trying to keep a
> secret, because I didn't think I was allowed to, and didn't
> want to live with the consequences of giving out any of that
> information. As soon as particular subjects came up, I had
> to find a way of vacating in case somebody asked me. So it
> was a lot of work. I didn't know how to tell people it was
> none of their bloody business. So for me choice and voice
> and being purposeful and being able to make that decision
> about when to speak and not to speak is such a huge part of
> my entitlement.

Another key element of coming into voice is that women define and claim their values and principles and limit the extent to which they are willing to take on responsibility for others. They spoke of opening themselves up to caring for themselves, not just others, and of taking personal responsibility for their future. They were starting to lift their heads up and see a bigger world of possibilities, opportunities, and relationships. The intention of their actions was to "protect" their emerging sense of self and give it a chance to grow without being shut down by others or re-submerged.

Jess described how she had lost her touchstone of values and principles in her intimate relationship and how this loss had made it difficult for her to assess what was right and wrong. She reflects on how important this touchstone is to her now and how she connects with other people who "live a principled life" as a way to receive reinforcement for following that path and not losing the connection to her self again:

> I'd lost that set of principles, which was where I was acting from before the relationship. I'd lost touch with what the bottom line was for me. And, when you're being treated in a certain way that is not okay, that doesn't fit with those, then you have a reference point. I've sort of just seen the value in that, in being grounded. Reminding myself of that and if something happens that's not right with me, or that doesn't sit right with me or a choice I have to make in my personal life, or whatever, that it's really about the larger picture, and that I have some kind of a reference point.

Women described how they had no boundaries around themselves and how they felt that they had to obey no matter what request was made of them. As they became more aware of their right to have voice, they were better able to create boundaries that distinguished themselves and their rights from those of others. They became aware that they could care for others as well as the self. This awareness of self and other, or self in relation to other, rather than focussing exclusively on the other, was experienced as very freeing. Karen had spent years trying to create a relationship with her mother that fit a certain image. She described learning new information in a psychology course on interpersonal relationships and becoming aware of what she was doing:

> I was really knocking myself out trying to have a good relationship with my mother, and it felt like I was the one

that was doing all the giving and wasn't getting much back you know and I had this conversation with the instructor and it was like those kind of "aha" moments. I saw better what I was doing in the relationship and how I had to change it some. I had to change how I was relating with her to some degree, but I also saw that there were some things here I just can't change. My mother is who she is and I am who I am and you know we can have a relationship, but it is not going to be what I'd like it to be ideally.

Suze described how, for many years, she felt very responsible for being "the Aboriginal voice" in situations where this vital perspective was missing. She was concerned about her community and she was a medium, as an Aboriginal woman, to bring the Aboriginal voice and perspective forward. This helped her in the journey to find her own voice:

Just starting to see myself as part of something, like a community that wasn't based on location, but in something else. My professor sort of said it was "finding my voice" but also writing myself into that larger dialogue. It shifted over time, because I got more comfortable. I stopped feeling so defensive. I think at first I was angry, like, "Why am I the only person saying something?" and then I started to just get used to it or something.

However, beyond "getting used to it," Suze also described a process of clarifying her personal boundaries and learning how to select what she said and in what contexts so that she could care for her self. When she first started to test her voice, she took on responsibility for being a medium through which the Aboriginal perspective was communicated and shared with others. Over time she has realized that "I'm not just a bridge, and I'm not just a tool." She is a talented and skilled person who can make choices about what she speaks about, and when and to whom, so that she can continue to care for and honour her self while also making a difference in her community.

Women described a variety of ways in which they became aware of their responsibility to either get out of or make something of their situation. Kate described becoming aware of what she needed to do for herself and her children:

[I recognized] that I was the only person that was really holding me back.... Being able to sort of understand it and take it apart afterwards, you know, was, well, that's a lifelong thing that I'm never quite done with. But recognizing that it was me that needed to make the shift there, it wasn't that I needed other people to do anything differently, or I couldn't rely on anybody, that it wasn't about other people.

The rest of the world wasn't going to change, so whatever it was, the barriers that I was thinking existed that prevented me from being able to step forward and be strong and say what I needed to say, do what I needed to do, they were artificial in some cases, because I perceived them to be there. And if they were real emotional barriers, then they were going to be there constantly unless I was prepared to dismantle them. So I needed to do it myself. I couldn't rely on being re-parented or having another childhood that was a more solid one or whatever. I had to take control.

Claire described her awareness that the experience of many Aboriginal adoptees was similar or far worse than her own. She had been fortunate to have a loving, caring adoptive family that gave her many powerful and important messages about her worth and value as a human being and her capacity to do and be whatever she wanted to do and be. Despite this, she had experienced confusion and doubt about herself and her place in the world and recognized this in other Aboriginal adoptees. She took on personal responsibility:

...and just in that year, I realized that I have something to say that needs to be said, and I think that I'm somebody who can say it so that it can be heard, and so that I can help mediate cultures, build a bridge, form foundations that somebody might be able to build a bridge over top of, those kinds of things. I was thinking about planting seeds as opposed to conquering nations, but I had the conquering nations in mind, but I knew the seeds had to be planted first.

Emotional and spiritual self-care often becomes more significant to women at this point in their voice journey. For example, Suze began to open up to her spiritual and emotional self and value her inner voice and consciousness:

I got sent to see a woman who's like a traditional healer, an Aboriginal woman. And she said, "You don't have to tell me anything…you don't have to tell me your story." She said, "I'm sure you've told it many times to other people. You tell it to yourself all the time, you know what your issue is, your problem, you talk yourself through, why, why aren't you doing. That's not the level that change happens on. It's at a deeper, spiritual, or emotional level that change has to happen." So the stuff we did together was not at all about talking. It was at a different level.

FINDING A PLACE TO SPEAK FROM

In speaking about the theme of finding a place to speak from, another dimension is added to the earlier image of floating down the river of emerging awareness and consciousness. Here the women find a place to stand, they gain their footing on a rock or on the bank of the river—they "locate" or situate themselves for a while. It is here and at this time that they integrate or re-integrate their sense of self and their sense of self in relation to others. This is a powerful shift in terms of finding voice, defining voice, and connecting to a sense of purpose. To refer again to the metaphor of the river, women have their feet on the ground and can see where they have come from and where they might be going, and they are beginning to gain a sense of confidence about their journey. There is a connection between self, voice, and purpose, or meaning, in relation to the larger context.

In conversations with Corinna, she described how her journey into voice really began when she "found a place to speak from" as an Aboriginal woman. Since then she has circled around the notion of identity and of finding a place to speak from. She described a continual process of re-locating herself and re-forming her identity:

> I think you always remake the place you're speaking from. The other day I was saying to my best friend, "I'm having an identity crisis again!" Like I go through times of thinking, "What am I doing? I'm not acting like myself. I'm doing these silly things that don't make sense to me intellectually." But that's just part of growth. I know that this is necessary in order to come back to something that's truer or whatever.

When Jess has had a sense of where she stands, her voice has been more accessible to her and stronger. When she has lost her footing and the "ground" of her principles, it has been more difficult for her to locate her voice.

Many women describe the relationship of voice to contexts and where we "locate ourselves" as we speak. They note the challenges of speaking about certain topics in certain contexts, such as speaking within Aboriginal or multi-cultural communities about issues that are uncomfortable to talk about, such as violence, sexual exploitation, substance misuse, and intergenerational abuse.

Working Around the Edges of Voice

PRACTICING AND EXPERIMENTING WITH VOICE

As women's connection to voice and self evolves, many women describe experiences that suggest that they are working around the edges of voice. As they become clearer about the need for change and their need to use their voices, they begin to consider how they would bring this about: what would they need to do in order to make it happen? These women are preparing mentally and physically for action and, in some cases, "convincing" themselves that they can do it and will make it.

The power of relationships once again shows up as women reach out to others for guidance, support, and encouragement. Tanya describes how she and her mom "practice" on each other as they are preparing to use their voice in new or different contexts, and when they are being silenced in one context they test their voices out with each other:

> How we assert ourselves with each other has always had a
> relationship to our other relationships. If I'm being silenced
> in my relationship, I'm really outspoken with my mom
> because that's a safe place. And she says the same thing.
> She says, "I'm putting a boundary." Like the other night
> I wanted to go to her house and she said, "I'm going to go
> to bed early, and I'm putting my foot down with you, but
> I know that I'm doing that as practice for putting my foot
> down at work."

Laura described how she practiced with her voice by writing university papers on topics that mattered to her once she'd located her self as an Aboriginal adoptee:

I was a C+/B- student before that. Then I became an
A student, because I had something to say. I would go to
class, they would say, "I want you to write a paper on this,"
and I would say, "Well, you know what? I'd like my topic to
be this, can I?" I wrote papers, I exercised making a voice by
writing papers and through my study.

Many years later, Laura is once again experimenting with her voice as she creates a relationship with her birth mother and tries to find her voice in the midst of a very complex situation.

Karen experimented with and tested her voice in new contexts, and through this became more acquainted with it and built some confidence in her ability to contribute to conversations and have something meaningful to offer. She described an experience as a member of a community board that worked on issues that were very connected to her experience as a marginalized woman. She tested her voice with the other women and learned that her voice and life experience (her self) was valued in some contexts:

When we talked about the issues and how we needed to
deal with things I often would feel at a fairly deep emotional
level. Everything was by consensus of course, any decisions.
And I remember this one particular time, I don't even know
what we were deciding on, and I just said, "It doesn't feel
right to me." And they said, "What is it?" And I said, "I
have no idea. All I know is my gut is twisting. It just doesn't
feel right to me, but I can't tell you why." And they said,
"Well fine. Until your tummy's okay we're not moving on
this." And we talked a lot and finally I was able to figure
out what it was that didn't sit right with me by talking it
through and everybody said, "Okay! Totally valid, totally
valid." Because I wasn't working from a brain place, I was
working from an emotional place, and they knew that and
they honoured that. They'd often say, "So how are you
feeling about this, Karen?" I wasn't always able to articulate.
But what I think was amazing was I had the confidence
when they said "We're not going to move until you can get
voice around this. We will wait," that I said, "Okay." You
know in the past I wouldn't have. I would've said, "Oh, I'm
being stupid."

Another dimension of working around the edges of voice and voicing was the shift that many women make from being "angry," "reactive," or "outspoken" to "having voice" or being "strategic" with their voices. Several women experimented with speaking and being outspoken in educational settings, and this enabled them to learn things about their voices and the impact that they could have:

> The reaction of how people accepted my words and interpreted them and held on to them and experienced them was so powerful for me. A dialogue was created, and it brought us to these new levels, and it brought me to new levels of understanding.

Through the process of experimentation and testing and reflecting on experiences, women have moments of realizing that their voices can make a difference.

WORKING THROUGH A LONG PROCESS

Women engaged in a journey from silence to voice often describe experiences of moving in and out of awareness about their voice and self, and that "coming to voice" is a long process for them that is still not over.

Tanya's story of moving in and out of voice over her adolescence and young adulthood, and in different contexts, captures well the fluidity and elusiveness of voice. Her story of not finding voice in the midst of her relationship with an abusive partner was particularly moving because her questions about why she couldn't find voice—why she didn't use voice, why she gave up her self and what mattered to her, what it was that kept her there when she knew that it was not healthy or right—describes that in-between place of knowing but not knowing, of knowing that something is terribly wrong, but not knowing how to get out of it. Being stuck but also aware enough to know that one is stuck and struggling.

Women's experiences of coming into voice and sense of self illustrates how—once we have a new scene before us—we cannot pretend that it does not exist. We may try to shift our gaze away from that which is coming into view, but it does now exist in our consciousness. Our existence and our experience are now mediated by our knowledge. To ignore what we have come to know is a conscious decision to suppress the self. As the next section describes, none of the women were willing to make that sacrifice any longer.

CROSSING THE LINE INTO VOICE

Amongst the women who have participated in my research, there is considerable diversity in their experiences of crossing the line into voice. However, there are also a number of connecting threads. One thread that connects experiences is that women are often engaged in a process, over years, of experiencing, reflecting, wondering, inquiring, and questioning about themselves, their voices, and their circumstances. These processes increase their awareness, sense of self, and, ultimately, their consciousness. As Tory said, "Well there's no going back, right? If you go back that's a conscious decision to suppress ourselves." After becoming conscious of voice, the women were less likely to question their voice, self, mind, or decisions.

The intellect is very much engaged in these processes. As people describe their movement from silence to voice, their language shifts from "I don't know" to "I thought," "I knew," "I got it," "It was in my mind," "I was clear in my mind," "I realized," and "I decided." They achieve a level of awareness about who they are (a sense of self), what is going on, what is at stake, and what is possible. They see things that they hadn't noticed before or that they had thought they just needed to accept, and they consciously realize that they can bring about change. Most are not clear at the outset how they will operationalize this understanding and resolve it, but they know they can do it and that they have to do it.

Taking Action

For most women, coming to this place of understanding and validating their voice does not immediately translate into "speaking out"; the voice that they have achieved is primarily a clear internal voice and a resolution to attend to it and honour it through their actions. They know that they need to act, although it is not necessarily clear what they need to do, how to do it, or when to do it. This can be a time of confusion and anxiety, as they try to work out the details. However, they plunge into the river and keep moving forward, taking action.

Claire described how she "didn't know how to say it, or when to say it…or what to say," but she knew that she needed to do something. Over time, she created a vision, with her birth mother, about how she wanted to tell others about the circumstances of her adoption and what she wanted to achieve, and since then she has started to take action and connect with others to bring this vision to life.

When Kate became clear that she needed to end her marriage and reclaim her self, she "vacated" her old position and began to create a new role and way of being. It took more than a year to finally separate from her husband, but throughout this time she was taking action on practical matters, establishing herself in a career, becoming more financially stable, and planning for what she had hoped would be an amicable separation. In addition to managing the practical aspects of the separation, she was also taking action to assure her family and friends that she could cope and would not be dependent on them for support. The effect of this was that she took action with her self; she convinced her self that she could make it through:

> So I was very anxious that people knew that this was going to be very different for me, but I don't know that I really believed it. I knew that I was going to have to do some persuading of myself and others that this was going to be okay. So I think in doing that it had the effect of preparing me mentally for it, so I was rehearsing for a year. I mean I don't think I ever really thought of that until this moment, but that's kind of how that worked.

> I just, I had *no* idea, really, how it was all going to work out. I was worried and very anxious about how it was all going to all fall into place, or not fall into place, but I just tried to convince myself that it would be okay. So, that was what got me through. I just did a sell job on my self. I was busy doing that for other people, so it was just, like, "Okay, let's keep going on this!"

Many women read literature, poetry, magazine articles, and books as means to gather new information and perspectives and to help themselves either in recovery, reclamation, or discovery. Joanne described the impact of taking this action: "C. S. Lewis said, 'We read to know we are not alone,' and reading for me was quite pivotal in that...I'm not crazy, other people are feeling that too."

ACHIEVING ALIGNMENT—VOICE AND SELF

As women choose voice and self, they create a space through which to come into their lives again or to do so more fully, with more intention and mindfulness. They often experience intense physical and emotional sensations. Some of these sensations feel positive: "being able to breathe again," "relief flooding over," being relieved of the "weight of the world," finding pleasure and joy in living again. Others are difficult: "reliving the years of abuse," and questioning what had happened to them and how it had happened, trying to recover their health and abilities, grieving their losses and experiencing tremendous sadness. Many women experience both extremes of sensation: they are relieved and they also need to grieve. Claire was both thrilled to find her birth family and devastated when she discovered the circumstances of her placement. She was clear in her self that she needed to find her voice, but she still needed to wade through intense feelings to discover how she would bring her voice out in the world. She describes the grieving process that she needed to go through in the following passage:

> I cried for three days straight after connecting with my birth family. [What triggered it was] being caught in the middle of two families, both of whom had been deceived. I cried for my parents being deceived and raising me all this time and thinking they were doing something good and beautiful and wonderful. Crying for my birth mother for having her baby stolen from her. Crying for the outrage that this government would allow something, this government, this country, this state would allow something like this to happen. Crying for the fact that they never searched for me for the 13 years that I've been searching for them. Crying for the fact that I had been beaten up before I was even born. Crying for the fact that I came from a place where that could exist.

Many women go through periods of questioning themselves and how they came to the place of being voiceless and silenced—where did they go? They wondered if they might lose their voice again and go back into voicelessness or selflessness in the same or other contexts. Karen discussed this:

> I went through about a year or two where I almost relived my whole life, but seeing it from this different view, right? I thought, "What an idiot. Why didn't you..." you know what I mean? I had to go through this whole process all

over again and I just spent a lot of time crying and, and being upset.

Two years ago when I changed my life and I moved back here, my body stopped functioning very well. It was like my emotional and mental world, my body also decided to match that and I lost tons of weight, and I just cried all the time and I felt sick to my stomach for a while. And then it was a process of coming back to life. I remember sitting by the water and reading this beautiful literature and there was one sentence that was so beautiful, and then this otter came out of the bush and went into the water. It was just like this picture-perfect sort of thing, and I felt this bubbling up of emotion and started crying. I wasn't sad or I wasn't thinking of anything bad, it was just like this bubbling up of living again. But I had to go through that, like, total dysfunction in order to, like, let myself really be in that place, in order to come to, to come back to life. It was like, just a big release or something, like "Okay! I'm here now." You know, somehow I'd shut things down enough to cope in that situation and then this process of coming back to life.

EMERGENCE AND CONGRUENCE

Women who have come into voice often share experiences of emerging more fully into themselves, of having a sense of possibilities and purpose, and of liking what they see. They describe "dis-integrating" their old ways of being and of creating space to "reintegrate" a new self. They describe "rising out of the ashes" and reclaiming their health, rights, identity, and self.

Meg recalled an image that she carried with her after she had reached her "no turning back point" and as she was in the midst of taking action and making the preparations for her future. Her description of the image illustrates the shift in how she saw her self and what she was capable of achieving:

I was with a teacher at my children's school and we were in the annex which was being renovated at the time. And we'd just gone up to look and see what progress they were making, and there were these huge beams and the enormous ceiling, the rafters, and we were up there and talking about what I was going to have to do through the separation, and this friend of mine who'd already gone through the process was really saying, "You know it sounds to me like you've reached that point and it sounds really clear and what's going to help you to do that? What are you going to attach yourself to?"

And I don't know what it was about the space that we were in, but everything was crystal clear for me at that moment. It was the image of an eagle…it's there but you're holding onto it…it's got to be freed. The image of an eagle flying. I had a pair of earrings, carved eagle earrings, and I remember I'd put them on and, I'd think "Okay, there we go! I'm going to stick with that."

And the light coming into the annex at the time, and something about the size of those beams and strength. I don't know what it was, but things came together. It was a powerful moment for me. So that was good, to be able to replay that one. [The] image of being able to soar above and rise above all that—that whole sense of being strong and competent and able to detach.

EVOLVING VOICE

The experience of coming to voice and bringing about significant change in their lives in one context does not mean that the "switch was flipped" and that women are able to claim or have voice in all other contexts, or even that it always remains true and confident in the initial voicing context. Returning to the image of the women's journey down the river, sometimes they experience times when they relax in the sunshine on the banks of the river, and at other times they plunge deep into the torrents again. However, they are never in the same place again and are constantly evolving.

The experience of coming into voice is also a process of coming into the self and into a heightened state of awareness and consciousness. Women describe how they have "reclaimed" or "recovered" or "discovered" the self in ways that had not been possible before they attended to and honoured their voices, and how they are better able to hold in balance both the interests of the self and the interests of others, including the people that they care about and people in their broader communities. They are both independent and closely connected; there is "self" and "relationship." They speak of being "more authentic," and "more my true self." They speak of "growing," "emerging," and being more proactive, open, and receptive to experiences and opportunities. As they describe who they are now, in contrast to who they were before they claimed voice and self, they use words and phrases that convey more energy, engagement (with self and others), clarity, and authenticity: "I think," "I feel," "I am aware," "I am passionate," "I am clear," "I am congruent in my self," "There's no pretending." Suze and Gabby comment:

> It's made me more myself. It's like being boiled down to your essence. I feel like I'm more my true self than I ever have been, and my voice is more authentic. I have better control of my voice. I can exercise my voice in ways that are more useful, purposeful, clearer, stronger. I can use less words to say more things, so it's richer. It's a richer voice. (Suze)

> I sort of think about a visual representation. It's sort of a small person that was backed into a corner, whereas now I'm comfortable in my own skin and able to hold my own and not apologize for my existence. So a real being able to move into my body and mind and fully engage in activities, and things that I want to [do], ways of thinking, without that being controlled or punished. The sense that in some way I'm doing what I like to do, or thinking the way I like to think, speaking how I like to speak. So huge. (Gabby)

Women describe how they have become more attuned to their inner voices. They have noticed that the self-critical inner "chatter" that they have listened and responded to in the past are often voices transplanted from other people, such as their parents and partners. When they go beyond these voices and discover and begin to listen to their own inner voices, they can be more authentic and true to self. The challenge is to "not put my inner voice down anymore. To listen to it. To let that voice be stronger than those other self-critical voices!"

Laura described how her inner voice and sense of self are intertwined:

> My voice is integral to my sense of self, clearly. I can't have one without the other, in both directions. I can't. Even if that voice is just to myself, it needs to be present. Could I be a whole person with my sense of self and a voice without a voice? No, I still need that voice to myself.

It brings everything that's back here, and brings it up front here, and makes it real. That's it. If I don't voice the thoughts in my head and bring them forward and front and centre, how can I manifest them? It's thoughts, paying attention to thoughts, right through to action, it's all connected.

It's actually consciously bringing the thoughts that happen way in the back, bottom, and giving them space and room to grow to come forward, and sometimes reaching back and pulling them out, and making them manifest. I think I'd be an empty shell without it.

Some women carry images of themselves and their connections in the world, and these images serve to encourage them and remind them of their strength and resilience. Jess's image illustrates how she locates herself contextually and in time—with connections to her past and to her future:

A lot of things that I speak about are so intimately connected with my heritage and my sense of community, and my role in that community. Because my family's from this island I think that I feel, I have this belief in having a purpose and being, not guided necessarily, but all around me are things that my family's been connected to for a long time, and that gives me a place—a sense of rootedness. If I need reassurance about anything, I just have to go to the water. There's that sound of the pebbles being pulled back into the water, and as long as that sound is being made, everything is okay. That sound has existed here on this island for longer than I can imagine, and it will continue on long after we're gone. And, that is a meeting place, and I see myself in that place because of my role of being mixed race. A lot of the issues that I speak up about I'm trying to be a bridge.

Many women describe how they are better able to sustain their voices, stand their ground, and be safe in the face of pressures and challenges to their voices, and also of how they have shifted the terms or nature of significant relationships over time. They are more sure of their voices and perspectives and "what I know." While they note the risks that they still face in losing their voices in certain contexts or having their voices challenged, there is an underlying sense of confidence that they are sufficiently aware of who they are, what they stand for, and what they are capable of that they will never again go as deep down into voicelessness and silence.

Connected to this sense of confidence is a sense of emotional and personal safety. Having come far enough along their journeys, they know they are not at risk of "going back in" to that place of silence or abuse, although they recognize that they may still circle around or move in and out of voice and silence from time to time.

Many shifts take place in relationships as women discover their voice and self. The relationships that many women have with their children, and with daughters in particular, evolve and are enriched because they are now stronger, healthier, happier, and more connected women and mothers than they were when they were in the midst of unhealthy situations.

Voice and Growth

My conversations with women about voice, silence, and self have been uplifting and inspiring, and it is fitting that this section ends with statements shared by many women, statements that capture the consciousness, courage, strength, spirit, and continued growth each woman manifests as she claims her voice, self, and mind:

> The threat to my voice and self is still out there, but I am
> a different person now and I see both the threats and a
> transformed self; I am conscious of the whole, not just
> the parts. I recognize my capacity to triumph over this
> new situation and continue the never-ending process of
> discovery. I am not alone in my experience of this process or
> in having gained this capacity.
>
> I can build my self up again to be resilient.
> I've come a million miles from where I was.
> I am well shored up.
> It makes you stronger within your self...this is who I am,
> and this is the way that it is, and this is what I want.
> I think our voices strengthen each other's voices.

IMPLICATIONS FOR CHILD AND YOUTH CARE PRACTICE

Opportunities and Engagement

New and different experiences, alliances, and relationships enable women to see and experience the world differently. By having new opportunities for different experiences and relationships, space is created for girls and women to discover new ways to integrate new beliefs, values, and perspectives that enable them to claim self and voice.

As Child and Youth Care workers, we need to consider how we bring ourselves into relationship with the people that we serve and how we support opportunities for girls and women to experience healthy relationships, new information, new opportunities, and a sense of belonging and affirmation.

A practical application of this learning is The Listening Partners Project (Belenky, Bond, & Weinstock, 1997). The project has illustrated the interactive power of relationships, social supports, and guided dialogue to contribute to growth of voice and mind, including the elements of confidence, motivation, reflective thinking, and collaborative problem solving (p. 74). A fundamental assumption of the model is

> that individuals' epistemologies or ways of knowing provide
> a framework for imagining the nature of relationships
> with others, including friends and children. A person's
> vision of the nature, role, and function of her relationships
> will simultaneously shape and be shaped by her own
> epistemological outlook and the interactions themselves.
> The Listening Partners Project was designed with the
> premise that these connections evolve in a dynamic
> and bi-directional way; that is, a woman's emerging
> epistemological outlooks encourage her to consider her
> relationships in more generative ways while her experiences
> relating with others in contexts of greater reciprocity and
> mutuality contribute to nurturing new epistemological
> perspectives. (pp. 74–75)

The learning of the Listening Partners Project and of my research challenge the typical efforts of "giving people voice," such as inviting people to "speak out" and "be heard" in meetings, focus groups, and other gatherings on selected topics. These approaches might create time for women's voices to be heard, but do not necessarily provide opportunity. Carol Gilligan noted that women involved in her research often spoke in terms suggesting that what they said was dissociated from who they were (e.g., "If I were to speak for myself"). About her research, in which confidentiality was assured, Gilligan (1993) writes,

> many women in fact did know what they wanted to do and
> also what they thought would be the best thing to do in
> what often were painful and difficult situations. But many
> women feared that others would condemn or hurt them if

they spoke, that others would not listen or understand, that speaking would only lead to further confusion, that it was better to appear "selfless" to give up their voices and keep the peace. (p. x)

What this suggests is that forums in which women are expected to "speak out" may be experienced as intimidating and risky, and whatever emerges in these contexts may be more attuned to "keeping the peace" than "telling the truth." Therefore, if we are to tap into and connect with the power that girls and women have to effect change, in their personal and familial contexts as well as in their community contexts, we need to consider alternative, relationship-based ways to support and create opportunities that allow for the emergence of self and authentic voice.

Knowledge, Skill, and Authenticity in Practice

Paulo Freire (1982) suggests that the ontological mission of each of us as a human being "is to be a subject who acts upon and transforms his world, and in so doing moves towards ever new possibilities of a fuller and richer life individually and collectively" (p. 12). Although attracted to the notion that each of us has a transformative mission, I am aware of the complex and multi-faceted nature of voice, self, consciousness, and action. How is the space created in which people can manifest their purpose? When the stakes are high, when the risk of harm or loss is huge, then what? What role does voice have in this equation, and what can having voice look like? What can I as practitioner do to create opportunity for the expression of voice? What are the strategies and tools for creating the dialogical encounter that facilitates people's reflection, acquisition of understanding, and, ultimately, the genuine expression of voice? I am curious about what knowledge, skills, and attributes I can bring into my practice that will support the conditions in which each of us can manifest our mission.

FAMILY TALK

We must consider the impact of the messages that children receive within their families—about themselves, their capacities and roles, and the rules to live by (Belenky, Clinchy et al., 1986/1997; Ungar, 2004). The messages received within the family are carried into adulthood and influence how individuals construct themselves, their relationships, and their perspectives on authority and expertise. One-way talk, inequality in parental communications, and discouraged questioning all contribute to the silencing of children's sense of self, mind and voice. Mutuality in communication, listening and dialogue, and respect for emerging ideas all contribute to a growing sense of self and voice. It is these lessons, learned in families, neighbourhoods, schools, and workplaces, that impact the development of self-confidence and sense of intellectual capacity (Belenky, Clinchy et al., 1986/1997).

The cyclical nature of family talk is also an important consideration for practice. Mothers who have a limited sense of self and voice are not in a position to create environments for their children in which self and voice can emerge, and thus a perpetuating cycle of silencing occurs (Belenky, Bond, & Weinstock, 1997). The influence of the early years is of particular significance to me as a practitioner in the field of Child and Youth Care. I question the effectiveness of programs and services that aim to tell marginally functioning parents how to be better parents, or protective care systems that engage in processes that perpetuate the silencing of both parental and child voices. Such systems reaffirm the voices of authority and do not serve to engage people in coming to know, inquire about, and become connected to self and others in healthier ways.

In my own practice, I have shifted my orientation from residual areas of practice (e.g., child protection services) to "wellness practices" (Bellefeuille & Charlesworth, 2004), including working within community contexts to introduce the notions of asset building to parents, neighbours, coaches, educators, police officers, and others who are or could be in relationships with young people (Benson, 1997). The attractiveness of this approach is that it validates what most people know at some level about what makes a difference (i.e., it draws on lived experience, and no expert is telling individuals how they should think and be), and it aims to create meaningful relationships between adults and children such that young people receive messages of being valued.

DIALOGUE

> Every human being, no matter how "ignorant" or submerged in the "culture of silence" he may be, is capable of looking critically at the world in a dialogical encounter with others. Provided with the proper tools for such encounter, he can gradually perceive his personal and social reality as well as the contradictions in it, become conscious

of his own perception of that reality and deal critically with it. (Freire, 1982, p. 13)

The way we can change our perspective happens through dialogue...if someone says something to me and they say something that's different a few days later, it might not be contradictory...through conversation they've changed their perspective or whatever.... That process happens for my self, having a conversation with my self...that's how my voice changes and how I understand my self. (Jess)

Both Paulo Freire and Jess recognize what an increasing number of leaders and social thinkers are coming to understand: conversation and dialogue are powerful means to create opportunities for individual and collective understanding and growth (Belenky, Bond & Weinstock, 1997; Kofman & Senge, 1995; Tarule, 1996; Wheatley, 1999). For women in particular, it is through conversation and dialogue that "the roots of their thinking are nourished...and...they apprehend new understanding and reinterpret their thinking and their ideas" (Tarule, 1996, p. 285). In my own practice I have become acutely aware of what I do and what I am a part of that either encourages or discourages conversation and dialogue. My aim is to do more of the former than the latter. Dialogue happens in the context of relationships, and a certain measure of trust is necessary for people to participate fully in a dialogic encounter. In my practice as a community facilitator, I ask myself what am I doing with others that creates safer places within which conversation and dialogue may occur. This requires attentiveness to myriad details, including physical environments, the ways in which I acknowledge and connect with each individual, group sizes, and so on; but while this attentiveness is intentional, it is not manipulative. Underlying these efforts is an authentic belief in the power of relationship and dialogue as means by which people are able to achieve ever higher levels of connectedness, purpose, and capacity for contributing.

Dialogue implies reciprocity and mutuality, wherein there is both speaking and listening. In my practice I ask my self, what am I doing to model this reciprocity? Mary Belenky and her colleagues (1997) make this observation:

The practice that most sets homeplace founders apart from traditional leaders has to do with the balance the homeplace women establish between speaking and listening.... The homeplace women are all highly articulate

> leaders—indeed most are extraordinarily gifted storytellers
> and spokespersons. Even so, when [they] talk about their
> own leadership styles they invariably emphasize listening
> at least as much as speaking.... [They] see themselves as the
> kind of leader who draws out the voices of people so that
> they might speak for themselves. (p. 266)

These observations illustrate the need for a different form or approach to leadership than is typical in Western society: one that "draws out" rather than tells girls and women what to think, feel, and be. It speaks to the need for more "discourse or interpretive communities" as described by Jill Tarule (1996, p. 286), and more courage to "invite disruption, disturbance or dissolution of the status quo [by supporting] the strengths, intelligence, resilience and knowledge" of girls and women (Taylor, Gilligan, & Sullivan, 1995, p. 203).

As described at the outset of this chapter, voice is a concept, a strategy, and an outcome. Effective Child and Youth Care practitioners, working in relational ways, are constantly and mindfully working in the domains of voice with the people that they serve. To illustrate, I will re-tell the practice story that was shared at the beginning of this chapter.

Practice Story

Ellen and I are making dinner together in the care home. The other residents are in the living room playing cards and the moment is quiet and safe. I remind Ellen that there is a case conference for her tomorrow. I begin to describe for her what the scene might look like—who will be there, what roles people will play, what might be discussed. We talk about this and play a game of guessing who will say what. I note that she will be asked for her views on how she is doing and what she needs, and I ask her what she would like people to know about her. My intention here is to create an opportunity in advance of the case conference for her to explore her sense of how she is doing and what she hopes for and needs from the adults and care systems that are in her life. I want to affirm her capacity for knowing what matters to her and create a space for her to experiment with her voice. Ellen doubts her value and worth and frequently discounts her thoughts and perspectives, with statements such as "What would I know?" "I don't know." "It doesn't matter." However, in these moments in the kitchen, she begins to share some of her thoughts. I listen. I ask questions. I pose possibilities for her to respond to. I suggest we write some things down after dinner so that she'll have something to refer to tomorrow.

As we move from preparing the salad to setting the table for dinner, I inquire about how she would like me to be in the meeting—where would she like me to sit, what would she like me to say, how could I support her in sharing her views? I let her know what I would like to say and we discuss how this fits for her. She is surprised that I believe that she has many strengths, and that I appreciate the way in which her aunt wants to be involved. I let her know that I am nervous about the conference and that I will probably struggle at times as I am so new to the team. We talk about ways to move through our anxiety and share our views, and we agree to signal the other if we need help.

I am under no illusion that either Ellen or I will miraculously find our voice in the conference and become articulate, passionate, and decisive, but we have learned more about each other, and we are both more conscious of our own thoughts and voice. We are on the journey.

The next morning, ten of us file into the meeting room. I bring up the rear with Ellen. Around the table is the guardianship worker from government's child protection service, the psychologist who has met with Ellen a few times, someone from the school, my team leader, Ellen's aunt (who is the one family member that has stayed connected with her), the outreach worker that has known Ellen the longest, and a few others that I don't even know. The coordinator calls the case conference to order and we proceed to discuss parts of Ellen's life—how she is doing in school, what the psychologist thinks, what has taken place in the care home and so on. Several times the coordinator asks Ellen a question or inquires about her views on what's been said. Each time Ellen looks down at her notes and in a barely audible voice, begins to tell the group what is working and not working for her at school and at home and what she would like. Several times she pauses and signals me for help. Inspired by her courage, I share some of my views, as does her aunt. I notice that the pace of the conversation shifts and slows down to create space and time for Ellen and her aunt to speak. The others are listening.

REFERENCES

Belenky, M. F., Bond, L. A., & Weinstock, J. S. (1997). *A tradition that has no name: Nurturing the development of people, families, and communities.* New York: Basic Books.

Belenky, M. F., Clinchy, B. M., Goldberger, N. R., & Tarule, J. M. (1997). *Women's ways of knowing: The development of self, voice, and mind.* New York: Basic Books. (Original work published in 1986)

Bellefeuille, G., & Charlesworth, J. (2004). Canadian social welfare policy: Toward community-based social wellness. *Social Development Issues: Alternative Approaches to Global Human Needs, 26*(2/3), 90–108.

Benson, P. (1997). *All kids are our kids: What communities must do to raise caring and responsible children and adolescents.* San Francsico: Jossey-Bass.

Freire, P. (1982). *Pedagogy of the oppressed.* New York: Continuum.

Gilligan, C. (1993). *In a different voice: Psychological theory and women's development* (2nd ed.). Cambridge, MA: Harvard University Press.

Kofman, F., & Senge, P. (1995). Communities of commitment: The heart of learning organizations. In S. Chawla & J. Renesch (Eds.), *Learning organizations: Developing cultures for tomorrow's workplace* (pp. 14–43). Portland, OR: Productivity Press.

Tarule, J. M. (1996). Voices in dialogue: Collaborative ways of knowing. In N. Goldberger, J. M. Tarule, B. M. Clinchy, & M. F. Belenky (Eds.), *Knowledge, difference, and power: Essays inspired by women's ways of knowing* (pp. 274–304). New York: Basic Books.

Taylor, J. M., Gilligan, C., & Sullivan, A. M. (1995). *Between voice and silence.* Cambridge, MA: Harvard University Press.

Ungar, M. (2004). *Nurturing hidden resilience.* Toronto, ON: University of Toronto Press.

Wheatley, M. J. (1999). *Leadership and the new science: Discovering order in a chaotic world.* San Francisco: Berrett-Koehler Publishers.

CHAPTER 9

Experiencing Differences

The Challenges, Opportunities, and Cautions

Marie Hoskins, PhD, and Frances Ricks, PhD

ABSTRACT

Child and Youth Care practitioners are often challenged by the differences they encounter in their work: differences in attitudes, traditions, habits, in the emergent self, and differences embedded in local and global changes. This chapter offers ways to consider what makes some differences more challenging than others. It also proposes an approach to deal with differences that are experienced as menacing and that threaten practitioners' sense of themselves and may immobilize them. We propose a reflective strategy for expanding our limited perceptions of, and values relative to, others with whom we work and those we serve.

INTRODUCTION

Differences are those determinations of mind that make something distinguishable in nature, form, or quality from another. They emerge through the everyday interpretations of experiences of others (Jack is hard working and John is not) and all aspects of the world that people encounter (roses are beautiful and pansies are cute) as they carry out their daily agendas at home and work.

The occurrence of difference depends entirely on whether or not, and how, people *see* it, whether they *pay attention to it*, and whether they are *motivated to do anything about it*. Individuals cannot deal with difference unless they perceive difference, and they cannot come to terms with difference unless they are willing to own that the difference exists because of personal, internal calibrations of what those individuals believe to be true. Many differences are *marginal*. People pay little attention to marginal differences because these types are barely noticeable—for example, hair colour, height and weight, or the use of verbal expressions such as *awesome*.

Other differences are *magnificent*. In this case, what is encountered is romanticized and made precious when people are not close enough to know and understand the more subtle, or not so subtle, troublesome differences embedded in what they are experiencing. Such instances may pertain to conditions for young children in distant lands who exhibit exotic clothing and dances, the experiences of foster care for a child uprooted from a traumatizing and life-threatening family, or the social and emotional changes encountered when one chooses to change gender.

The more challenging kind of differences are those that are *menacing*. Menacing differences challenge how people think the world should be, what they think they know or, more importantly, who they are. When dealing with menacing differences the stakes are high because reality is not as it appears, and people have to examine what is personally at stake if they are to come to terms with and live more creatively with the difference that has challenged them. Adversarial or bullying behaviours in others (enemy stances), for example, are rooted in making a progressively bigger and bigger deal out of differing points of view about how things should be. One or more people make "the difference" into a problem that results in a conflict that one must win at the other's expense. Conflicts might take the form of determining who to hire, which family to serve, or what disciplinary action to take, if any.

Coming to Terms With Differences

The challenge of coming to terms with differences requires up-front clarity about the desired end result. What is the value in coming to terms with differences? What are we trying to achieve? What is driving our need to accommodate some of the differences in current times?

First, as the world increasingly becomes a global village, people face several challenges as they leave their countries of origin to study abroad, or they move to avoid political consequences or to take advantage of better employment and lifestyle opportunities. Neighbourhood schools are multicultural; universities have larger numbers of foreign students (whom we no longer think of as "foreign students"). Countries with declining populations are recruiting professionals to work inside their borders and to become citizens, and local schools are dealing with language and cultural differences as a result. More than ever before, people have the ability to travel worldwide, especially those who have the economic means to do so. The world over, people are exposed to diverse customs, values, politics, and social and cultural differences. Through the use of advanced technologies, there are now long-distance connections to friends and loved ones, and there is contact with aspects of the world not previously encountered. Cell phones and computers function in almost every corner of the world.

As a result of this broad and growing exposure to differences, and due to emerging cultural awareness of differences generated by advocacy movements that address gender differences, sexual minority differences, cultural differences, ethnic differences, religious differences, and differences of persons with disabilities (to name just a few categories of difference), people are re-examining their beliefs, values, and ethics. Further, they are beginning to question what is true, what matters, and how they ought to engage with each other.

The language people use to express their beliefs, values, and ethics is also being re-examined because there is greater understanding of and appreciation for how diverse, rich cultural languages are linked to highly specialized versions of reality and systems of social relations (Nowak, 2007). As realities change due to globalization and increased connectedness, people are challenged to re-examine old assumptions about differences as expressed through language, especially those assumptions that equate differences with deficiency, pathology, and disorder.

Collectively, human beings are grappling with profound questions such as these:

- When dealing with differences, do we seek genuine commonality and solidarity with others?
- Is living in a pluralistic society a good thing, or does it lead to irreversible social disintegration and fragmentation?
- Do we have to accommodate condemnatory judgments that affect our self-esteem and self-identity, or do we have to give up our condemnatory judgments of others?
- Who gets to question, define, and enforce normalcy in the very diverse world that is now our community? Is normalcy an *old world* concept?
- Does dealing with difference simply require personal and community understanding, or does it require personal and community change?

These are the kinds of questions that need to be grappled with by individuals, members of local and global communities, and Child and Youth Care practitioners. Whether people are conscious of them or not, the tensions that provoke these questions show up in the various challenges found in every practice setting—between individuals, and when working with families, communities, and institutions.

Understanding the Occurrence of Differences

We contend that it is crucial for Child and Youth Care practitioners to understand and manage the occurrence of differences within Child and Youth Care practice. Two key aspects of current times demand these qualities: (1) Child and Youth Care practice environments are ever-changing and reflect the on-going changes of global economies and shifting populations, and (2) the cultural nuances of equity, diversity, success and achievement, and family are evolving and emerging around the world. The field and practice of Child and Youth Care need to evolve and respond to these emergent and complex changes.

Many theorists have offered solutions for understanding and managing the occurrence of differences, particularly when dealing with cultural, gendered, and ethnic diversity. Several of these models, frameworks, and strategies tend to locate solutions outside of the self; proposed solutions often includes special programs, the establishment of quotas for those from minority groups, the development of policies to mandate inclusion, and the provision of financial aid, to mention a few. All of these strategies are intended to establish a practice of inclusion and mutual respect (Bomzar, 2007; Cox, 1994; Cushner & Brislin, 1996; Robin, 2007; Smith & Wolf-Wendel, 2005; Vargas & Koss-Chioino, 1992).

Although many of these ideas and strategies have been successfully integrated into workplace and academic settings, the personal aspect of engaging with differences has tended to be minimized. One of the dangers lies in thinking that if certain policies are in place, individuals can carry on as usual without inconveniencing themselves. Equity plans are in place; therefore, reflecting on individual responsibility to change does not need to happen. We argue that without a careful and thoughtful exploration of how one's self is experienced, implicated, and ultimately held responsible for dealing with differences, these programs will fall short of achieving meaningful change in coming to terms with the conflicts that arise, especially when menacing differences are experienced.

From our perspective, then, the personal experience of engaging with differences needs to be moved to the foreground to understand more fully how to proceed. Coming to terms with differences in Child and Youth Care practice is personal because practice depends on individual perceptions or awareness (Descartes, as cited in Davies, 1990), apperceptions or self-awareness (Leibniz, 1925; Locke, 1959), and self-consciousness or awareness of being aware (Gennaro, 1995; Lycan, 1996) of differences. Individual perceptions, apperceptions, and self-consciousness are related to self-identity and how people think they are and should be. Coming to terms with differences is about coming to terms with one's self because differences are experienced with and through others.

We offer ways to think about this challenge and propose a reflective strategy for expanding limited perceptions of, and values relative to, others with whom we work, whether they are colleagues or those we serve. The strategy requires Child and Youth Care workers to function at a higher level of consciousness with respect to differences and their personal relationship to them. But before describing our strategy, it is important to grasp more fully some of the complexities that underlie the challenges of engaging differences.

Personal and Limiting Perspectives

What is it that makes understanding and valuing differences so challenging and formidable? Despite all of the rhetoric and scholarship on accepting, tolerating, and celebrating differences, why, when push comes to shove, are the up-close-and-personal instances of difference so overwhelmingly stressful and downright unwelcome? In pursuit of answers to these questions, we have reviewed the literature and found some important clues in a recent article, "Thinking Outside the Box Can be Dangerous," by Neil Agnew (2008).

In his article, Agnew discusses what are considered to be insurmountable challenges that scientists encounter when critically reflecting on their own biases and assumptions. Agnew emphasizes that the capacity of people to step outside of their own perspectives has limitations when it comes to making any claims about what they assume to be true. Although he speaks specifically about failing to reflect critically on biases and assumptions within scientific research, we have found his ideas to be relevant and particularly informative when attempting to understand the complexities and challenges of working with differences in practice. In light of Agnew's ideas, the question for us becomes this: What gets in the way of overcoming our biases and assumptions when faced with menacing differences, and what impedes our ability to truly understand one other?

Bounded Rationality

The main culprit, according to Agnew, is contained within the concept of *bounded rationality*. For hundreds of years, people have been seduced, he argues, by the dream that if they can think more clearly, more rationally, will they then be able to solve most of life's dilemmas. This seduction of reason—that is, the belief that people might be able to think their way through and beyond complex issues—has dominated Western collective consciousness for several centuries.

According to many contemporary thinkers (see for example, Agnew, 2008; Gergen, 1999; Haraway, 1988; Harding, 1991; Hawking, 1988; and Mahoney, 1991, to name just a few), the idea of rational thought as a panacea for all that is wrong with the world has been widely refuted. In other words, relentlessly pursuing a transcendental Truth will not lead us to nirvana, especially when it comes to working with differences. To begin, there are cognitive constraints that interfere with moving beyond what is comfortable and familiar. Although the mind is fairly flexible, it can only stretch so far. Without diverging too far from our topic, a brief summary of how the brain sorts information is needed.

In order to make sense of something or someone, it is necessary to organize a multitude of bits and pieces of information that are encountered in daily life. To do so, systems need to be developed (often referred to as *construct systems*, [Kelly, 1955]) for managing details, determining what will be taken as evidence, making distinctions, and creating categories. Without a system for organizing, sorting, and categorizing information, the internal world of an individual would be a chaotic mixture of random, contradictory, and disorganized thoughts. The desktop on a computer is a good example. When documents are not filed or organized, they sit randomly on the screen. Without a filing system of some sort, documents cannot be retrieved easily, nor is it simple to recall why they are there, their purpose, and their relationship to other documents. Many times, filing systems are created after data are collected, not in advance. Cognitive systems work similarly, in that they have feedback mechanisms that are created to organize thoughts and experiences that occur in response to the world. When an unanticipated event happens, the cognitive system is activated to make sense of experiences and interactions. These systems also function proactively, in that people learn to anticipate events and, in doing so, invoke feed-forward mechanisms that are applied to in-the-moment experiences.

In practice, every time a Child and Youth Care practitioner meets with a family, these systems for making sense are called upon. *Who is this family? What is going on in their lives? Is this child safe? What can I do to help?* These are the kinds of anticipatory questions that construct frameworks for thinking about how to proceed. All of these cognitive systems and their feedback and feed-forward functions serve people well when faced with the complexities of practice and everyday life.

Despite the ways in which these systems simplify life, there is a downside to construct systems. In fact, there is something risky and sometimes dangerous about them, because they can also prevent people from seeing beyond their own beliefs and values, and the assumptions they have used to construct the system based on their experiences and interactions. Unfortunately, individuals are always trapped within their own ways of organizing and making meaning of events. They are both the guards and prisoners of their own construct systems (Mahoney, 1991), so there is a Catch-22: people need their construct systems to manage the complexities of life, but these same construct systems also curtail capacities to think differently and thereby step outside of the box.

 Further, Agnew (2008) reminds his readers that there are no assumptions, or no "premises without bias" (p. 108). All of what can be taken to be true is built upon layers of assumptions and presuppositions, making knowing always partial, subjective, relative, and contingent. Citing a wonderful example of the idea of the layering of beliefs and assumptions, he borrows an excerpt of Stephen Hawking's bestseller, *A Brief History of Time* (1988). Following a public lecture given by Bertrand Russell on the solar system, Russell accepts questions from the audience:

> A little old lady tells him that he's got it all wrong. The earth doesn't circle around the sun; everyone knows it sits on a giant tortoise. Smiling patiently Russell asks her upon what does the tortoise sit. The old lady replies: "You're a very clever young man, but it's turtles all the way down." (p. 28)

This anecdote captures several ideas, but the point we want to make is that all knowledge is constructed and such constructions are built upon layers of assumptions about reality, and the multiple interpretations that can be formulated in response to any thing or event.

How, then, you might wonder, can people ever escape their own biases? If they can never move beyond their own assumptions, what does this suggest about the limitations of understanding another person's perspective? Are all people doomed to just orbit around their own beliefs, values, and assumptions? If rationality itself is bounded, how tightly bound are individuals? What happens when what binds their assumptions together begins to loosen?

One positive outcome is that when frameworks are stretched, people can accommodate, as Piaget reminds us, more distinctions and therefore more differences. In these moments of expansion they can even adjust and/or revise *what they assumed to be true* without too much difficulty. In fact, these moments of expansion can be exhilarating as new insights are formed. Such changes can be considered *first order* when there are minor revisions to what one thought was true.

There is also another effect of stretching personal frameworks that is not so pleasant. When construct systems are stretched beyond what they can bear, or what they seem able to accommodate, the experience is not so comfortable. In fact, as Kelly (1955) so aptly stated, "Anxiety exists when we are caught with our constructs down." Niemeyer (1995) compares this kind of experience to the experience of snorkelling near the edge of a reef where, on one side, there is comfort in knowing there is—and seeing—a visible bottom to the ocean floor; once outside the reef, however, the shelf drops suddenly into a black, seemingly bottomless ocean. It is in this moment that the adventurer grasps the terrifying experience of being suspended over an abyss in which there is nothing to connect oneself to the safety of the shore. Niemeyer writes:

> My clearest, starkest memory…is of holding onto the drift line with one hand and stretching out toward the void beneath me to see the fullest extent of the light's revelation. Unprepared for the outcome, I drew back in horror. There the lights ceased to penetrate; a thousand watts fell dead in space, failing to reveal what lay concealed in the vast depths before me. (p. 112)

Most of us are inclined to prefer the safer location where the bottom is perceived or known. Gently stretching one's perspective, in contrast to being thrown into the deep end without a life preserver, is also preferred. We contend, however, that as uncomfortable as it may be, at the heart of those difficult times, falling into the abyss is absolutely necessary, especially for those working in Child and Youth Care.

Agnew offers an important idea when it comes to avoiding deep waters and stretching one's perspective. Having a high-trust to low-doubt ratio, he contends, is important in order to function in an otherwise chaotic world. For the most part, people do trust that most of the time *things work as they should*. Planes will stay in the air, people will obey traffic lights, ships will stay afloat, and so on. In other words, they trust the assumptions that support their views of reality, their perspectives on how the world should be, and what they deem valuable in life. Trust helps people contend with how random life may be by allowing them to act "as if" (Vaihinger, 1952) things are predictable and, therefore, within their control most of the time.

When people surround themselves with like-minded people who think like them, value what they value, and share their visions for how the world should be, they keep this high-trust/low-doubt ratio in place. To keep their assumptions well shored up, they constantly search for supporting evidence. In our case, for example, spending time with people whose ideas resonate for us, such as those experienced within Child and Youth Care, helps to provide support for our beliefs, values, and assumptions. Although we are relatively few in number, we tend to orbit around similar attractive ideas, such as the value of the therapeutic relationship, working from a strengths-based perspective, and the necessity of working in the life space of the child.

This is all well and good until differences become too "different" and the capacity for handling or accommodating outliers begins to diminish. People may not have the same ideas about therapeutic relationships, strengths-based perspectives, and what constitutes the life space of a child. What often lies beneath handling outliers is a fear that if the differences become too vast, then the centre (or in this example, the essence of Child and Youth Care) will disappear. So, in response to these threats, people tend to spiral inward in an attempt to protect that which they cherish. This movement inward happens at many levels of human experience: from the intimate relations between self and other, within the boundaries of disciplinary groups, within racial and/or marginalized groups, within religious organizations, and so on.

It is this same phenomenon, fear of losing the centre or essence, which some may equate to a loss of self, that may be the heart of the difficulty. If I accept your truth, I may have to abandon my own. Or perhaps even more threatening, I may lose my identity as a professional, as one who is *supposed to know*. Ultimately, I may even have to reflect on whether or not I am who I think I am or what others believe me to be. Difficulties related to identities are not mere idle pastimes; a strong sense of self is so important for wellbeing that if identity issues are not resolved, they can create serious problems, such as despair, alienation, and loss of meaning or purpose. No wonder people find ways to minimize, retreat, avoid, and/or persuade others to think in similar ways.

So far we have mentioned the cognitive and emotional strains that occur when working across differences, and we have discussed why it is so difficult to get enough distance to objectively examine cherished personal perspectives that differ from others'. Yet working with the complexities of human experience found within the practice of Child and Youth Care requires practitioners to overcome these limitations. But how? What can be done to stretch capacities for working with difference? How can practitioners best prepare themselves?

Agnew presents key constraints of the capacity to think outside the box: bounded rationality, bias, and the propensity of human beings to survive by protecting and living within the reality they have constructed. On the other hand, Agnew, as the joker, cites McIlwain (2007)—"we are not only knowers but wanters" (p. 529)—making the point that emotionality plays a central role in overcoming bounded rationality. He goes on to say that "anyone who has fallen in love with a person or a theory appreciates that *wanting* trumps *knowing* almost every time." This suggests that *wanting to understand and live with differences* opens a necessary window to pursue a different truth—one that is based on what we call *co-created consciousness*.

USING *WANT* TO CO-CREATE CONSCIOUSNESS AND A *DIFFERENT REALITY*

While the essence of consciousness has been debated for many lifetimes longer than any of us reading this chapter have been around, a public recognition and understanding of consciousness and how it relates to the social and the interpersonal (Gennaro, 1995; Heidegger, 1927/1962; Perry, 2001) is relatively new. Even newer is the idea of applying this kind of knowledge to everyday interactions to co-create a different reality. Further, the articulation and use of requisite skills to manifest the co-created reality is just emerging (Ricks & Nicholson, 2003; Sharmer, 2000).

We refer to the kind of people who *want* this way of being to exist in the world as *sophisticated self-observers*; they have the capacity to take inner stances while recognizing how they influence and are influenced by what goes on around them in the moment. Working from an awareness of co-created consciousness, they structure their experiences and reality with others by constructing and deconstructing their beliefs, values, and assumptions.

We suggest that the sophisticated self-observer lives the following statement made by Robert Kegan:

> Transforming our epistemologies, liberating ourselves from that in which we're embedded, making what was subject into object so that we can "have it" rather than "be had" by it—this is the most powerful way I know to conceptualize the growth of the mind. (Kegan, as cited in Anderson, 2003, p. 127)

Being mindful in these ways of knowing and being requires people to be resourceful, creative, and ingenious when inventing and co-creating themselves and others in each moment. They must be resourceful, creative, and ingenious because this practice requires using one's mind differently to *change one's mind* about *what is* in order to co-create *what might be*.

When people are resourceful they generate practical ingenuity and the art of being open and frank to create or bring something into existence. They are co-creating an experience and creating more from what might naturally exist. Further, they are attempting to understand what is, as well as aspects of the self and other, in a new way. Being resourceful requires an optimistic attitude that frames anything as possible; people have strengths and capacities to get things done, act differently, and to respond to difference. There is a collective attitude that recognizes and promotes infinite possibilities to work together on a common goal or vision to live with differences.

We visualize co-created consciousness as *needing to deal with the deep waters on the other side of the reef* described so well by Neimeyer (1995). Rather than circling around and getting nowhere or lapsing into despair, individuals need to challenge themselves to co-create an alternative experience.

We see the different aspects of the sophisticated self-observer as being deliberately accessed, interactive, and self-managed so that these individuals can encounter differences and generate a different meaning and understanding, shifting from *what is* to *what might be*. We are mindful that to engage in this process involves a personal choice and motivation to engage in a discovery process that explores and determines what is at stake for each person. This also requires a sophisticated self-observer's skill set, which transcends skills taught in most professional training programs.

Our objective is to pose a strategy and identify the skills required to co-create consciousness and mutually determined realities. We apologize for exploring each of the aspects of sophisticated self-observers in a linear fashion; please recognize that we are explaining a complex and generative process that represents the chaos of change and co-creation that results in a co-created reality. It is not tidy and is certainly neither linear nor predictable!

Figure 1.

Figure 1.

EXPLORING THE EXPERIENCE OF DIFFERENCE

Our visualization of the sophisticated self-observer is reflected in Figure 1.

Figure 1 captures the experience of floating in the dark waters of uncertainty, change, and possibility while acknowledging and experiencing a menacing difference. In order to navigate, one needs to be a sophisticated self-observer who, through self-awareness, holds one's inner stances while noticing how he or she is influencing and being influenced by others and events within the larger context. Collaborating with others, the self-observer becomes aware of the other's consciousness and engages the other in a mutual restructuring of the experience. This is accomplished by sharing understandings of what is and then deconstructing these understandings in order to consciously co-create a shared explanation. We will now take each aspect of this strategy and make explicit what it takes to be a sophisticated self-observer.

Sophisticated Self-observers

Sophisticated self-observers notice aspects of the self, such as these:

- thoughts (i.e., writing this chapter will never end)
- feelings (i.e., *tired* of writing this chapter)

- acts (i.e., sitting at the computer many days in a row)
- motives (i.e., get the book completed so students can access it)
- character traits (i.e., dogged determination, energetic, funny, hard worker)
- situations in which they find themselves (i.e., work, work, work)
- repeated patterns that involved similar relationships such as relationships with boyfriends or husbands, girlfriends or wives, teachers, or friends (i.e., too many projects on the go while saying that we are going to slow down)
- capacity to learn (i.e., unending)
- skills (i.e., writing, thinking, reflecting, co-creating, co-consciousness)
- assets (i.e., lots of support)
- deficits (i.e., out of time)
- likes and dislikes (i.e., love to learn, love to work with others and co-create, hate being late)
- beliefs (i.e., this will be a contribution to the field of Child and Youth Care)
- values (i.e., it is important to change curriculum and prepare for changing times), personal rules of comportment (i.e., look smart by being smart)
- reactions (i.e., frustration)
- justifications (i.e., it must be done)
- rationalizations (i.e., the grand children are important too)
- compromises (i.e., not enough time together as authors)
- lies (i.e., none that we know of)
- fears (i.e., no one will understand this)
- work habits (i.e., work your fingers to the bone…what do you get? bony fingers), and more.

Sophisticated self-observers understand the complexity of the self and how aspects of self are related to each other, how they emerged historically and are manifest in certain circumstances. They also understand that there is no such thing as an isolated individual who can make decisions without considering others. Selves are always relational and, in this sense, all people are highly intersubjective beings who only know themselves in relation to others. That said, whether they have actual conversations with others, or conversations with internalized others (my deceased grandmother, or my best friend who died last year), they are always relating to more than just their own inner dialogue (Hermans & Kempen, 1993; Gergen & Gergen, 2004). Needless to say, self-observations are always in relation to both self and other. One does not go it alone.

Inner Stances

Inner stances can be abstract moral positions about something and an imaginal way of thinking about how one might proceed. Such a priori stances, or positions, refer to the kinds of standpoints that people take when thinking in advance about how they *should* act. These often come from moral reflections about what is real and good. Conceived in the abstract, they may or may not be *applied* to any given situation. At the cognitive level, inner stances help people to describe how they think they would like to act, their justifications for doing so, and their perceived hunches about what the consequences might be. Taking a slightly different perspective at this point, we want to focus on applied stances: stances that arise in the moment, especially when differences emerge.

Applied inner stances are dynamic, in-the-moment positions about one's self and the other, taken in light of reacting to what is happening within a process of inquiry, participation, observation, and reflection. Here, we will focus on the pragmatic aspect of acting from an inner stance. Naming one's inner stance is a valuable first step, but imagining the impact of such a position requires much more reflection, which we will guide you through once we have added a few more details about stances (see Figure 2).

Figure 2.

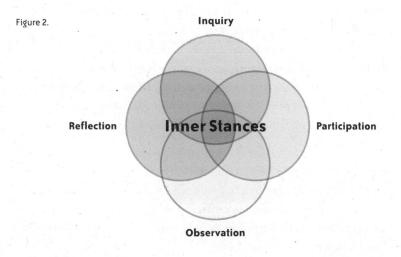

Inquiry

Reflection   **Inner Stances**   Participation

Observation

First, stances are functional; they serve a particular purpose. When differences emerge that are seemingly difficult, people return to their own stances. Stances occur within the context of inquiry, participation, and observation and are noticed by paying attention to one's reactions (feelings, thoughts, and actions). In doing so, and in relation to stances, one attempts to explain one's position to oneself (and sometimes to others) in various ways. Some of these explanations attribute responsibility to others, such as "*they* must not understand," "*they* are not behaving the way they should," "*their* beliefs are outdated," "*their* values are not really very good," or "*their* inner stances are self-serving." Other explanations are self-deprecating, such as "*I* must be stupid," "perhaps *I'm* not the good person I think I am," "*I* haven't really thought deeply about this issue," or "*I* am not really worthy of belonging, being accepted, or being loved." Conversely, these inner stances, whether "other"-blaming or self-deprecating, can act as lifesavers for people when they are faced with the uncertainty of the abyss, that is, with differences that are seemingly incomprehensible. In Neimeyer's analogy, inner stances are like tethers that people hold onto temporarily while allowing themselves to play with what might be different and threatening.

Underlying these stances are some core beliefs that may manifest in the following kinds of statements: "My values are well thought out. I act accordingly. I have a worldview that is ethical." These are the core beliefs, values, and rules about self and other that people cling to while initiating inquiry into other points of view. We contend that it is important to become more cognizant of what some of these inner stances may be so that, as Kegan (as cited in Anderson, 2003) reminds us, *we can "have [them]" rather than "be had" by [them]*.

Ask yourself, "what stances do I hold onto when I am faced with a challenging difference?" Here it is important to reflect on what you believe and why, without becoming lost in the quagmire. It may be merely the best understanding you can come up with at this point in time; nevertheless, it is better than nothing at all.

Consider the following questions:

- What stances are life-sustaining and enduring? *For example, if I believe that people are basically good and we have the capacity to get along together despite our differences, how does this perspective show up in my daily interactions with others and in my Child and Youth Care practice situations?*

- What stances would be the most challenging to change? *For example, based on the stance above, and if I am constantly faced with experiences of violence and discrimination, how would I hold onto these beliefs despite evidence to the contrary? What might it be like to revise this stance, and what might be the consequences for me in my work, my family, with friends, and so on?*
- What stances would I find almost impossible to revise or abandon? *If I find myself in a situation where I am obligated to adhere to local customs and traditions, and I find myself confronted with instances of violence and discrimination against women, how would I handle such a situation? What would be the costs to me personally? What might be the cost to others if I refuse to oblige?*

Once you have identified what stances you cherish most, you need to be able to hold them up to scrutiny to understand how they work for and against you. In order to reflect on the following questions, think about a recent experience in which you were faced with a conflict between yourself and another person. Now that you have recalled the experience, consider these questions:

- When I am faced with a difference that negates mine, do I engage in blaming others, or do I reflect on the viability of my own inner stance?
- What benefits do I receive from blaming others?
- What benefits do I receive from blaming myself?
- During these times, can I actually think relationally instead of thinking of victim and perpetrator?
- What are the consequences of thinking in *either/or* ways?
- Am I able to hold two competing stances simultaneously and appreciate their differences?
- Where does my mind go as I entertain these questions? What statements do I make about myself?

Stances are central to one's self and are conceptualized in various ways. Some people refer to these stances as a centre of knowing (an intuitive and inner knowing), a way of being (grounded), an inner truth or a meta belief about the self (Life Is Good). Stances do not always present themselves when they should (or could), and they sometimes become illusive and ill-defined. They may become manifest in surprising ways, and an immediate response may be, *You want me to explain why I believe what I do? I don't really know.* People sometimes say that they know intuitively when something is very close to their heart. For example, it is often said that something just feels like the right thing to believe, value, and do. On the other hand, when people behave counter to their espoused stances, they describe such experiences as being out of balance, off centre or out of sync, and respond with feelings or statements like this: *This uncertainty is wearing me out. I will just keep quiet and avoid this issue, situation, or person. This is just too painful and it's not worth it.*

Sometimes inner stances (what some may also consider to be moral codes or orientations) act as buffers against too much difference or change or, put more succinctly, too much *uncertainty.* Emotional responses like these—*Not so fast. Slow down. Keep calm*—might ensue. We have found that in the literature on diversity and difference, there is little acknowledgement of the emotional impact of dealing with difference, especially on a person-to-person level.

It is important to realize that emotional engagement with one's stance when faced with difference can be upsetting. When stances are challenged, a certain amount of emotional stability is needed to stay in the moment of difficulty. For example, when in the midst of a heated debate, one needs to be conscious of emotional reactions. Most people have, too often, allowed intense emotions to run amok when what was needed most was thoughtful and "sophisticated" self-observation. Feeling uncertain is bound to be a frequently encountered feeling. For example, these may be some internal reactions: *My heart is pounding; I want to end this conversation. I'll just agree for now and then deal with this later. I don't know what to think or do.* Sometimes emotional reactions will be attributed to something physical: *My asthma is acting up. There must be something in the air.* Other times may pose a complete mystery and offer the opportunity to learn: *What's going on here? This is different.* Or, *Darn, here we go again; why does this keep coming up?* Attending to one's emotional barometer can lead to new insights about oneself and others.

Equally important is paying attention to others' emotional reactions. How is this person experiencing my emotions? What might be occurring for them at this moment in relation to the stance I am taking? Instead of thinking, *Wow, what a weird reaction*, assumptions need to be checked out: *Are you really upset about this or is something else bothering you?* Or, in ideal interactions, individuals embrace the challenge of trying to

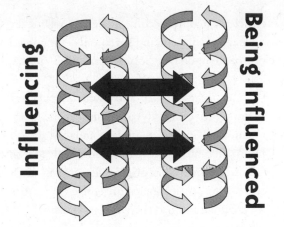

Figure 3.

Influencing

Being Influenced

understand each other in that moment: *Aren't our differences interesting. What can I learn from this person's perspective?*

Knowing when and how to deal with reactions that arise requires careful attention to reactions and responses that are embedded in emotions. In other words, it can be helpful to consider how much of the reaction is related to the discussion, and how much might be carried over from another situation. It is all too easy for people to take a victim stance: *No one understands me.* Equally problematic is taking an all-knowing stance: *We feel exactly the same and there really are no differences.*

A final caution regarding stances is that the use of stances needs to be flexible if they are going to be life-sustaining or something to hold to while other points of view are entertained. On the other hand, too much flexibility can lead to a stance that has minimal utility when it comes to considering differences that are life- or self-threatening. When relying on stances within a particular moment of reflection, there is an interesting paradox to consider: stances need to be fluid and flexible and, at the same time, solid and dependable.

Influencing and Being Influenced

This idea of influencing and being influenced recognizes that people are constantly engaged in the change process. The change process results from personal interactions when people act and react with others taking in what each has to offer without feeling the threat of losing their "selves." Through a process of inquiry into what the other perspective offers, individuals are provided with opportunities to experiment with a different stance. Moments of change can be microscopic or they can be akin to an epiphany. Nevertheless, people become different whenever they engage with others. Influence and influencing surrounds everyone daily, whether they are conscious of them or not. Sophisticated self-observers are aware of influence.

The cycle of influence (see Figure 3) by which a person is changed by another person's perspective or way of being can be both positive and negative. Less favourable situations, understandably, are those in which a person uses his or her power of persuasion to lead someone astray. Needless to say, there are many historical and contemporary examples of the kinds of leaders who can influence an entire population to think or behave in ways that run counter to their inner stances.

There are also positive examples that can influence the interactions between individuals. For example, although the student–professor relationship is full of power differentials, one small favourable shift in attitude on the part of the professor can change the quality of the interaction. Similarly, a Child and Youth Care practitioner can engage with families in a facilitative rather than adversarial or officious way. Rather than resort to bureaucratic statements, like "The policy states that you must do the following or else there will be consequences," practitioners can work collaboratively with families to respond to and bolster the values embedded within such policies. Both approaches—facilitative and adversarial—influence human interactions, yet they can generate very different outcomes depending on the individuals involved and the attitudes they hold.

Being aware of how individuals influence others and are influenced *by* others poses the opportunity to explore other options. A wise friend once mentioned that she refused to allow someone else's cruel behaviour to shape how she wanted to be. This undesirable behaviour was an influence this friend could actually choose to avoid. By staying with her stance regarding friendship, she could maintain her own values without feeling the need to revise them so that she could engage with a person who held a different stance about how friends relate to each other.

To better understand influencing and being influenced, think of an example of a conflict you have experienced with someone, and ask yourself the following questions:

- How does the quality of this interaction influence my inner
  stance? *For example, do I feel guilty for not adhering to my own*

Figure 4.

inner stance? Do I respond with a statement like, "I hate it when I do this"?

- What happens for me on a personal level when I relate and respond to this person in this way? *For instance, do I express thoughts like this: "Oh, I'm such a fraud—I wonder if she's noticing too"?*
- What choices do I have to act differently? *For example, have I even considered that there may be other ways of responding that could be more generous and generative? I could...I could...I could...because many are the ways.*
- What parts of myself can be positively affected by staying open to the other person's perspective? *In other words, perhaps I could learn something here, such as...*

Co-created Consciousness

Co-created consciousness is an awareness of self in relation to others. It is a way for people to think relationally by being conscious of their own inner stance, but only in relation to how it affects others and vice-versa (see Figure 4). It is challenging to accomplish because people not only have to be aware of their stance and all of the emotions that arise when meeting difference, but they also need to be mindful of how all people exist within networks of relationships. It is important that people become aware of their capacity to self-observe, identify their inner stances, and become aware of their participation in influencing and being influenced.

Thinking relationally sometimes means putting one's own immediate needs aside to connect with the experience of someone else. This takes energy and commitment, and it is usually much easier to focus inward instead. Leaving one's own experience at the door means that something cherished, such as one's inner stance, may not have centre stage. In essence, one has to honour and appreciate a different location—a space that sits between self and other. Take, for example, a heated debate in the classroom. Each person is vying for a winning argument—so much so that the debaters listen only for the purpose of composing counter arguments to persuade others to support their side. Although people sometimes treat each other with respect, there is nothing generative about this type of debate. Each person hangs on firmly to their inner stance of what is *right*. Influence and persuasion surround the discussions, but not in the spirit of collaboration that aims to enrich everyone's understanding and generate a new formulation of what might be.

Reflect on a recent time when you came away from a conversation feeling energized, understood, and respectfully challenged. Consider the following questions:

- What might it be like to have interesting discussions that become generative rather than adversarial? *What conditions were present that allowed each of us in this situation to collaborate rather than compete?*
- What would I need to think, feel, and do to make those kinds of conversations occur more often in my life? *What did I think, feel, and do in this situation? How can that be re-created in other circumstances?*

The saying that "it takes two to tango" is relevant to what we are describing. The dance requires all partners to willingly engage and work to synchronize their movements. When the rhythm is off, the dance feels discordant, with raw edges at every turn. Often, this sort of experience occurs when differences cannot be understood or reconciled. Common ground cannot be reached because sharing (and therefore, learning) does not take place. People retreat to what is familiar and, although there is still change, the change is minimal. While co-created consciousness may be present, the gap between individual perspectives may be too vast to bridge. Despite people's best intentions, generative dialogues may fall short or fail to develop at all.

As indicated in the following graphic (see Figure 5), people who understand co-created consciousness have the capacity to create something

Figure 5.

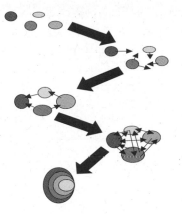

more generative than an individual could ever engender alone. Most people have these kinds of experiences in various contexts, but sadly they are more rare than common. Even in the most intimate relationships (such as those between a husband and wife, or between long-time friends), these interactions may not be as frequent as one would hope.

Paying attention to the idea of co-created consciousness can also produce guilt when one has a heightened self-awareness that reveals aspects of the self, and the other, that one may not want to know. For any of you who have seen the movie *Blood Diamond*, it is easy to see how actions in developing countries can be linked to capitalism in the West. As Western adults we are all responsible, despite where we happen to live. What exactly are our responsibilities? What might we do? Once global or co-created consciousness is understood, it can be disconcerting because being "relationally responsible" (McNamee & Gergen, 1994) calls people to a new kind of inquiry and, in turn, to a new kind of responsibility. It is the difference between knowing that actions have immediate consequences and knowing these interactions affect others who may not be physically present. Given that all people are interconnected, the ripple effects can be far reaching. Take, for example, a child who is removed from her home. Not only are both the child and parent affected, but so are the extended family members, the local school, the community that she may have been a part of, the protection workers who may now be held responsible for her well-being, and so on. Actions taken, no matter how singular and unobtrusive they may seem, have a way of moving far beyond two individuals dealing with differences. This relational awareness requires thinking globally while acting locally. Co-created consciousness means being aware of the relational aspect of one's actions. This understanding can be useful when coming to terms with difference because it serves as a reminder that no one is entirely separate from that which they critique.

In light of co-created consciousness, consider the following questions. Again, these may be easier to answer honestly if you call to mind a particular experience in which you were faced with difference:

- How willing are you to put your own emotional needs aside when differences arise? *For example, are you able to take a meta perspective of yourself to better identify patterns and processes of engaging with others?*
- Are you able to recognize your emotional reactions when faced with a threat to your own inner-directed stance? *For example, can you observe your own emotionality without running away from the conflict?*
- What strategies do you draw upon when faced with irreconcilable differences? *For example, can you identify possible strategies for dealing with differences that would either prevent you from avoiding, minimizing, or negating your own or another's perspective?*
- What stops you from using those identified strategies? *For example, are you unable to live with ambiguity, paradox, confusion, uncertainty, or all of these aspects of experience?*
- How do you determine when to let differences just be and when to attempt to engage honestly with someone else's perspective, despite how it contrasts with your own? *For example, when do you stop working so hard at something and just "go with the flow"? How do you come to this kind of decision?*

Constructing and Deconstructing Interpretations

Constructing and deconstructing interpretations means engaging with another person to explain what is happening and what it all means. Operating independently, people readily construct what is happening and what it means to them; they rarely do it with others. Even more rarely do people deconstruct what is happening and what it means in light of their previous constructions. This is because constructions grant individuals a false sense of security that *this is the way it is*—because they say so.

Perhaps people are reluctant to deconstruct their explanations because most have been inherited from family, religion, and other aspects of their cultures; such bodies of knowledge are often considered sacred territory. Some cultures allow adolescents to challenge what is true, others do not. As maturing persons, some adolescents are rarely encouraged to "wonder at" or "inquire into" the truth of *what is*. We frequently hear words to the effect that something *just is that way and has been forever and ever. What's to challenge?* Some people wander far from home and encounter differences that are alarming and lead to a path of questioning, such as may occur when a student goes on an overseas exchange. Other examples could include a blended family that integrates a new parent figure who has a different view of parenting and household management, or a high school graduate who goes away to university and discovers fields of study and points of view previously unexamined or unknown.

To explore ideas about constructing and deconstructing interpretations, you may begin to consider questions like these:

- How do I know what I know?
- What do I take as evidence for truth?
- Can opposing points of view both be true?
- Who gets to decide what is true?
- Who determines what goes into textbooks and eventually becomes part of my education?

Such experiences and questioning can be confusing and may, in dramatic cases, cost some people their relationships with family members or community. (Fear of death is second to our fear of not belonging!) On the other hand, the negation and denial of such experiences and the suppression of questioning may cost us our lives, in the sense that we merely adopt what we are told to believe and do not take the opportunity to become sophisticated self-observers.

It is personal constructions, however they are established, that become the "truths" that people readily defend and seek to impose on others, and vice-versa. These constructions are created from the truths people have been taught and the experiences they have—experiences from which they draw conclusions about *what is* and *what it all means*. For some, these realities become a ball and chain, while for others they are instigators of freedom.

Sadly, people do not often talk about the construction of their truths while constructing them. They hold onto them and live by them and carry them around until they are challenged—*if* and *when* that happens. Not surprisingly, people are unpractised in this business of constructing and deconstructing *what is* and, consequently, learn little from the many others who have different experiences and learning. Life feels comfortable and safe when one's interpretations and explanations are congruent and remain uncontested, even though this minimizes opportunities for new learning.

People rarely pause to reflect on whether or not, and how, their constructions or explanations are similar and different to those of others. Nor do they learn enough from others to reconstruct a mutual truth. Most young people are taught well in school how to be good, compliant students rather than critical thinkers who can think "outside the box," as Agnew reminds us. Worse yet, such behaviour is rewarded with A-pluses for reflecting that which is presented to us in classes. After years of reinforcement of compliance at school, in hospitals, in playgrounds, in the military, in government services, and, well, just about everywhere, why would we expect people, and how could we expect them, to engage in a different game of inquiry?

We have the technology for new understanding and meaning-making, whether it is based on quantitative or qualitative research, or storytelling and sharing. Each day is filled with opportunities to co-create. But usually we do not consider that we are co-creating the day through this kind of inquiry.

One of us (Ricks) had a co-created experience while attending a friend's funeral on a sunny day with a warm breeze in the air.

> When I walked into the foyer I said to her husband: "What a beautiful day for Madelane's funeral. She would have loved it and thought it was a great day to celebrate her life." Overcoming his initial shock, he smiled and responded: "You're right, it *is* a beautiful day for her funeral, and she would have loved it."

This is just one example of how situations do not merely exist, inertly, waiting for us to pass through them; they are co-constructed in each moment, and understandings shift and change through dialogues and interactions.

EMBRACING UNCERTAINTY, EXCITEMENT, AND POSSIBILITY WITH OTHERS

What we have described in this chapter are possibilities and hopeful, optimistic approaches to experience difference in Child and Youth Care practice in a new light. We have sought to emphasize that overcoming differences requires people to be sophisticated self-observers who have the capacity to take inner stances while recognizing they influence and are influenced by what goes on around them. Engaging in co-created consciousness, sophisticated self-observers structure their experiences and realities with others by constructing and deconstructing their beliefs, values, and assumptions. This is an ongoing process when people choose to engage in it; it is not necessarily an easy process. Some people prefer to live a less risky existence and opt to leave unexamined what they hold to be true. On the other hand, truly grasping that people can co-create realities in each and every moment can help people understand the magnitude, hopefulness, and responsibility of engaging with others. And, if each and every person were to begin to work on being sophisticated self-observers in their daily interactions with themselves and others, they might be better able to engage with respect and excitement what is unfolding and what is possible. No doubt, such an effort would result in infinite possibilities for creativity, communion, and compassion. This way of interacting demands from everyone the capacity to be helpful and merciful in understanding themselves and others in the moment.

REFERENCES

Agnew, N. (2008). Thinking outside the box can be dangerous. *Constructivism and the Human Sciences: Co-creating Worlds of Meaningful Connection, 12* (1&2) 100–119.

Anderson, W. T. (2003). *The next enlightenment: Integrating east and west in a new vision of human evolution.* New York: St. Martin's Press.

Bomzar, D. (2007). *Diversity: Does it mix?* Retrieved January 2, 2008, from http://sciencecareers.org/career_development/previous_issues/articles/2380/diversity_does_it_mix, p.1–3.

Cox, T., Jr. (1994). *Cultural diversity in organizations.* San Francisco: Berrett-Koehler Publications.

Cushner, K., & Brislin, R. (1996). *Intercultural interactions.* Thousand Oaks, CA: Sage.

Davies, C. G. (1990). *Conscience as consciousness.* Oxford: The Voltaire Foundation.

Gennaro, R. (1995). *Consciousness and self-consciousness: A defense of the higher-order thought theory of consciousness.* Amsterdam and Philadelphia: John Benjamins.

Gergen, K. J. (1999). *An invitation to social constructionism.* Thousand Oaks, CA: Sage.

Gergen, K. J., & Gergen, M. (2004). *Social construction: Entering the dialogue.* Chagrin Falls, OH: Taos Institute Publications.

Haraway, D. (1988). Situated knowledges: The science question in feminism and the privilege of partial perspective. *Feminist Studies, 14*(3), 575–599.

Harding, S. (1991). *Whose science? Whose knowledge? Thinking from women's lives.* New York: Cornell University Press.

Hawking, S. (1988). *A brief history of time.* New York: Bantam Books.

Heidegger, M. (1962). *Being and time* (J. Macquarrie & E. Robinson, Trans.). New York: Harper and Row. (Originally published in 1927)

Hermans, H. J., & Kempen, H. J. (1993). *The dialogical self: Meaning as movement.* New York: Academic Press.

Kelly, G. A. (1955). *The psychology of personal constructs. Volume 1: A theory of personality, Volume 2: Clinical diagnosis in psychotherapy.* New York: Norton.

Leibniz, G. W. (1925). *The monadology* (R. Lotte, Trans.). London: Oxford University Press. (Original work published 1720)

Lycan, W. (1996). *Consciousness and experience.* New York: Wiley.

Locke, J. (1959). *An essay on human understanding.* New York: Dover. (Original work published 1688)

Mahoney, M. J. (1991). *Human change processes: The scientific foundations of psychotherapy.* New York: Basic Books.

McIlwain, D. (2007). Rezoning pleasure: Drives and affects in personality theory. *Theory and Psychology, 17*(4), 529–561.

McNamee, S., & Gergen, K. J. (Eds.). (1994). *Therapy as social construction.* Thousand Oaks, CA: Sage.

Neimeyer, G. (1995). The challenge of change. In R.A Neimeyer & M. J. Mahoney (Eds.), *Constructivism in psychotherapy* (pp. 111–126). Washington, DC: American Psychological Association.

Nowak, M. (2007). Dealing with difference: Diagnostic labels, the hunter–farmer metaphor, and self-referential terms of identity and affiliation. *New Horizons for Learning.* Retrieved January 2, 2008, from http://www.newhorizons.org/spneeds/adhd./nowak2htm

Perry, J. (2001). *Knowledge, possibility and consciousness.* Cambridge, MA: MIT Press.

Ricks, F., & Nicholson, D. (2003). *Caring to question: A guide for participatory inquiry in child care communities.* Ottawa, ON: Child Care Federation of Canada.

Robin, D. (2007). Part 13: Dealing with differences in a world of diversity: A better workplace. *Leadership in Action Series.* Retrieved January 2, 2008, from http://www.abetterworkplace.com/081.html

Scharmer, C. O. (2000, May). *Presencing: Learning from the future as it emerges. On the tacit dimension of leading revolutionary change.* Paper presented at the Conference on Knowledge and Innovation, Helsinki School of Economics, Finland.

Smith, D. G., & Wolf-Wendel, L. E. (2005). The challenge of diversity: Involvement or alienation in the academy? *The ASHE Higher Education Report*. Hoboken, NJ: John Wiley and Sons.

Vaihinger, H. (1952). *The philosophy of 'as if': A system of the theoretical, practical and religious fictions of mankind.* [Translated from the 6th German ed. by C. K. Ogden] London: Routledge and K. Paul.

Vargus, L. A., & Koss-Chioino, J. D. (Eds.). (1992). *Working with culture: Psychotherapeutic interventions with ethnic minority children and adolescents.* San Francisco: Jossey-Bass Publishers.

Marquis Book Printing Inc.

Québec, Canada
2008